Geoffrey & Shar

The Property Handbook

Your Essential Guide

How to

Buy, Renovate, Stage, Sell & Move

Packed with insider tips, checklists and tools to fast track your property success

www.gsansellproperty.com

ISBN: 978-1-9993470-0-0

First published in 2018 by G & S Ansell Publishing.

Copyright © 2018 Geoffrey & Sharena Ansell. All rights reserved.

All rights reserved. Apart from any permitted use under UK copyright law, no part of this publication may be reproduced or transmitted in any form or by any means, electronic or mechanical, including photocopying, recording, or any information, storage or retrieval system, without permission in writing from the publisher or under licence from the Copyright Licensing Agency Limited. Further details of such licenses (for reprographic reproduction) may be obtained from the Copyright Licensing Agency Ltd, Saffron House, 6-10 Kirby Street, London EC1N 8TS.

Typeset for G & S Ansell Publishing.

Printed in Great Britain for G & S Ansell Publishing.

DISCLAIMER

Every effort has been made to ensure that the information in this book is correct at the time of publication. The Authors (Geoffrey and Sharena Ansell) and publisher (G & S Ansell Publishing) do not assume and hereby disclaim any liability to any party for any loss, damage or disruption caused by errors or omissions, whether such errors or omissions result from negligence, accident or any other cause.

HOMAGE

To My Mother, Prem Prabha Azam
An Extraordinary Woman

Thank You for bringing me up
For taking such remarkable care of me
Throughout Your life
With such devotion and love
So single-handedly
Against such immense odds.

Whilst You have flown to Your bliss
You remain
For me
An outstanding, awe-inspiring and timeless icon
Of courage
Of strength
Of determination
Of perseverance
Of survival itself.

My eternal love and gratitude to You, my Amma.

DEDICATION

We dedicate this book to one another.
Without one, there is no other.

TESTIMONIALS

I have known Geoff and Sharena for many years now and had the pleasure of seeing their houses evolve and witness the creative process from the start until completion. My company has been lucky enough to have assisted in buying and selling two houses in Rickmansworth, Hertfordshire for them. I can say without hesitation they research their market place and produce an end product tailored to achieve the best price. They create well designed and presented living spaces that appeal strongly to the target audience. They have always been transparent and easy to do business with. Once a sale is agreed and the sales process starts, they are quick and effective in responding to legal queries and questions. They always appear to be one step ahead of the process which helps push sales to conclusion faster than most. I can highly recommend their knowledge of the residential property market.

Nicholas Walker, Director, Robsons Estate Agents, United Kingdom

Between them, Geoff and Sharena have vast experience in project management and delivering on time. They are also exceptionally stylish in their property presentations. The homes they create have a very functional flow which encompasses clever and thoughtful extras, providing a very desirable result. They are a thoroughly methodical and practical team, paying particular attention to ambience and detail, with the kind of panache that is usually hard to find.

Christine Brien, Entrepreneur, Property Investor & Developer, New Zealand

I have known Geoff and Sharena for many years in professional and personal capacities. Every property I've seen them working on has been very skilfully renovated and beautifully staged to a stunning, show-home finish. In fact, I have always asked for their guidance on houses I've been involved with regarding decorating and the best use of space and found them very thorough; their attention to detail has really helped to transform my properties. It is then I noticed why so many people have sought their guidance within this arena and hence why they come highly recommended. They helped me immensely in dealing with various teams and tradespeople. Their input was extremely useful as I managed to always get the best out of the teams and ensure I completed my renovations on time and in a cost-effective manner. I advocate using them for your property needs if you are looking for a striking and impressive property within budget and on schedule.

Kamal Radia, Property Investor, United Kingdom

ACKNOWLEDGEMENTS – A BIG THANK YOU TO:

Richard McMunn, Joshua Brown and Jordan Cooke at How2Become for patiently assisting us through our writing and the self-publishing process, and for bringing our book to you.

Michael Snooks and the team at Robsons Estate Agents for their assistance with the assignment of rights to us for the professional photographs of our property.

Adrian Palmer and his team at Blaser Mills Law Solicitors for constructive reviews of the *Buying* and *Selling Chapters*, and for providing information which added important content.

Paloma Harrington-Griffin for allowing use of Home Staging Association UK material, and for her invaluable reviews of the *Staging* and *Interior design and decorating Chapters*.

Stas Prokofiev and Daniel Davies at Fast Track Success for their expertise and patience with the build and support of our website and social media platforms.

Simon Coulson and his team at the Internet Business School for their valued tuition for our Internet Marketing Diplomas, and our talented IBS Diploma colleagues for their advocacy.

H Akademy's Eric Ho for providing clarity and establishing the value we bring in our service to others; Stephen Gwilt for aiding us in uncovering our impact and providing branding and design expertise; Harriet Bratt for identifying the right people to help us.

John Assaraf at NeuroGym for being the finest mentor, and for coaching and inspiring us in our personal development so that we are the best versions of ourselves.

Our dear family, friends and associates for all their encouragement, advice, reviews and feedback – there are too many of you to name, but you know who you are!

And a massive thanks to you for buying our book! We hope you enjoy it and find it engaging and helpful, and that it enables you to be better informed to successfully navigate the buying, renovating, staging, selling and moving home phases.

We wish you the very best of luck with your property adventures!

Welcome

Dear Reader,

What is it about homes and property that we aspire to owning these?

Abraham Maslow, the Jewish American psychologist and professor, created a prioritised hierarchy of intrinsic human needs within a pyramid and introduced it in 1943 in his paper titled "A Theory of Human Motivation". Maslow's hierarchy put shelter on the first tier and property on the second tier of the pyramid, relating these to our essential physiological and safety needs. Property enables physical survival for us. It is also an asset which is expected to increase in value, offering security during the property owner's lifetime, as well as an investment providing for the future of beneficiaries.

When we left New Zealand in search of adventures abroad, little did we know the extent to where our journey would take us. We have now lived in the UK and worked in the IT sector in London, Europe and the Channel Islands for the past 20 years. Our work as project management consultants largely within the oil and gas, banking and financial services sectors has equipped us with valuable knowledge and expertise, and we have combined this with our passion for buying and transforming properties, fulfilling our desire for a creative channel. Our Interior Design and Decorating Diplomas have further inspired us and aided in creating functional and stunning spaces.

What this really boils down to is that we have learnt to be meticulous in our planning, thorough in defining and documenting our requirements, accurate in managing our budget and time, and effective in communicating with people working on our projects. But some questions remain. In New Zealand, we have purchased and sold properties within just a few weeks. Throughout our property purchases, renovations and sales in the United Kingdom, we continue asking *"Why the long phase?"* as these take so much longer.

During the last 15+ years, we have bought, renovated and sold many properties in the UK and NZ, discovering different types of houses and having fun with our projects. However, our property journey in the UK did not start out auspiciously. Cowboy builders wrecked our first house. It was winter, and we had no heating, insulation, power or even a kitchen. It was a Christmas surrounded by rubble. The builders had packed up and walked off the job, abandoning us. This was supposed to be our dream home, but we were left devasted and running out of money. You may be in this situation and know what it feels like.

That encounter taught us a great deal. And now having been through the dodgy seller, the ghost gazumping and the cowboy builder experiences, as well as survived the IT management consultancy sector, we have developed resilience and wisdom. So, we thank those who have impeded us on our journey as they have made us stronger, smarter, sharper and more determined to succeed.

Our family and friends frequently suggested we should write a book to document our experiences, communicating our knowledge to help others with their property journey. We have applied the steps and processes in this book to great effect on our own properties. Our system has enabled us to buy property more easily, renovate creatively, sell quickly and for top money using key staging techniques, and move home smoothly. We have secured an average of 31% uplift on the prices we paid for the properties within 9 to 24 months of buying, renovating and selling each property in a variety of economic markets. Not everyone intends to buy, renovate, sell and move on as we have, but this illustrates that when you get the formula right for any of the phases, you can really benefit.

Our experiences have enabled us to offer valuable guidance, intended to lead you through the different phases of property ownership, saving you money and time while reducing issues and stress. During these demanding phases, readily-available information that has already been distilled and collated from years of hands-on experience in one book is helpful. Having the crucial knowledge to help you navigate these phases before you approach them is vital, rather than learning what you should have done after the fact.

When you are buying your home or investment property, there are many potential pitfalls to be aware of, as well as many activities that you and others will need to undertake. We have developed procedures, tools, administrative structures and systems to progress through all the steps required because we now know what to expect and how to navigate through the issues to find resolution.

We are bringing you information on how best to plan your property purchase, detail your requirements, conduct your search and undertake pre-offer due diligence. This book also contains information on how to present yourself to a lender as a good prospect, and how to communicate your suitability as a good buyer to the agent and seller. You will learn how to navigate and negotiate through the buying process up to exchange and completion of contracts.

We alert you to the many factors to consider when renovating your property and provide you knowledge and tips for the activities required to successfully complete your property's refurbishment. This book also assists you to plan your time, budget and tasks efficiently and effectively during a renovation. We provide you with valuable information on how to renovate cleverly, creatively and also how to do it on a budget.

We have provided you with a chapter on interior design and decorating. This describes the importance of colour in your design scheme, as well as how to develop your own unique design style and make the most impact cost effectively.

Staging your property for sale appropriately is crucial in assisting a potential buyer to visualise themselves living in a property without clutter, distracting and polarising features and lack of designated spaces. Staging is also critical for selling your property quickly and as close to the asking price as possible. The information in this book provides you with staging ideas to transform your home, give it the wow factor and make it appealing to your potential buyers.

When selling your home, you need to understand your finances. You also need to be aware of external influences, along with key infrastructure changes, that could impact your sale. Be proactive and responsive throughout this process and move speedily. While it can be seen as a positive change when you're upsizing, selling your home can also be a stressful time. And it can be a particularly emotionally challenging time if you are involved in downsizing. We will guide you through all these processes.

Moving home can also be really stressful. We have moved home over 20 times. We have also assisted our parents with downsizing and moving, so we know the physical challenges of this significant undertaking and the emotional difficulties of the process. We provide you with useful information to help you prepare, organise and complete this stage as smoothly and comfortably as possible, whether you are using a professional moving company or undertaking the move yourself.

Busy lives are ramped up further when engaged in any of the property phases. These phases can be overwhelming, confusing, stressful and expensive experiences. If you do not educate yourself with how best to approach these phases, you may spend more money than you need to, or end up losing money. As described already, our property journey has been full of high and low emotions, excitement and stress. To deal with this rollercoaster, we have developed resilience and built solid structures to support us. In this book, we have dedicated a chapter to dealing with stress, issues and conflict resolution. We have also provided a Q&A section to address common renovation problems.

Additionally, we have created comprehensive and detailed checklists to summarise what you need to do to maximise your chances of success in all these phases. We have also provided useful links and resources to help you to quickly navigate to the relevant web portals for further information.

We created this book with the responsibility of sharing with you our knowledge and experience. We also want to share with you the joy of property ownership, communicate the beauty of our creative experience and provide appreciable value to you. We have collated and provided information, guidance and steps you can implement immediately to enable you to increase your knowledge and fast track yourself to successfully buy, renovate, stage, sell and move home.

We hope our stories, experiences, ideas, processes, tools and references will enable you to be more informed, confident and successful in your property journey. Our vision is to help educate and provide guidance to as many people as possible.

Through buying, renovating, staging, selling and moving home many times, we have had tremendous opportunities to be imaginative, inventive and creative. We have met some wonderful people and had immense fun. We wish you the same on your property journey!

For further information and photos, please visit our website on www.gsansellproperty.com. If you would like help with any aspect of buying, renovating, staging, selling and moving home, please email us at contact@gsansellproperty.com to discuss the services we offer. We would love to hear from you.

To your success,

Geoffrey and Sharena Ansell

TABLE OF CONTENTS

CHAPTER 1 BUYING YOUR PROPERTY ... 15
Overview ... 16
Plan your property purchase ... 16
Detail your property requirements ... 39
Start your property search ... 41
Pre-offer due diligence ... 49
Offer and acceptance ... 56
Plan your move ... 61
Prepare for exchange of contracts ... 61
Gazundering, gazanging and gazumping ... 66
Exchange of contracts ... 68
Prepare for your move ... 70
Completion of contracts ... 70
Moving ... 71
Post-completion activities ... 71
Checklist – Buying your property ... 73

CHAPTER 2 RENOVATING YOUR PROPERTY ... 75
Overview ... 76
Plan your renovation project ... 76
Gather your requirements ... 81
Decide on your build team ... 86
Organise your budget and finances ... 92
Planning and consents ... 96
Project management ... 102
The renovation project ... 109
Our renovation project photos ... 132
Checklist – Renovating your property ... 134

CHAPTER 3 INTERIOR DESIGN AND DECORATING ... 137
Overview ... 138
Interior design elements ... 139
Interior design principles ... 142
Interior design styles and themes ... 144

Colour theory.. 149
Mediums to transform your walls 157
Utilise fabrics and soft furnishings 161
Choose works of art.. 162
Design and decorate in a day 163
Design and decorate on a budget... 164
Summary of dos and don'ts.. 166
Checklist – Interior design and decorating... 171

CHAPTER 4 STAGING YOUR PROPERTY 173
Overview.. 174
Key activities that help sell your property 177
Plan your home staging... 178
Professional versus DIY home staging... 180
De-clutter 183
Repair and redecorate... 185
Plumbing and heating 188
Lighting and electrics 188
Flooring 189
Clean, clean, clean 189
Give rooms a function 193
Prepare individual rooms 193
Exterior and curb appeal... 202
Take professional photographs... 203
Viewing day 206
Checklist – Staging your property... 208

CHAPTER 5 SELLING YOUR PROPERTY 213
Overview.. 214
Plan the sale of your property... 214
Prepare and stage your property for sale 220
Fixtures, fittings and chattels 221
Disclose material information 222
Property valuations and agent's costs.. 223
Understand your finances 224
Confirm your asking price 226

Decide how you will sell your property 227
Your sales brochure 236
Viewings 236
What to do if your property is not selling 238
Offer and acceptance 240
Complete conveyancing questionnaires 243
Negotiate the draft Contract 244
Plan your move 244
Make yourself available 244
Gazumping, gazundering and gazanging 245
Exchange of contracts 247
After exchanging contracts 249
Prepare for your move 249
Completion of contracts 249
Moving 250
Checklist – Selling your property 251

CHAPTER 6 MOVING HOME 255
Overview 256
Plan and prepare for your move 256
Coordinate your move 275
Activities for your moving day 280
Checklist – Moving home 286

CHAPTER 7 MANAGING STRESS, ISSUES AND CONFLICT 291
Overview 292
Managing stress 292
Issue management and conflict resolution 294
Questions and answers (Q&A) 298
Checklist – Managing stress, issues and conflict 303

CHAPTER 8 USEFUL LINKS AND RESOURCES 305
Reference list 306

ABOUT THE AUTHORS 314

Chapter 1

BUYING YOUR PROPERTY

Overview

Before you start the process of buying your home, plan ahead and consider the individual elements of the purchase. Investing your time in planning is hugely beneficial as buying your home is the most expensive purchase you are ever likely to make.

Decide on your strategy and budget, positioning yourself as the best possible buyer. Ensure that you detail your property requirements as clearly as possible. Conduct research and due diligence thoroughly on your chosen properties. Make yourself available and keep communication flowing with all parties throughout the buying process.

Plan your property purchase

Thorough planning and having clear, detailed requirements for the purchase of your property will help you to move through the buying process more effectively and efficiently.

The buying timeline and process

The end-to-end buying timeline can be relatively fast or can take a considerable amount of time. The duration of each stage within the buying process will depend on how long it takes you to identify the property you want to buy, any conditions set by any of the parties, the length and complexity of a chain, or how responsive all the parties are, including the buyer, seller, solicitor, agent, surveyor and mortgage provider. The diagram below illustrates approximate timing for the main stages within the buying process:

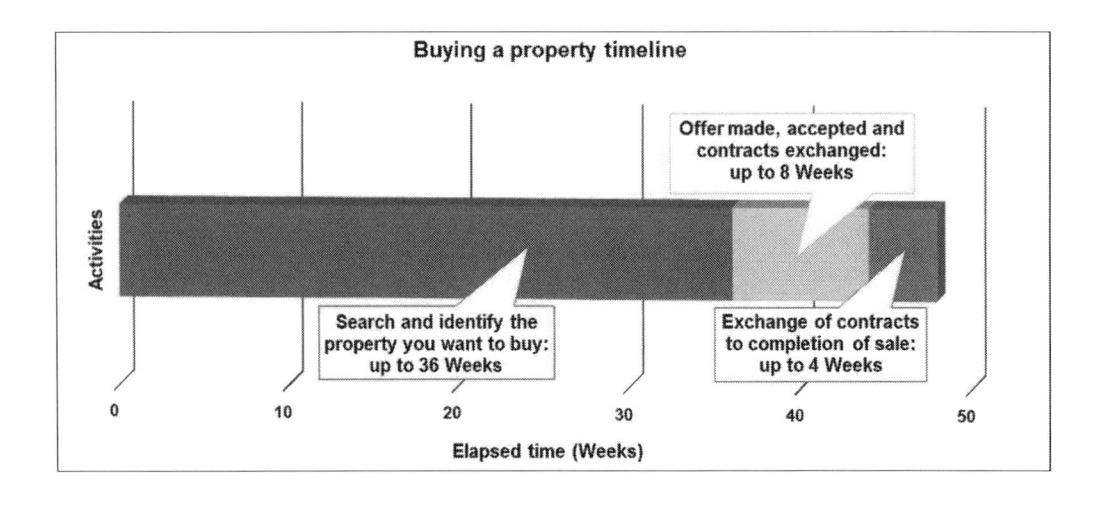

Buying a property timeline

- Search and identify the property you want to buy: up to 36 Weeks
- Offer made, accepted and contracts exchanged: up to 8 Weeks
- Exchange of contracts to completion of sale: up to 4 Weeks

Elapsed time (Weeks): 0, 10, 20, 30, 40, 50

Chapter 1. BUYING YOUR PROPERTY

Being aware of how long this whole process can take enables you to plan accordingly and allow sufficient time for each phase. From start to completion, each phase can take:

- Up to 36 weeks for searching and locating your desired property.
- Up to 8 weeks for offer, acceptance and exchange of contracts.
- Up to 4 weeks for completion of contracts

Also, be aware of the step-by-step process for buying a property as illustrated below:

1. DETERMINE IF YOU ARE READY TO BUY
Assess if you can afford to purchase a property at this time.

2. PLAN FOR YOUR PURCHASE
Confirm your requirements and familiarise yourself with the property market.

3. CONSULT YOUR BANK OR MORTGAGE BROKER
Obtain a Mortgage / Agreement in Principle.

4. START YOUR PROPERTY SEARCH
Register with local estate agents and view properties.

5. ENGAGE A SOLICITOR OR CONVEYANCER
Agree a fee and instruct them to act on your behalf once an offer is accepted.

6. MAKE YOUR OFFER TO PURCHASE
Identify your target property and make your offer to purchase.

7. ACCEPTANCE OF YOUR OFFER
Instruct your solicitor and advise your mortgage broker to request the mortgage provider to arrange a loan valuation / survey of the property.

8. YOUR PROPERTY SURVEY
Instruct your surveyor to assess the condition of the property and determine if this will affect the offer you have made to purchase.

9. OBTAIN QUOTES FROM REMOVAL COMPANIES
Agree a quote and date for your move.

10. EXCHANGE OF CONTRACTS
Searches are completed by your Solicitor and enquiries answered. Contracts are exchanged, making the purchase legally binding for all parties.

11. COMPLETION OF CONTRACTS
Legal ownership of the property is transferred to you and the house move can take place.

12. POST COMPLETION ACTIVITIES
Evidence received from your solicitor of the Registered Title and Stamp Duty payment.

Your reason for buying

Consider your reasons for buying, along with the type of property you are interested in owning. Along with your essential need for a home, understanding your specific reasons for wanting to buy a property helps you to define the type of property that will best suit your needs and your budget. The reasons for your intended purchase may include:

- Buying a property to move into or for investment purposes
- Moving from your parents' home to buy your first home.
- Moving from your rental property to purchase a home.
- Rightsizing by upsizing or downsizing.
- Relationship or job changes.
- Financial difficulties or needing a home with lower running costs.
- Change of scenery or lifestyle.
- Moving from one country to another.

Sharing ownership

You can either own your property on your own (sole ownership) or enter into a contract with another party as a joint or co-owner. Decide whether you are buying on your own or sharing the purchase and ownership of the property with your family and friends. The legalities of co-ownership are complicated, so ask your conveyancer or solicitor to explain your rights to you before you commit to this arrangement.

Your property strategy

Once you have ascertained your reason for buying, consider what category of property you are looking to purchase and the budget you have.

A renovated property

You may pay more for the property, but this can be absorbed into the mortgage without you needing to find additional money for a refurbishment. You then have the luxury of enjoying a renovated property from the time you move in. The downside of this is that you may not like the colour scheme, but this can be individualised over time.

Chapter 1. BUYING YOUR PROPERTY

A refurbishment project

Do you have money set aside for this type of property, or is this a future, long-term project you are confident you will have sufficient income, budget or savings to cover? Depending on how run-down the property is, you may end up spending a lot more money and time on it than you expected to, especially if you are not experienced in assessing properties. Ensure you have a detailed survey done (this is detailed further in a later section). You may also wish to commission specific reports from tradesmen and professional bodies to further ascertain costs and the degree of work to be completed before you exchange. The upside is that you end up with exactly what you want and how you want it to look.

Buying a new property from a developer

You may wish to buy a new home from a property developer where you can benefit from your legal fees or Stamp Duty being paid as an incentive. You will also be the first to live in the property, you can generally select fixtures and fittings to your own taste (if you are purchasing early enough in the property development process) as well as benefit from lower energy bills. Repairs and redecoration should be minimal for several years and the property will come with guarantees and a National House-Building Council (NHBC) 10-year warranty. The downside is that you could be living on a building site until the entire development is completed. Also, the property might look good value, but may take some time to rise in value.

There may be issues with the mortgage as mortgage offers are typically valid for six months and your property in the new build development could exceed this timeframe. There may be snagging issues and faults with the property and / or fittings that need to be remediated, although the NHBC can step in within the first two years if the developer does not undertake this work. Ensure you purchase through a reputable developer by making use of online forums to investigate any known issues with development companies.

Rightsizing or change of area

If you are expecting to start a family, or have children who have outgrown their space, you could either be looking to extend your existing property or look to buy a larger property to move to. Similarly, if you have family members moving in with you, they will also need their own space, so you will need to consider upsizing or rightsizing your home to accommodate them. If your current neighbourhood no longer suits, or you want to move to a better school catchment area, you may choose to target a different neighbourhood.

Purchasing land to build your property on

This may be a good solution if you want to self-build or have your dream home built to your specifications. Keep in mind you will need to purchase the land, making sure that you check there is legal access to the land, and to water and sewage, or if you are required to obtain permits and make separate provisions for these. You will also need to secure the services of an architect, a builder, along with all the other elements of the build, e.g. plumbers, electricians and tilers. You will need to take into account the higher costs and longer timeframes required to build a house from scratch, as well as outgoings on accommodation in parallel to the build.

A retirement property

The reasons for downsizing are numerous. These include properties which have become too large to manage or are too geographically isolated, parents have become empty nesters because children have left home, or people wanting to move closer to family. People are now downsizing and moving into smaller homes whilst they are still able to manage the move themselves rather than relying on family members to help.

The stigma attached to retirement homes is not as it used to be. There are more and more developments being created now so there is a choice of flats, houses and bungalows for independent living where you can have shared communal areas like a garden, restaurant and library. If you are looking to retire, or downsize to a retirement property, areas that are relatively low in price could be attractive so keep a lookout for retirement hotspots. Some places allow you to keep a pet while others have good parking facilities as a lot of people will still be driving their own cars. Living in a retirement village also caters for later requirements so that as the need for care grows, the transition from independent living to more specialised care can be easily managed. There are different management fees associated with the facilities, so investigate these before fully committing to one. If you are looking for sheltered housing, you can contact Help the Aged in your area to find out about properties that may be suitable for your requirements.

A property to flip

Flipping is where you purchase a property with the objective of selling it at a profit as soon as possible. There is a natural tension between getting as much profit as possible versus selling it quickly so that your capital isn't tied up for long and you don't keep paying ongoing costs like Council tax and utilities. Educate yourself thoroughly, getting input from your solicitor and accountant, before you enter this market as there are a number of legislative rules around flipping real estate. Look into the Stamp Duty Land Tax (SDLT) surcharge, which was introduced in 2016 and is a 3% surcharge added to the stamp duty if you already own your own home (making this investment an additional property). Stamp duty and surcharges need to be paid within 30 days of completion or you will pay penalty charges and interest.

You will need to pay income tax on any capital gains when you sell the property, or even Capital Gains Tax (CGT) up to 40% if you have kept the property for a longer period (and already own your own residence). Be aware that if you have a mortgage on the property, you may need to pay early repayment charges if you sell the property before your mortgage end date. Also, real estate fees will need to be paid on the resale if you are using an agent. The combination of these can be hefty enough to make a large dent in your profit. Choose your mortgage carefully and include the length of time you will need to complete the sales process. If you are going to be entering the market to flip properties on a regular basis, reach an understanding with a real estate agent who may be willing to drop their fees in exchange for your continued business.

Buy-to-Let

There are various strategies under buy-to-let. Information is provided below to help you to identify your preferred scheme.

Buy-to-Let investment property: Short term lets

This is a lucrative market for landlords as there is a premium on the rental of short term lets, which can command up to 30% more than long-term lets. Short term lets are used by business travellers as much by holidaymakers.

But there is higher risk and more effort required to maintain short term lets, especially with the constant changeover. Before embarking on this, discuss it fully with the local council, including finding out what the restrictions are on minimum rental terms. If it's a leasehold property you are looking to let, ensure you also discuss this with the free-holder otherwise they can seek to stop you.

Investigate specialist short term let insurances as the usual buildings and contents insurance will not be sufficient. Find out about additional cover as well before proceeding, e.g. public liability and loss of income insurance. Once you have all your costs collated (including furniture and furnishing, utility bills, council tax and cleaning), you can make an informed decision as to whether this type of investment is right for you.

Air BnB

Air BnB has certainly been a major force in disrupting the market with this strategy. It is an online marketplace and hospitality service whereby people rent out their entire properties, or just spare rooms, for short term stays.

If you are looking to enter this short-term rental market, ensure you are up to date with all the costs. For every booking, Airbnb currently will take 3% commission from hosts, as well as between 6% and 12% from guests. And as a host, you will receive your money 24 hours after guests check in, even though they have paid in full at the time of booking.

Buy-to-Let investment property: Single-let

This type of property allows one tenancy and has an individual, couple or family renting one property solely for themselves. The benefits are influenced by the fluctuating costs (e.g. stamp duty changes and mortgage rate increases) but if you thoroughly research the property area, target market, available mortgage products and rental yields (which is the annual rent as a percentage of the purchase price of the property), and consequently buy appropriately, there is still a profit to be made.

Buy-to-Let investment property: HMOs

A Buy-to-Let property with a multi-let tenancy has at least 3 unrelated tenants sharing the communal lounge, kitchen and bathroom or just stairwells and landings. A large HMO is rented to 5 or more people who form more than 1 household, where the property is at least 3 storeys high and the tenants share toilet, bathroom or kitchen facilities.

Residential properties with multi-let tenancies are called Houses of Multiple Occupancy or Houses in Multiple Occupation (HMO). While the 1985 Housing Act introduced the concept of HMOs, these multi-lets have become more popular in recent years due to the realisation of increased rental income compared to the usual Buy-to-Let investment properties.

Check with your local Council whether you need a licence for renting out your HMO. If you are renting out a large HMO, you must have a licence valid for a maximum of 5 years for each HMO you are running. You can be prosecuted for running an unlicensed HMO as this is deemed a criminal offence.

Depending on how much work needs to be done to the property to convert it to an HMO or large HMO, you may need Council planning permission to be able to make specific changes or make the property habitable for more tenants. Check planning permissions and building regulations with your local Council as all councils don't have the same criteria, so there may be other things you need to consider to be compliant, e.g. ensure that a valid Gas Safety Certificate is sent to the Council each year and smoke alarms will need to be installed and safety certificates for electrical appliances must be available on request.

Resale and profit gains for Buy-to-Let properties

There are incentives from property developers to help you get into the Buy-to-Let market. However, unless you are a cash buyer, the mortgage on these types of properties is more difficult to obtain. Additionally, there is higher Stamp Duty attached to this investment.

Be diligent and thorough in doing your planning, looking into mortgage products and understanding the Buy-to-Let market, including return on investment (ROI) and yields. ROI is a calculation of the ratio between the net profit and cost of investment; a high ROI means your investment is more profitable. Gross yield (before costs) refers to the percentage annual return on your investment, calculated using one year's rental income divided by the cost of the property. Look out for competition from Airbnb property owners as there is an increase in short-term lets due to good returns; if the Government and HMRC introduce licencing and tax in this sector, this could lower the competition you face.

Resale and profit gains on your Buy-to-Let property can occur in diverse ways. Some of these are noted below:

- If you have purchased a property off-plan from a developer, you can sell your purchase contract when the build on the entire development has almost completed as prices are likely to have increased by then. Check that your contract can be assigned for resale otherwise you will not be able to flip this property. You can secure this investment on the payment of a deposit, with the balance payable when you take full ownership (completion of the purchase), and you will not need to obtain a mortgage until then. This means you won't need a mortgage at all if you sell before you pay for the full purchase price of the property; as well, you won't be paying for the stamp duty as you have not purchased the property in full.

- You can obtain bridging finance and sell the property before taking full ownership. The developer may be able to assist you with obtaining a buyer if there has been interest from other people following the sale of all the properties in the development, especially if you are looking to invest your profits with the same developer again. Developers have an interest in cultivating a waiting list of prospective purchasers as they move from completing one development to starting the next (or have several developments underway simultaneously).

Only take the calculated risks that you are prepared for – if you haven't found a buyer at the right price and can't really afford the mortgage at this stage of the purchase process, then this can turn your gain into a property flipping loss.

- Selling the property once you have completed the refurbishment. What you spend on a project like this is dependent on what the purchase price of the property is (along with other costs like stamp duty, purchase costs and insurance), what money you have remaining for refurbishment and what amount of profit you will deem acceptable after the sale.

Properties that have been partially completed before sale don't have as much appeal because buyers know that they will need to finish the work but are still paying over the odds as part of the refurbishment has been completed. These properties tend to sit around for longer than those which are tastefully and fully refurbished to a high specification. As well, prospective buyers are inclined to negotiate hard on the purchase price, especially if other properties on the market, similarly priced, illustrate that they are fully refurbished.

So, if this happens to be the case for you, you will need re-think what profit margin you will tolerate just to move the property on.

Buy to let re-mortgaging

The information in this sub-section is provided courtesy of Scodie Deyong LLP, Chartered Accountants.

The number of landlords looking to re-mortgage has risen to an all-time high, as many seek to mitigate higher tax costs.

A survey by Paragon of around 200 mortgage intermediaries found that as a proportion of the buy-to-let market, re-mortgaging increased from 49% in Q2 2018 to 57% in Q3 2018.

Meanwhile, the proportion of first-time landlords fell from 14% to 10%, and landlords looking to expand their portfolio declined from 23% to 19%.

Landlords have been hit by a series of tax changes in recent years, including the phased withdrawal of mortgage interest relief.

Chapter 1. BUYING YOUR PROPERTY

Before April 2017, landlords could offset their entire mortgage interest against rental profits, at which point the Government began phasing this out and replacing it with a phased in tax credit at the basic rate of income tax (20%).

In 2017/18, it was possible to deduct 75% of your mortgage interest. This went down to 50% in 2018/19 and will hit 25% in 2019/20, before being eliminated altogether by 2020/21.

John Heron, managing director of mortgages at Paragon, said:

"Landlords are investing less in the private rented sector which, in time, is going to make it more difficult for tenants to find a property at a rent they can afford. "Tax bills due in January 2019 will include the first-phase impact from the withdrawal of mortgage interest tax relief and landlords are preparing carefully for the next stages ahead."

Affordability and budget

Before you start the process of buying your home, it will be useful for you to plan ahead and consider the individual elements of the purchase. We have found planning to be a crucial part of our search for properties. Investing your time in planning is hugely beneficial as buying your home is the most expensive purchase you are ever likely to make. It's vital to investigate all the elements of your purchase before making a decision regarding your affordability and the property you will be happy to purchase.

You will also need to decide if you are going to use your existing property to fund your next one, either by selling it, or leveraging against it (releasing the equity or re-mortgaging it). If you are selling your existing property to fund your next purchase, ensure it has been valued as soon as possible so you are aware of your equity in your current property, and how much additional funding you will require for your next property.

It's advantageous to put your existing property on the market before you start searching for your next property. Otherwise you may find a property you really like, but potentially lose out on it because your own property remains unsold, or you are under pressure to take a lower price on your existing home as you have so much vested interest in the property you have identified, and you don't want to miss out. If your house is not on the market before you find your next property, it may delay your purchase. You may also not be a buyer of choice for a seller who wants a quick completion. However, most people are in a chain and this is not unusual.

Monthly costs

Your budget needs to take into account what you can afford to re-pay monthly as mortgage payments (if you are getting a mortgage), along with other monthly expenses, including building and contents insurance, utility bills, Council Tax and any parking fees or parking permits for each vehicle in the household, as well as living expenses.

Consider whether your monthly costs could be met by letting out a spare room. Be aware that if there is a change in the way your home is going to be used (i.e. rented out, as opposed to being owner-occupied), then your mortgage loan may need to be changed as different mortgage products apply to different types of housing. Discuss this with your mortgage provider in advance.

You could also investigate Government schemes for first home buyers and existing homeowners, e.g. Help-to-Buy or Shared Ownership.

Deposit

Confirm what your total budget is. Consider the deposit you will need to pay on exchange of contracts, which is usually 10% of the purchase price of the property. The seller may agree to a lesser amount of deposit being paid on exchange, but if you fail to complete the purchase, the seller is still entitled to receive 10% of the value of the property from you.

Stamp duty

Stamp duty is payable by you on the completion date of your property purchase and you will need to provide these funds to your solicitor. You may be able to negotiate on this to your advantage with some new-build developers. The amount of the Stamp Duty is according to the agreed purchase price of the property. Use an online Stamp Duty calculator to confirm the amount you need to pay your solicitor prior to completion.

Payments are all progressive (calculated on a tier basis) but vary throughout the UK:

- In England, the stamp duty thresholds range from £125,000 to £1.5 million. First-time home buyers do not pay stamp duty on the first £300,000 of their home purchase and they can claim a discount or relief of 5% on the portion from £300,001 to £500,000. For Buy-to-Let properties and second homes, purchases now attract an additional 3% stamp duty surcharge. Along with other new measures in place for lettings, the introduction of this surcharge on second properties has meant that landlords are no

- longer find smaller properties attractive and are therefore not competing as much in this market with home buyers.
- In Scotland, stamp duty has been replaced by the Land and Buildings Transaction Tax (LBTT) which is a progressive tax with thresholds ranging from £145,000 to £750,000. The Scottish Government has introduced a new tax relief, the First Time Buyer relief, and increased the initial LBTT threshold to £175,000 for first time buyers.
- In Wales, stamp duty has been replaced by a new Land Transaction Tax (LTT). LTT is also a progressive tax and has thresholds ranging from £180,000 to £1,500,000. No additional relief is available for first time buyers in Wales under the LTT scheme.

Survey costs

Property survey costs may need to be paid for when you proceed with an offer to purchase a property. Some mortgage providers pay for the basic valuation report or survey they require (to provide security against the mortgage loan) while others don't.

Depending on the state of the property, you may wish to request a more detailed report (a Condition Report, Homebuyers Report or a Building and Structural survey) so you will need to pay for this report yourself. Confirm the cost of your report of choice with the survey company before you proceed.

Conveyancing fees

Conveyancing is the process via which the title and ownership of your new home is legally transferred to you from the seller. Establish whether you will use a licenced conveyancer or a solicitor to undertake your property conveyancing. Licensed conveyancers are specialist property lawyers and are regulated by the Council for Licensed Conveyancers. solicitors are regulated by the solicitors Regulation Authority and offer other services e.g. representing you in court. They will both undertake the same conveyancing work. It may be costlier to instruct a solicitor rather than a licenced conveyancer, but if the purchase is complicated (e.g. if a leasehold property is involved) and there are issues that need to be resolved in court or require further expertise, a solicitor may be the appropriate choice.

We have used our local solicitor since 2001. He has completed the purchase and sale of all our properties in the UK. His conveyancing has always been thorough, timely and complete and he has always provided us with good advice.

Your conveyancing fees and the associated charges for buying your home will also be due before the completion of the purchase of your property. The associated charges include costs incurred when doing searches and making telegraphic transfer payments when completing your purchase. Ask your solicitor or conveyancer for an estimate. Some solicitors will cap the cost of the conveyancing, so it can assist you to budget if your solicitor is able to do this for you.

Contingency funds

Have some contingency money set aside in case there is an overrun on the costs during your purchase, e.g. in case you need to increase your offer or want to obtain a detailed survey report.

Credit score

Find out what your credit score is so that you are aware of any errors or anomalies, including those involving historical bank accounts and credit cards. You are then able to address or correct any issues in advance. A negative credit report can affect your chance to obtain a mortgage and affect the amount of interest you pay on a loan if you are perceived as a high-risk borrower. You can obtain a copy of your credit report from various online credit score companies, e.g. Experian. Ensuring that your credit score is high means you can have more confidence during the mortgage application process and a higher likelihood of having a positive outcome by securing a good mortgage product.

Mortgage providers

Determine in advance who will provide your mortgage. Investigate mortgage providers in the market, including your bank or building society, other banks and building societies offering competitive products, or use the services of an independent broker who can offer free advice and has access to a broad mortgage market (their fee is usually paid for by the mortgage provider, but you will need to confirm this beforehand).

> Your mortgage provider will require you to provide the following information when applying for a mortgage, so be prepared and have this available:
> - Proof of ID: a passport or driver's licence showing your photo.
> - Proof of address: utility bills or bank statements showing your current address
> - Proof of earnings: pay slips or company accounts

- Recent bank statement: usually dated within the last 3 months, though it could be as much as 6 months old (depending on your mortgage provider's requirements).

Mortgage in principle

Discuss obtaining a pre-qualified mortgage agreement or letter from your broker or mortgage provider. The aim of the document is to show that you have been assessed by your mortgage provider and that you are able to obtain a mortgage of up to a certain amount. This agreement is not a legal and binding contract – your mortgage will need to be appropriately qualified and quantified by your mortgage provider when you apply.

The mortgage will need to be issued against the specific property you wish to purchase, and this can only be done once you have identified the property. You will find this letter valuable when you get to the offer stage as it will show an advantage over other buyers if they are not similarly prepared, presenting you as a serious buyer in a good position.

The pre-qualified mortgage agreement is known by different names, e.g. Agreement in Principle (AIP), Decision in Principle (DIP) or Mortgage in Principle (MIP).

You will need to provide the proving documents to obtain this letter (i.e. confirmation of ID, address and income).

Mortgage products

There are numerous mortgage products in the market and these change on a frequent basis. There are different interest rates, terms and duration (years) offered with individual mortgages. Most mortgage products allow you to overpay by up to 10% annually without early repayment penalty. These overpayments may be subject to rules, e.g. the overpayments may only be made in a certain month, so check this out to ensure that you make your overpayments in time.

Ascertain which mortgage products you are eligible for e.g. fixed rate, variable rate, standard variable rate, tracker, offset, first home buyers, Buy-to-Let, etc. Ask your mortgage provider or broker to advise you of the advantages and disadvantages of each of the applicable products and see if you can narrow your choice to one product (you can always change your mind later when it comes to obtaining the actual mortgage loan). Often, the higher the deposit you can pay, the better the interest rate you can obtain from a mortgage provider.

Before you decide on your mortgage provider, find out what is being paid for, as well as what fees and charges you are expected to pay – this will help you to decide which mortgage provider you will approach for a mortgage.

Below is a summary of the of the types of mortgages available in the market:

MORTGAGE PRODUCTS
Variable-Rate Mortgages - Tracker Mortgage The interest rate of your mortgage product tracks the Bank of England base rate (currently 0.5%). As an example, if your mortgage rate is 3.5% plus the base rate of 0.5%, your total mortgage rate will be 4%. In the current mortgage market, you will likely take out a tracker mortgage with a deal for an introductory period. After this, you will be moved on to your lender's Standard Variable Rate. There are a few lifetime tracker mortgages where your mortgage rate will track the Bank of England's base rate for the full mortgage term.
Variable-Rate Mortgages - Discount Mortgage You pay the lender's Standard Variable Rate with a fixed amount at a discounted rate. For example, if your lender's standard variable rate was 3.5% and your mortgage had a 1.5% discount, you'd pay 2%. Discounted mortgage deals can be stepped, you might take out a three-year deal but pay one rate for six months and then a higher rate for the remaining 2.5 years. Some variable rates have a collar, which is a rate below which they cannot fall, or are capped at a rate that they cannot go above.
Standard Variable Rate Mortgages Each lender has its own Standard Variable Rate (SVR) that it can set at it's own level. It is not directly linked to the Bank of England's base rate. The average SVR at the start of April 2018 was 4.99% which is higher than most mortgage products on the market. Lenders can change their SVR at any time. If you are currently on an SVR mortgage, your payments could go up. When a fixed, tracker or discount mortgage product completes, it is most likely that you will be automatically transferred to your mortgage lender's SVR.
Fixed Rate Mortgages With fixed-rate mortgages, you pay the same interest rate for the entire mortgage product period, regardless of interest rate changes elsewhere.
Interest-only and Repayment Mortgages With an interest only mortgage, you only pay interest on your mortgage. The monthly repayments are cheaper but you will not have paid off any capital at the end of your mortgage term. With a repayment mortgage, you pay off the money you borrowed.
MORTGAGE FEATURES TO CONSIDER
Flexible Mortgages Flexible mortgages allow you to overpay as well as underpay. You can take payment holidays and make lump sum withdrawals. You can also pay off your mortgage early and save on interest. Many mortgage products allow you to pay off up to 10% more each year. Other types of flexible mortgages include offset mortgages, which is where your savings are used to offset the amount of your mortgage you pay interest on each month. Alternatively, current account mortgages combine your current account, savings and mortgage into one, so all your credit balances offset your mortgage debt. Flexible mortgage products can be more expensive.
Offset Mortgages An offset mortgage can be linked to one or multiple banks or savings accounts. With a standard mortgage, your mortgage lender calculates the interest you owe based on the total amount you have borrowed. With an offset mortgage, the interest calculation is based on the total amount borrowed minus however much is held in the linked account(s). Offset mortgages typically come with slightly higher interest rates than ordinary repayment mortgages.
Cash Back Mortgages Some mortgage deals offer you cash back when you take them out. The deals are not always the cheapest once you have factored in the fees and the interest rate you are expected to pay.

Definitions of fixed and variable rates

The mortgage rates are further defined below for clarity:

- Fixed rate mortgages: the rate is guaranteed not to change during the term of your mortgage. You always know what your repayments are, and you will have the same outgoings each month during the term of your mortgage.

- Variable rate mortgages: the rate will change during your mortgage term, so it will either increase or decrease. These mortgages can be cheaper, but your repayments are impacted by changes made by your lender on the Standard Variable Rate (SVR) and when the Bank of England (BoE) base rate changes. The changes are dependent on the economic cycle we are in, but your repayment is most likely to increase. The following are the main types of variable rate mortgages:

    o Tracker Mortgages: these follow the BoE's Base Rate (e.g. 0.50%) plus a percentage set by your mortgage lender (e.g. 4.0%), making your tracker mortgage 4.5% for your chosen term (e.g. 5 years).

    o Lifetime Tracker mortgages: these will track the BoE Base Rate for the full term of the mortgage.

    o Variable rate mortgages: follow the SVR of your mortgage provider. SVRs differ from lender to lender because the rate is set by each individual lender and not linked to the BoE base rate. SVRs can also change at any time.

    o Discount mortgages: follow the SVR which is then discounted for your particular mortgage product so that you are not paying the full SVR.

Repayment and interest only mortgages

With repayment mortgages, you pay off your entire mortgage loan by the end of the mortgage period. With interest only mortgages, you only pay interest on your borrowing for the mortgage period, with the capital still due at the end of your mortgage term. Interest only mortgages are much cheaper than repayment mortgages. You will need to show your lender that you have sufficient funds, assets or pension to pay off the capital when it's due at the end of your interest only mortgage term.

Flexible mortgages

Flexible mortgages can allow you to underpay, have payment holidays and make withdrawals. They are more expensive than traditional products. They include the following offset mortgages: Current account mortgages, where your current and savings account are added together, and your mortgage payment is offset against this amount.

Offset mortgages

An offset mortgage can be linked to one or multiple banks or savings accounts. With a standard mortgage, your mortgage lender calculates the interest you owe based on the total amount you have borrowed. Interest calculation is based on the total amount borrowed minus however much is held in the linked account(s). Offset mortgages typically come with slightly higher interest rates than ordinary repayment mortgages.

Cash back mortgages

Cash back mortgages are where your lender will give you some cash back in exchange for taking a particular mortgage product. These mortgages are also relatively expensive because they incur interest and fees. Add up the total cost of the mortgage before committing yourself so you know what you are expected to repay.

Buy-to-Let mortgages

Most Buy-to-Let mortgages are generally interest only. You are not paying off the capital, so the cost of repayment is lower and limited to the monthly mortgage interest. As you will still not own the property at the end of the mortgage term, you will need to re-mortgage further, sell the property or find other monies to pay off the mortgage. You should be able to claim a percentage of your mortgage interest against your tax.

Lenders will usually look at your potential rental income, rather than your salary or wages, to decide whether you can afford the loan. However, if it is your first Buy-to-Let mortgage, they may look at income from your employment as well.

Because Buy-to-Let mortgages are riskier for lenders, you will generally need a bigger deposit than with residential mortgages, typically a minimum of 25%, although many of the best Buy-to-Let mortgage products require a 40% deposit. The rates for these types of mortgages can vary and are dependent on how much risk exists, how much deposit is available and how strong your credit score is. These mortgages are only issued when a bank or building society thinks they are affordable. An affordability calculator is used that assesses your personal income, along with the expected rental income, against the value of the property. Most lenders will require the expected annual rental income to equate to at least 125% of the annual mortgage repayments.

Help-to-Buy mortgages and loans

The Government has a Help-to-Buy property ownership scheme (launched in April 2013) which includes, amongst others, incentives under 'Equity Loans' and 'Shared Ownership'. Educate yourself on the latest costs, criteria and benefits. Determine how well these incentives will work for you in your geographical location. Investigate house price growth in the area to confirm that the particular incentive scheme you are considering is working positively and will benefit you, and that previous buyers within the scheme have not been pushed into negative equity.

As things change regularly, refer to the Government's website as well as other links in the Useful links and resources Chapter of this book, and complete your research before you make any commitments. This will also help you to ascertain the types of housing available under these schemes (leasehold or newly built homes) as well as confirm exactly when the payment to the Government is due after the interest-free period is up.

Most lenders will offer Help-to-Buy mortgages. The following are some of the schemes currently available:

Mortgage Guarantee Scheme

The Mortgage Guarantee element of Help-to-Buy was designed to give those first-time buyers and home movers with a small deposit an improved likelihood of obtaining a mortgage. Under the scheme, buyers only needed to raise 5% of the property value, while the government provided a guarantee to the mortgage lender for up to a further 15%. This gave banks and building societies the peace of mind to lend larger mortgages. This guarantee scheme was closed to new applicants in December 2016.

Equity Loan Scheme

The Help-to-Buy Equity Loan scheme is designed for those first-time buyers and home movers with a deposit of at least 5% buying a new-build home worth less than £600,000 (£300,000 in Wales). The Government will lend you up to 20% of the property price and this loan is interest-free for the first five years. The loan allows you to access cheaper mortgage products as you only need to borrow 75% of the purchase price of the property (the maximum you can borrow). This scheme only applies in England and Wales and is scheduled to run until 2021.

The amount you owe the Government will need to be repaid when the mortgage matures, or if you sell the property. The 20% repayment amount depends on the property's value at the time the mortgage is settled. Interest payments are paid on the initial amount you borrowed, and not on the repayment amount at the maturity of the mortgage.

Your local Help-to-Buy agent will be able to assist you with the following:

- Your initial property search.
- The interest rate that is applied from year 6, along with the other measures that relate to the rate for every year of your mortgage after year 6. Measures include the Retail Price Index (RPI) and the percentage point added.
- Approvals for any changes or alterations that you make to the property (you will need to request permission beforehand).
- Approval for the price you sell your property for.

London Help-to-Buy

From the 1st February 2016 the Government increased the London Help-to-Buy Equity Loan scheme's upper limit for loans from 20% to 40% for buyers in all the boroughs within London. These loans are available to first time buyers as well as homeowners looking to move to another property. The criteria for securing the loan is that the home you want to buy must be a new build with a maximum price of £600,000.

You will be required to provide a 5% deposit on a newly built home and the Government will provide an equity loan for up to 40% of the purchase price. Properties under the scheme cannot be sublet or be used for a part exchange deal on your old home. Under this scheme, you must not own any other property at the time you buy your new home.

Financial institutions offering London Help-to-Buy loans are:

Aldermore	Lloyds	Santander
Bank of Scotland	Nationwide	Teachers Building Society
Barclays	NatWest	
Halifax	Newcastle Building Society	TSB
Leeds Building Society	Royal Bank of Scotland	

Chapter 1. BUYING YOUR PROPERTY

The London scheme is run by the Help-to-Buy London agent, appointed by the Government. They are available to take you through your purchase, from providing general information as well as dealing with your application. The Help-to-Buy London website provides the information you need for the agents and the schemes.

Scotland Help-to-Buy

If you want to buy a new build home in Scotland but cannot afford the total cost, you may be able to obtain help through the Help-to-Buy (Scotland) Affordable New Build scheme which is available for first time buyers as well as for existing homeowners. It assists you with up to 15% of the purchase price of a new build home. There are two types of Help-to-Buy (Scotland) scheme:

- The Affordable New Build scheme.
- The Smaller Developer scheme.

Both schemes work in the same way, and the Buy-to-Let agent who handles the schemes will tell you which one you need to apply for (depending on the home you wish to buy). You will need to submit your application no more than 9 months in advance of the date you expect to finish buying the property.

If you apply to the scheme, you will need to ensure the following:

- Your mortgage and deposit cover a combined minimum 85% of the total purchase price.
- Your mortgage is not an interest only mortgage.
- Your loan is a repayment mortgage for at least 25% of the purchase price.
- The value of the new build doesn't exceed the maximum threshold price of the scheme.
- Before you apply to the scheme, you have spoken to either a lender or an independent financial adviser.

You will be required to pay a minimum of 85% of the home's total purchase price. The Scottish Government will enter into a shared equity agreement with you and it will hold the remaining % share. You will have the complete title to your home and your name will be on the title deeds, but there will be a mortgage on the home to make sure the Scottish Government's share is protected.

If you want to buy a new build home in Scotland using the Help-to-Buy scheme, the property purchase price cannot be more than the threshold price. The threshold price is £200,000 for the financial years 2018 to 2021.

If you want to apply for funding through the Help-to-Buy scheme in Scotland, you will need to contact a participating home builder in the first instance. Then speak with either a lender directly, or to an independent financial adviser, who will discuss your current financial position and your ability to obtain a mortgage.

There are currently the following 9 lenders offering mortgages for the Help-to-Buy scheme:

Barclays Glasgow Credit Union Leeds Building Society	Lloyds Banking Group Nationwide Scotwest Credit Union	Skipton Building Society TSB Virgin Money

You will need to reserve the home and get a full reservation agreement by the builder. (you may need to pay a reservation fee). Then, apply for funding through the administering agent for your area. You can visit the Help-to-Buy Scotland website for further details.

Armed Forces Help-to-Buy

Armed forces personnel can take advantage of the Forces Help-to-Buy scheme, which is a £200 million scheme made available to assist them with getting on the property ladder. To enable Armed Forces personnel to buy their first home or move to another property on assignment, they can borrow up to 50% of their annual salary up to a maximum of £25,000 and this is interest free. This borrowing can be used towards their deposit and any other costs and fees, e.g. for solicitors and estate agents.

Those eligible to use the scheme include all regular personnel who have completed the required length of service and have more than 6 months left to serve at the time they apply. They also need to meet the right medical categories.

Service personnel can apply for the loan online through the Joint Personnel Administration system. They can also seek advice through their chain of command and personnel agency in relation to their application.

ISA

If you are saving to purchase your first home, the government will top up your ISA savings by 25%, up to £3,000. If you are buying with someone else, they can also get a Help-to-Buy ISA (which you do not have to pay back). The first payment you make to your ISA can be up to £1,200 and then up to £200 each month. When you purchase your property, your solicitor will apply for the extra

25%. To be eligible for this, the home you purchase must have a purchase price of up to £250,000 (or up to £450,000 in London). It must also be the only home you own where you intend to live. You can use the scheme with an equity loan.

Starter Homes Initiative

The Government has announced a new Starter Homes Initiative in England that aims to help young first-time buyers purchase a home with a minimum 20% discount off the market price. Buyers will need to be aged between 23 and 40, will need a mortgage and have a maximum household income of £80,000 (£90,000 in London). This initiative will enable first-time buyers to purchase new homes priced up to £250,000, or £450,000 in London, at below market value.

Many of the new homes will be built on underused or unviable brownfield land (vacant space that has previously been used for industrial or commercial purposes), which the government will release to developers free from planning costs.

Shared ownership

Shared ownership properties are sold through housing associations. These types of properties are for people who would like to own their own home but cannot afford to buy on the open market. They are leasehold properties with a monthly service charge. You buy a stake in a property between 25% and 75% of the property's value, using a deposit and a mortgage. You pay rent on the remaining share, which is owned by the local housing association. The amount of rent you pay can be up to 3% of the housing association's share of the property's value.

Anyone with a household income of less than £80,000 outside London (£90,000 inside London), is eligible to buy a shared ownership home if they fit the following criteria:

- A first-time buyer.
- An existing shared owner.
- Owned a home previously, but now cannot afford to buy one.

If you are aged 55, or over, you can buy up to 75% of your home through the Older People's Shared Ownership (OPSO) scheme. Once you own 75% of the property, you will not pay rent on the rest.

Disabled people can apply for a scheme called Home Ownership for people with a Long-Term Disability (HOLD), if other Help-to-Buy scheme properties do not meet their needs (such as the need for a ground floor property). With this scheme you can buy up to 25% of your home and you can also apply for the general shared ownership scheme and own up to 75% of your home.

It is possible to buy a greater share of your property at any time from the housing association, and this is called 'staircasing'. The cost of increasing your share will depend on the current market value of the property. To staircase, you will need to pay for the housing association to carry out a valuation of the property. You will need to make sure you have the cash or mortgage finance in place to pay for the extra share.

Each housing association will have different rules, but if you do want to staircase, you will generally have to buy a 10% share as a minimum. If you want to buy a share of more than 10%, that is possible as long as it is in 5% increments (e.g. 15%, 20%, 25% and so on). Many housing associations will only permit you staircase up to three times. Some housing associations will only allow you to staircase a third and final time if you intend to buy the entire remaining share of the property. This would take your ownership up to 100% of the property and you are effectively buying the housing association out.

If you own a share of your home, the housing association has the right to have first refusal to buy it. They also have the right to find a buyer for your home. You can sell your shared ownership property at any time, but the housing association has the right to try to find a buyer before you put it on the open market. The amount that you and the housing association will receive from the sale will depend on the current market value of the property. If you own 100% of your property, then you can sell it yourself.

For the information on any of the schemes, refer to the Government's Help-to-Buy website.

Comparison sites are also useful for investigations into the right mortgage for you as they provide information on the various mortgage products in the market. There are a number of these, including Moneyfacts, Money Saving Expert and Compare the Market. Once you have identified the product you are interested in on the comparison website, contact the actual mortgage provider directly to ensure that you have the most up-to-date information.

Detail your property requirements

> As part of planning the purchase of our new home, we always write a list of detailed requirements for what we must have and what would be nice to have in our new property. This helps us to determine, very quickly, if properties meet our needs or not. The list is an active document and is refined and updated as we proceed with our viewings. Sometimes we see something we like in a property that we had not previously considered, so we add this to our list. Conversely, there may be things we come across that we don't like, so again, we refine our requirements. An example of this is when we viewed two properties on a desired street where the property on one end of the street was on very steep incline, whereas the property at the other end was on a flat stretch of road. We refined our requirements by including flat access and excluded properties within a certain house number range on that road.

Decide on what your requirements are and confirm your prioritised list of must-haves, along with a list of nice-to-haves, for your desired location, property type and budget:

- *What is your price range for the deposit you have?* For some properties and mortgage products, you may be able to put down a smaller deposit and can therefore afford to purchase a better property (though your monthly mortgage repayments will be higher, so you will need to take your affordability into consideration).
- *What is the upper limit of your monthly costs?* Council tax, as well as home and contents insurance, may be affected by a change in location. Do you have Automatic Payments or Direct Debits that will be on-going after you have purchased your property, and if so, have you taken these into account? Can you afford an increase in mortgage payments compared to what you are currently paying in rent or mortgage?
- *Which location do you work in and how far would you be willing to travel from your home?* Once you move into your new home, there will still be the daily travel to your workplace and you want to ensure that the distance doesn't become an issue, so make proximity to transport links or motorway access a must-have if you need them to be easily accessible.
- *Which location would you prefer to buy in?* What areas do you wish to consider extending your search to if you cannot find a property within your budget or in your desired location? Desired areas with dream properties may not be reasonably priced so you may have to look at the next best thing you can afford.

- *Will you buy a freehold or leasehold property?* Dealing with freehold properties is easier than leasehold properties. With leasehold, there are several additional, complicated and lengthy processes, arrangements and management structures to consider and administer the purchase through. This can also impact your solicitor's time and costs. We initially withdrew our offer on a property that had leasehold attachments (along with another 35 properties), but the sellers were prepared to convert these to freehold by merging the leasehold and freehold titles, so we proceeded to purchase the property.

- *What style and size of home and garden are you looking to buy?* Is it a flat, terraced, semi-detached, detached, cottage, bungalow or retirement home? Ascertain if stairs are going to be an issue for any members of your household as this could direct you to purchasing a bungalow or a flat; otherwise, check that you have the space to install a lift or fit a stairlift. Decide if you want a large garden for children to play in, or ample outdoor entertaining space, or a modest and low maintenance space outside.

- *How many bedrooms do you need in your home?* Will young children be sharing bedrooms? If you have people staying over regularly, you may want to have a permanent guest room set up.

- *Do you have other dependants who have specific requirements or special needs?* Disabled or elderly relatives may need ground level accommodation.

- *Does the property allow you to live the way you would like to?* Decide on the layout you prefer, e.g. check that there are open-plan living spaces, large windows / doors opening out to the back garden, or a south-facing garden you can spend time in during most of the year; confirm that there is easy access onto the property and ascertain if it has sufficient storage, out buildings or an external home office that you may require. Also verify that there is adequate parking and garaging available on or near the property. You may wish to develop the property later, so check that there is potential to extend.

- *Do you wish to live in a bustling locality with a café culture or are you noise sensitive and require a quiet environment?* Be alert to loud music, barking dogs, intrusive noise through party walls, etc. We asked the sellers at one of the properties that we later bought whether they knew of any noise issues. It turned out that there were noise issues, and these emanated from their own dogs which the neighbouring households had complained about and were pleased to see the back of!

- *Do you have children who are have particular schooling requirements?* Are there schools that fulfil their needs in the catchment area you are looking to purchase in and move to? This may be one of those requirements you may not be prepared to compromise on. If it is an investment property you are looking to buy, keep in mind that your rental market may be swayed by the same decision process to determine whether they rent from you or not. We always purchase properties close to transport links and in catchments areas for the best possible schools in the area to ensure that we appeal to a wider audience when the time comes to sell.

- *When do you expect to move?* If there an urgency to your move, or a date you must move by (e.g. for the start of the academic year), determining this in advance will help with your property search start, exchange and purchase completion dates.

Start your property search

Determine whether you really know the area local which you are looking to purchase in, or if it will take you time to become familiar with it. When we are unfamiliar with an area, we take several drives and walks around the vicinity of the property to locate the streets that we will be happy living in. And to get a feeling for the neighbourhood, we often start up conversations with people in our desired streets. When we view properties that we are interested in pursuing, we take time to speak to the neighbours to obtain their view of the neighbourhood and local area.

We do a lot of research to determine if prices have risen or fallen in the last 5 years in our preferred location. We find out what has sold, when, and for how much in neighbouring streets. We investigate crime rates and transport links as well as where schools and other local amenities (e.g. libraries, banks and supermarkets) are located in relation to our desired neighbourhood.

We also look into areas that are undergoing upgrades and are having (or have planned) infrastructure improvements to new industries, housing developments, schools, supermarkets or transport infrastructure. Be aware of projects such as such as the new Crossrail Elizabeth line in London, the HS2 route and whether there will be a station close to your desired location. From late 2019, the Great Western mainline electrification will result in 57 trains in service, which means areas like Bath and Bristol will have faster journey times into London and these trains will also hold an increased number of passengers. Both these upgrades provide an option of a daily commute into London to home buyers in these areas and can impact the quality of your life and property values.

Use websites such as Findahood, Propertytribes, Streetcheck and Crime-Statistics to obtain information on crime rates, house prices and population density in the area.

Use local professionals

While there can be a cost benefit for using service providers in lower cost areas, we have found that using professionals based in the area local to where you are looking to buy is more useful as they have information and know details about the location that those outside the area may not be aware of. These include mortgage providers, real estate agents, surveyors, solicitors and licenced conveyancers (for the purposes of this book, we will use the term *solicitors* to cover both *solicitors* and *licenced conveyancers*). The benefit of this is that they can all engage with each other quickly and easily. So where possible, use local professionals.

Identify a local solicitor to undertake the conveyancing work for your property purchase. While the conveyancing process doesn't start until your offer is accepted by the seller, you may wish to prepare in advance and choose a solicitor beforehand so that you can contact them and ask if they will represent you. They can also provide you with information on fees and costs and you can use this information to update your budget. The Law Society and Rated Solicitors are useful for locating a local solicitor.

Local surveyors are also useful as they are likely to know the history and local considerations (e.g. whether the property is in a conservation area). Your mortgage provider may instruct a specific company to survey the property, e.g. Esurv for property valuation purposes. The survey company will provide a surveyor who is as local as possible to the area. If you have concerns about the property, you may wish to go further and advise the same survey company to conduct a more detailed survey (e.g. a Homebuyer's Report) than what is being requested by your mortgage provider, which is a simple survey for valuation purposes. The survey company can then plan to conduct both surveys simultaneously as this is a more efficient use of time. The additional survey will need to be paid for by you, so ensure that you have put aside money for this. Contact the surveyor beforehand and find out what their lead times are on conducting surveys.

It is also useful to contact the local branch of your mortgage provider where possible. This is beneficial in case you wish to discuss your application or deliver documents (rather than mailing) to clarify or hasten the process during your purchase. Dealing with specific people at your local branch can help to build relationships. You can then refer back to these precise individuals if there are any issues as your application details will be known to them, rather than explaining your situation several times to different people who may be based in a call centre and have little knowledge of your particular application.

Speak with local estate agents who can assist you with providing local area information. Additionally, speak with locals and potential neighbours so you can gather more information to help you to assess the neighbourhood and local area.

Register your interest

Once you have confirmed your preferred location and property requirements, share this with the agents, sellers and / or property developers you are engaging with so that they are aware of your crucial requirements. They can also work with you to meet your budget and any necessary dates or advise if there are any issues as you progress with your home search and purchase with them.

You can register your interest as follows:

- *Existing networks* – inform your family, friends, work colleagues and associates that you are looking to purchase a home and the locations you are interested in. They may hear of properties that could be of interest to you.

- *Real estate agents* – visit local agencies so that you can meet the agents and convey your requirements to them face-to-face. This familiarises both you and the agency staff and starts to build relationships. You have more chance of being top-of-mind when a property suiting your needs comes up. We work to build good relationships with the local agents and keep in touch with them regularly during our search for a new home.

Discuss with the agents your specific needs, rather than your dream property. Use your list of detailed requirements for the agent to best assist you. Also show the agents proof of your pre-qualified mortgage agreement from your mortgage provider as this provides evidence of you being in a strong position to have your mortgage approved. It also shows that you have planned ahead and are a serious buyer. If you are looking for a property as a Buy-to-Let investment, ask the agent to provide or recommend a lettings service who you can engage with. You can then enter into a dialogue with the letting's professionals about potential lettings, expected rental for the type of properties in the area you are considering, as well as what services they can provide you. This will assist you in creating a relationship with the agency, as well as confirming what rental you can expect to achieve for the area, budget and type of property you are considering.

- *Online* – register your details on as many property search engines and websites as possible. These include Rightmove as well as sites like Emoov (which is a fixed-fee agency). While registering your interest on the sites, set up your property alerts according to the urgency of your requirement (e.g. as soon as properties are registered, or every 24 hours, etc).
- *Auctions* – if you can act fast, then you may wish to consider buying at an auction. If this is the way forward for you, familiarise yourself with the auction process, attend a few auctions and find out what is expected of you if you make a winning bid. You will then know how the system works and what the costs and commitments are. Auctioneers in the UK include Auction House and Allsop.
- *Private sales* – you can also buy your home privately instead of going through estate agencies. The main advantage is that the seller has no agent's commission to pay and may be more negotiable on the asking price. The disadvantage is that without an agent involved, there is no middle person driving your purchase through to completion and dealing with the links in a chain (if there is one). Houseweb and Houseladder are examples of websites where the private sales of properties are listed.

Consider extending your search area if you can't find anything within your budget and preferred location.

Viewing properties

When you have shortlisted the properties you are interested in, re-check that your budget aligns with the price of the property, along with your monthly costs (e.g. Council tax and home / contents insurance, which may be affected by a change in location).

Do your research

We use Google Maps, Google Earth and Streetview to obtain an initial perspective of the individual properties we are interested in and to identify any obvious issues with access, available parking, what the neighbourhood looks like, whether the property is under pylons, near nightclubs, noisy bars, cafés, takeaway shops, noisy roads, refuse / recycling station, industrial premises or any other impediments. This saves you time and effort and will assist to confirm your decision to proceed with the viewings.

To ensure you don't waste time viewing an unsuitable property, check the following:

- If it's in the right catchment for your preferred schools via the Admissions Day website.
- Whether it's near required amenities and transport links.
- If the property is on a flight path by using Webtrak.
- Whether it is in a conservation area.
- If the property is in a flood zone.

These investigations will help you to refine requirements and assist with deciding which properties to view. An example of this is when we found a great property in a wonderful location, but it was near an electricity pylon and a sub-station, so we didn't view it.

Decide how much time you can fit in for viewings and whether you can do these during the week or in the weekends only. If you are only available on weekends to view, it would be prudent to ask someone to view on your behalf during the week and provide you with feedback. This will ensure that the agent keeps you in the loop if an immediate offer on the property is made. We have missed out on viewing properties that went under offer within a few days of being presented to the market as we were unavailable to view immediately.

We view properties at different times of the day, and on different days of the week, to assess the neighbourhood, traffic density and road noise. Driving past your preferred property over several evenings is useful for checking out noise from neighbours, e.g. if there are (late) band practices or frequent parties at the home of someone who could be your immediate neighbour, it may be an issue for you which could influence your decision to proceed further. If you already have queries about the property, note these and take them with you so that you remember to ask the agent or the seller during the viewing.

Assess the property exterior

Plan time during your viewing to assess the exterior of the property to check the following:

- If the property environment suits you (i.e. a quiet area or if there are unacceptable levels of noise from party walls, neighbours, loud music and barking dogs).

- Parking and pedestrian access onto the front of the property, as well as access to the rear of the property.
- The condition of the drains and gutters and whether they are damaged, as well as signs of overflowing and damp staining.
- Obvious signs of subsidence (where the ground sinks) which may show as cracks near doors and windows and on walls.
- The state of the roof, whether there are any damaged or missing tiles, and the condition of the chimney to ensure it's not damaged or leaning.
- The potential to extend the property if required.

When viewing a property, the condition of the garden and outbuildings can often be overlooked because there is so much to take in. So, keep a note of these by examining the condition of the garden, outbuildings and any basement space.

If there is work to be done, then take this into account where your purchase price or renovation budget is concerned. You may even choose to make the property purchase subject to certain work being completed by the sellers so that the external property is in a condition you can enjoy when you move in. For example, there may be large patches of dead grass which need to be replaced, or a dilapidated shed to be removed, or even a shed to be installed (along with the appropriate base it would need to sit on). All these cost money as well as time and effort to be completed. So, take these into consideration when you get to the stage of making an offer because it's likely that the external area will be neglected once you have purchased the property as all your time, money and effort will go into the internal requirements of your home.

When friends of ours purchased their home, they decided not to have any parties until they had smartened up their garden. Unfortunately, due to a change in their work circumstances and personal lives, they didn't have the funds for their garden, and it's been a number of years since they purchased their home. This is not unusual because money and effort usually go into the interior of the property before work on the exterior is visited.

Also check the neighbouring properties and how well these are maintained. If drains and gutters are blocked, it could impact the property you are viewing.

We constantly refer to our detailed requirements and use our Buying Checklist to ensure that enough of our needs are being met in the properties that we are viewing. If we find that the current list of properties doesn't meet our needs, we

Chapter 1. BUYING YOUR PROPERTY

re-assess our requirements, along other properties that we have selected to view, and refine our list. We also advise the agents of any changes that we have made and update our online preferences.

Inspect the property interior

When you are inside the property, check the following:
- The general condition of the property and décor, and whether there is work required to repair or renovate.
- Damp smells, patches of damp, recently painted or wallpapered areas as these could be masking existing damp in walls, floors or ceilings.
- The age of the boiler and the condition of the radiators, as well as the location and number of radiators in the property. Check that there is a radiator in each room otherwise it could be a very cold house in winter.
- The condition of the windows, any condensation and whether they will need replacing.
- The amount of insulation within the property, including the roof space and walls.
- The state of the kitchen and bathroom, and whether these will need to be replaced.
- The flow rate of the water by turning on a tap on each level of the property.
- The condition and type of appliances included in the sale of the property (e.g. the cooker or fridge / freezer) and whether any of these will need replacing imminently.
- The amount of daylight in the property and direction of the sun.
- The amount of storage available throughout the property, especially in the kitchen, bedrooms, bathroom and loft.
- The mobile phone signal quality (in case you need to get broadband fitted and / or change service providers).
- Anything else that is on your requirements list that you deem critical or important.

All this is expected to be picked up in a survey if you proceed, but this early assessment may determine whether you make an offer or not. It may also affect how much you are prepared to offer if there are repairs and maintenance that will require investment after you purchase the property.

It is challenging to ascertain the size of a room, the entirety of the space available, and the layout of rooms if a floor plan is not provided. Sellers are not always keen to spend money to pay for a floor plan to be drawn up, so if you are particularly interested in the property, ask the agent if the seller will provide a floor plan. Otherwise, you may choose to pay for one yourself if this helps you to make the right decision about the property.

It can be difficult to visualise how you will live in a property if it is empty when you view it. We use measurements of our furniture and fittings, along with paper templates of the width, depth and height of the larger pieces of furniture (e.g. beds, wardrobes, sofas, dining table and chairs) to assist us during our viewings. We place the templates on the floor to confirm how and where our furniture and fittings will be placed in a room, as well as throughout the property, and how much space these will take up.

The use of the templates is also valuable in illustrating the movement in a room and whether there will be a natural, easy flow. If your furniture and fittings are too small or too large for the property, this exercise will also help you to develop your shopping list of items you may need to purchase to live comfortably in your new home. We find that on moving day, we can put items into their designated places without wasting time thinking about where things will go.

Full disclosure requirements

Caveat Emptor (*let the buyer beware*) is not an effective defence for the seller or the agent. It is no longer up to the buyer to ask the questions and the seller or their agent to give honest answers. The Consumer Protection Against Unfair Trading Regulations (CPRs) now require a seller to inform their estate agent, and any potential buyer, of material information that may affect a buyer's decision. This refers to buying a property as well as a potential buyer's decision to view a property.

Estate agents are required to reveal any material information that they are aware of or should be aware of. For instance, if a previous sale has fallen through because of defects that came up on a survey, they must disclose this. The agent cannot make misleading statements or fail to mention key information that could influence a buyer's decision.

Some sellers may consider being economical with the truth, but this can backfire even after a seller has moved out. An example of this is when a seller states there are no issues with a neighbour when there is actually an ongoing dispute, such as with a boundary. This is likely to come up in the conveyance process, but if this does not come to light until after the new buyer has moved in, the buyer may still have recourse to the seller.

Chapter 1. BUYING YOUR PROPERTY

If the seller is aware of major works carried out on the property before they purchased it, and states that no works have been carried out while they have owned the property, this can be considered a misrepresentation and the seller can be legally prosecuted.

To protect all parties in the transaction, provide and obtain as much communication, and as many agreements as possible, electronically or in writing (emails, texts and letters) rather than relying on verbal discussions and agreements.

Pre-offer due diligence

Don't feel pressured or bullied into making an offer to purchase a property until you are ready and certain that the property is the right one for you. It's very easy to get caught up in the emotions of the purchase, but stand your ground, be clear about your requirements, and try and make the right decisions for yourself and your family calmly and professionally.

Sites like Nethouseprices provide information on houses for sale and those sold. They inform you of prices paid for individual properties previously and the date the properties were last sold. This information can be used to confirm if prices have risen or fallen in your desired street. Undertake a comprehensive appraisal of the property you are intending to purchase before making your offer.

Initial checks

Ask the agent for comparable examples of similar properties in the location of your intended purchase: either those homes which are currently on the market, or preferably those that have sold recently where the sold prices are not yet publicly available. You can then make an informed decision about your offer price.

Ascertain if the property is listed (you can check this with English Heritage). Any changes that you may wish to make to a listed property will be scrutinised by the local Council, and you will need to budget for the cost of those changes. It may also impact on the types of mortgage products available to you and the insurance premiums you need to pay.

Also investigate if the property is in a conservation area. If so, additional planning controls and considerations may be required if you want to work on the exterior of the building, or cut down, top or lop any trees on the property if the trees are affected by a Tree Preservation Order.

Calculate the cost per square foot of the property (the sale price of the property divided by the square footage). Check that it is in line with similar properties sold recently in the same location. If there is a significant variance, discuss with the agent why this is. An increased cost per square foot could be the result of your desired property having had a large extension completed, along with the entire house being fully refurbished with high value fixtures and fittings. You can then assess whether the neighbourhood is in line with the money you are looking to invest in the purchase, and the possible renovation or extension, of the property.

After the initial checks, obtain the following information before making your offer:

- Where a floor plan exists, confirm that:
    o The layout is how you would want to live in the property or whether alterations will need to be made to reflect this, including an extension (if needed).
    o The layout corresponds to what you have viewed. From our experience, this can vary, especially the placement of walls, bathrooms and chimneys.
    o The measurements are correct and according to the details provided to you, even if you have to measure the rooms in the property yourself.
    o The floor plan provided to you corresponds with the details being held by the local Council for the property and takes into account any extensions or changes to the original building.
- The full Energy Performance Certificate (EPC) for the property. This will assist you to ascertain what energy-saving improvements need to be made and how expensive the property will be to run in terms of gas and electricity bills. This could provide early indications of the extent of work to be done. If you decide to proceed with the purchase, you can also obtain quotes for any works required and assess these in view of your offer price.

Also ask the agent and the seller if they have any information on the following:

- Whether the correct approvals have been obtained for building works such as a loft conversion or extension.
- Any major defects that they are aware of for full disclosure.
- Issues with boundaries or disputes with neighbours.
- Notices of any developments nearby.

Evidence of completed works

Request evidence of key documents for the completion of any work completed, such as:

- Evidence of Planning and Building Regulation Consents, along with the relevant Completion Certificates, for alterations, extensions or work completed on the property. While this is to assist the conveyancing process later, at this early pre-offer stage, it will give you comfort that you will not have to go through a prolonged process and period trying to prove work or have to pay for documentary evidence yourself if the seller refuses to. You can also ascertain when these works were done and if there is a requirement to have them re-done, e.g. installing a new boiler. Again, this may assist your negotiation and influence your level of offer.

- An electrical certificate for electrical work done as part of the UK national standard, BS 7671 (Building Standards Requirements for Electrical Installations). There should be an Electrical Installation Certificate (or a Minor Electrical Installation Works Certificate) that confirms the work meets this standard. There should also be a Building Regulations Compliance Certificate confirming the work meets Building Regulations.

- A Building Regulations Compliance Certificate from a Gas Safe registered engineer for the installation of a heat producing gas appliance in the property, e.g. gas boiler, fire, cooker or hob.

- Certification for the replacement and / or installation of new windows, doors, roof windows and roof lights (FENSA reports) if installed or replaced in the last 10 years.

- If the property is under 10 years old, a copy of your New Home Policy and Warranty documents, including the National House Building Council (NHBC) warranty or another recognised Certificate (i.e. Architect's Certificate).

- Any guarantees for recent damp-proofing, the boiler and new appliance installations.

- Records for the servicing of the boiler.

- Details of any service or maintenance contracts in place, e.g. cost and type of cover for the house alarm.

- Insurance paid for the property to help you to assign these costs. Also find out details of the doors and windows fitted. All the door and window key locks will need to be according to British Standard (BS) so that later you can get contents insurance. Without BS keylocks, insurance companies will not provide insurance against theft, or if they do, it will be very expensive.

Obtain insurance quotes from different companies so you are aware of the different types of cover and the costs related to them.

Leasehold properties

- If it is a leasehold property you are looking to buy, obtain details on the following:
    - What the body corporate fees and other maintenance, service charges or ground fees are for your share to maintain the building, garden and common spaces (e.g. hallways).
    - If there are any other monthly or annual costs, or associated fees.
    - How long the remaining lease is for and what the process is for extending the lease.
    - The cost of extending the lease.
    - What ownership and decision-making powers are included in the leasehold.
    - Whether the other properties are owner-occupied or tenanted.
    - If rooms can be sub-let.
    - Who the freehold belongs to.
    - Details of the managing agent.
    - Whether there is adequate residents and visitors parking.
    - Whether you can keep pets on the property.
    - The time expected to take to complete the purchase. Leasehold chains are notorious for taking additional time to complete due to the intricacies of this type of purchase (e.g. lease extensions and management changes).
    - Speak with one of the other leaseholders who lives full-time in the property (as opposed to one who rents their property out) to discuss what the experience is like of owning and living in that particular property. You can ascertain whether your neighbours will be friendly and helpful, as well as what the environment is like to live in. Discuss party wall noise with the neighbours and try to find out whether there are any particular owners or tenants you need to be alert to as they could be your immediate neighbours.

Chapter 1. BUYING YOUR PROPERTY

The seller's situation

Ask the agent to advise you on the seller's situation:

- *Why are they moving?* They could be downsizing, looking for a larger property, moving in with a partner, having issues with neighbours, or looking for a quieter environment. An answer here could indicate how soon they need to sell.
- *How motivated are they to sell and are they negotiable on the price?* If you know why the property is being sold, this might give you an indication of how negotiable the seller is, for example:
  - If a couple are splitting up, they may want a quick sale, so a discount might be possible. However, if they do want a quick sale, they might only look at cash offers, or prefer buyers who have nothing to sell, or those who are well advanced in the sale of their own property. Conversely, they might need as much money from the sale as possible and will hold out for the asking price, or close to it, especially if one of the partners is reluctant to sell. Be aware that your purchase could be delayed if other parties are not communicating.
  - The seller has found a property they want to move to and need to sell their home in order not to lose out on their next property.
- *What type of buyer are they looking for?* Ask your agent for an indication of what sort of buyer the seller prefers. Sellers who are highly motivated and need to sell quickly will be more attracted to unencumbered buyers with nothing to sell, or cash buyers, or those not in a chain. Cash buyers are becoming increasingly attractive as sellers are aware that they are not likely to be impacted in the sale as these buyers are not subject to the strict lending standards being put into place. However, buyer confidence is being swayed by Brexit. To date, each time we have sold our home, we have rented a property to move to as this has been the most convenient thing for us to do. As renters we have been unencumbered buyers, and this has been very attractive to sellers.
- *How many viewings and repeat viewings have they had?* Knowing the traffic that has been through the property will assist you in determining the level of interest. If there have been a lot of viewings and low, or no offers, this could signal issues with the sale. If the property has been on the market for a while, you could ask the agent if surveys have been conducted by potential buyers and if so, whether any issues have been discovered.

- *If the seller has current offers on the property already:*
    - *If so, when were they made?* Current offers on the table mean they are being considered by the seller. You may choose to see how any current offers develop before making your own offer, or you may decide to put your offer forward immediately. An agent will sometimes ask all interested buyers to submit a sealed bid by a set date or ask buyers to submit their best and final offer by a certain date.
    - *Did any offers fall through and why?* Offers made on a property, and then subsequently withdrawn, could indicate there are issues with the property that the other prospective buyers were not prepared to compromise on. It may also indicate that the asking price for the property is too high or that a mortgage application was unsuccessful.
    - *Where do the offers stand with the seller?* Although a seller may be considering offers currently on the table, a buyer should not be put off, especially if they are well prepared and in an unencumbered position (i.e. they have nothing to sell). This may prove to be the point of difference when the seller is deciding which offer to accept.

        During one buying process, we were advised that the property we were interested in purchasing had just gone under offer. We decided to leave an offer on the property with the agent in case anything changed with the existing offer and sale. As it happened, the existing buyer was unable to proceed, and our offer was accepted. If you are in a similar position, advise the agent that you are interested in offering on the property and leave them with your offer in case a sale collapses. You are then most likely to be the first person contacted by the agent, particularly if you are in a good position to proceed.
    - *What are the conditions on the existing offers?* Offers made can range from offering the asking price (or more) but with a property to sell, to a low offer from a cash buyer who is able to move to exchange and completion quickly. Knowing what conditions exist in the current offers helps you to decide what you can offer and the conditions you attach to your own offer, such as a quick completion.
    - *Are there any dates that they looking to sell, move or avoid?* The seller may need to move by a specific date. This could be due to the milestone dates agreed for a property they are moving to, or dates agreed to in a chain. They may be taking a holiday or have teenagers taking crucial exams and don't want any conflict during this time. You will need to be aware of these dates, plan for them against your own commitments and work with the seller so you can accommodate each other.

- o *How many parties are in the chain?* Every party in a chain can impact the time and complexity of the entire transaction. If you are in a long chain selling your own property, this could be off-putting to a seller. It would depend on how much success the seller has had in obtaining an offer and how motivated they are to sell. You may need to put a strong case forward that would appeal to the seller, letting them know how keen you are to buy their property, what you would like to do with it (e.g. keep it as a family home) and how much you would like to live in that particular street.

  Equally, if a seller is buying their next property, and that purchase is in a long chain, it could influence your decision to offer as a chain can collapse at any stage, leaving you with an expensive outlay and possibly delays to acquiring your home. If you have had previous negative experience in a chain, you may decide not to progress with making an offer, though this may be influenced by how far advanced the chain is.

  Ask the agent whether they can ensure that the chain is managed end-to-end and if they are able to communicate with each link in the chain to ensure progress is maintained. If there are a number of different types of properties involved (e.g. leasehold and freehold), along with various agents, solicitors, mortgage providers and surveyors representing each buyer in the chain, the purchase is expected to be more complicated and lengthier. We have experienced the effect of being in a multi-link and complicated chain, but we were fortunate to have an agent who managed the chain end-to-end towards a successful conclusion.

- *Are the sellers still living at the property or have they moved?* The agent will have this information and it may be that the seller has found another property and already moved into it, or the property may have been rented and the tenants have vacated. If the property is empty, you will be able to more closely determine the condition of the property and how much work needs to be done. This could influence how much you decide to offer or whether you will offer at all.

- *What is included in the price?* It is important to know what you are expected to pay for. Sellers may include chattels in the sale that you may or may not want. Additionally, there may be items not listed that you would like, but unaware that they form part of the fixtures and fittings that you are paying for (e.g. whiteware that is bolted down). This is a point of discussion and negotiation and could affect your offer price. Ensure that what is included, along with what is not included, is clearly noted so that all parties have the right expectation and there are no issues after completion has taken place.

  Chattels do not attract stamp duty, but if it's a costly chattel then it's important to obtain clarification on this from your solicitor. The HMRC can enquire into your property purchase within 9 months of your completion date, so your decision to include a chattel as such (and not pay tax on it) needs to be shown as 'just and reasonable'. To clarify, fixtures and fittings are attached to the property and are expected to be part of the purchase price (e.g. affixed bookshelves and garden sheds), whereas chattels are easily removable, so they are additional items for sale (e.g. curtains and blinds). Refer to Government guidelines on whether the items you are considering are chattels or fixtures and fittings.

Offer and acceptance

Make your offer

The information you gather in the section above could potentially affect your budget and subsequent offer. Before you make your offer to purchase, consider the timeframe and completion date you would like to purchase the property by. Plan for counter offers from other parties as this could take up a lot of time, especially if the property you are interested in has several potential buyers, or if the sellers are not in a hurry to move.

While you may informally find out about previous or current offers, it is illegal for an agent to disclose the value of any offers that have been made on a property. But it is worth asking the agent to indicate what level of offer would need to be made to be taken seriously. If you find out that you need to increase your offer, you may wish to consider using some of your contingency budget to negotiate with.

Once you have made the decision to make an offer, advise the agent that you are interested in buying the property and provide the amount of your offer. Let them know that your offer is reasonable and fair so that they can convey this to the seller.

Also remind the agent if you are a first-time buyer and unencumbered if this is the case. If you are encumbered and your purchase is dependent on you needing to sell your current property, your offer will need to be made conditional on this. If your current property is not on the market yet, you may choose to list it with the same agent as they will have better visibility of the chain. If you are unencumbered, let the agent know that you do not have property to sell and will therefore not be part of a chain. If you are in rental accommodation currently, advise them what the notice period is. If you can move to a quick completion, highlight this to the agent as well.

Provide the agent with as much information as you have available as it formalises the seriousness of your offer. This includes the names and contact details of your solicitor and your mortgage provider. Also provide your pre-qualified mortgage agreement and the letter from your bank or solicitor confirming the amount of your deposit. Inform the agent if a co-ownership agreement will need to be drawn up if you are buying the property with others.

Discuss with the agent the indicative dates you will be working to for exchange of contracts and completion, especially if there is a date that you need to move by. Confirm this with your solicitor beforehand to ensure the proposed dates are reasonable and achievable. Let the agent know that if your offer is accepted, you will be wanting to obtain an indication of dates of when the seller will be unavailable (e.g. during school exams or overseas assignments) so that you can have this in mind for exchange and completion dates.

> You can make your offer conditional on a number of things, including the survey, your final mortgage approval, selling your property and / or subject to the property being taken off the market.

Acceptance of your offer

Once your offer to purchase the property has been accepted by the seller, remind the agent to take the property off the market immediately and ensure an exclusivity period for you so that you can get the initial purchase activity underway (e.g. the survey). Your offer may be subject to change based on the outcome of the property survey and the search results obtained by your solicitor.

If the agent has erected a board outside the property, this should be updated with *Sale Agreed,* or *Under Offer* or *Sold Subject to Contract*. All these terms mean that the sale has been agreed, but contracts have not yet been exchanged. Once contracts have been exchanged, the signage will change to Sold.

Ask the agent to ensure that the property is no longer available on the agency website and other websites as a property for sale. The agent will also need to update the information on the various property websites (Rightmove, etc.) so that the property does not attract any further interest. This means that the status of the property online will also need to read *Sale Agreed,* or *Under Offer* or *Sold Subject to Contract*, or the details of the property removed from the websites completely. The agent must confirm to you that the property will not have any further viewings by any interested parties. The agent will also need to update anyone else who viewed the property to date and showed interest in purchasing it so that they are aware that the property is no longer available to be offered on.

If you are obtaining a mortgage, contact the mortgage provider or broker to advise that your offer has been accepted and that you would like to formally apply for a mortgage. Your mortgage provider will then arrange to send out a surveyor to complete a valuation report on the property to confirm whether the mortgage amount you are borrowing is appropriate. At this stage, you will need to pay for the survey if the mortgage product you are interested in obtaining does not have the survey cost paid for by your lender.

You can discuss with the mortgage provider what additional level of survey you would like to have completed (alongside the basic valuation requested by the bank). You may wish to request a Condition Report, Homebuyer's Report or Building / Structural Survey. You will need to pay for this additional survey.

Notify your solicitor of the acceptance of your offer. They will ask you to complete a number of documents and provide information to address money laundering regulations. These include proof of identification, e.g. passport or drivers' licence, proof of address, e.g. utility bills or bank statements, single or joint accounts, showing your name and address. Your proof of address documents should not be more than 3 months old.

At this stage, your solicitor will provide you with documentation for client care details and standard terms of business, which will detail the responsibility of your solicitor, hours of work, fees and what form of communication will be largely used (e.g. emails).

Your solicitor will also issue you with an Instructions Letter confirming you have requested them to act on your behalf, granting them authority to exchange contracts and transfer funds. You will be asked to provide your contact details, current address, date of birth, National Insurance number and the address of the property you are purchasing.

Additionally, your solicitor will ask you to confirm the ownership or share of the property and whether you will have sole or joint ownership:

- Sole ownership means your home is owned solely by you. In this case, you can leave the property to anyone in a Will or Trust.
- Joint ownership means two or more people own a property. You will need to advise you solicitor whether the property is to be held in equal or unequal shares (e.g. if one person is investing more than the other, this can result in an unequal share). There are two types of joint ownerships:
    - Joint Tenants means when one owner dies, their share in the property will automatically pass to the surviving owner.

Chapter 1. BUYING YOUR PROPERTY

o Tenants in Common means each individual owner hold separate shares (so they can use their Will to dispose of their interest in the property), therefore the property will not automatically pass to the surviving owner. If there is no Will, then Intestacy rules will apply. Intestacy law refers to statutory and case law that determines who is entitled to the property from the estate under the rules of inheritance (estate includes all assets e.g. property, shares and cash). Your solicitor will be able to advise you further on this and is likely to recommend that you make a valid Last Will and Testament, especially if your home ownership is held under Tenants in Common. Refer to the Citizens Advice Bureau (CAB) free service for clarification

Your solicitor may request a payment on account of costs at this stage to start acting on your behalf to cover the costs of initial searches. During this phase, your solicitor may set up an electronic file for the purchase of your home and send you a link to share your files. If your solicitor has done so, you will be sent instructions on how to download your file and retrieve your documents. You can then access your file at any time to get an update on the purchase of your home. This will also allow you to receive automated messages e.g. when contracts have been exchanged and when your solicitor has completed on your purchase, so you will know when you can collect the keys to your new home.

Agree initial milestones and dates with your solicitor and then communicate these to the agent so that there is a consensus regarding activities and timelines for the following:

- *The Memorandum of Sale.* This letter, provided with the property particulars, confirms that your offer has been accepted. This is sent by the agent to both sets of solicitors so that all parties are introduced formally and can subsequently be in contact with each other to progress the transaction.
- *The Mortgage Valuation.* This is the survey that is requested by your mortgage provider to check if the property is appropriately valued (with reference to the mortgage application you have made). The agent and seller will expect you to book the survey within 7 days of receiving the Memorandum of Sale.
- *The draft contract issued / received.* Once the seller has completed the required forms (including the Fixtures and Fittings Form), a draft contract is sent from the seller's solicitor to your solicitor.
- *Searches completed.* These are undertaken by your solicitor, including:
    o Local authority searches can take from one to six weeks to complete and cost up to approximately £400. These searches reveal information held by the local authority such as planning consents, Building Regulation approvals, confirmation of any notices or orders issued in respect to the

property, as well as who is responsible for maintaining roads and paths adjoining the property.

o Land Registry official copies of the registered title are legally required for the sale and prove that the property seller is the legal owner of the property.

o Environmental searches establish whether the property you are buying is built on, or near, contaminated land or water, or whether there is a risk of flooding.

o Water authority searches confirm matters concerning sewers and drainage, showing their position on a plan and whether the property is connected to the mains water supply (the routes indicated on plan). They also reveal whether there are any public drains on the property (this could impact potential building work, e.g. an extension).

o Location specific searches are additional searches particular to the area you are buying in e.g. checks on subsidence risks.

o Chancel repair searches establish whether or not your property lies within an area where you could be liable for the cost of repairs to a parish church. You may be advised by your solicitor to take out Chancel Repair Indemnity Insurance. The cost of this insurance will be based on property value and type of cover. Your solicitor can obtain this insurance on your behalf. This cover is highly recommended as chancel repairs could be expensive.

Preliminary Enquiries / Enquiries about the searches, the draft contract, or any other matters (e.g. Right of Way) will be raised by your solicitor to the seller's solicitor when the search results have been received back by your solicitor.

Indicative dates for exchange and completion are agreed so that all parties are aware of the dates being worked to.

Chapter 1. BUYING YOUR PROPERTY

Plan your move

Refer to the *Moving home Chapter* in this book for detailed information on planning for your move.

Prepare for exchange of contracts

Conveyancing

Your solicitor will deal directly with the seller's solicitor to obtain all the relevant documentation and details for the purchase of your home. Agree regular updates on the progress of enquiries and searches. You can request copies of all communication between solicitors and keep yourself in the loop, along with receiving automated updates from the electronic portal set up by your solicitor (if you have been offered this facility).

You will receive all the legal documents and relevant information from your solicitor for the purchase of your property, including a report explaining the mortgage and the property Title, which details the legal title and also local search results.

You will also receive the following information which you will need to carefully review:

- A Co-ownership Agreement, drawn up by your solicitor, if buying with another party.
- Council permissions obtained, and details of the work completed if substantial work has been done during the term of the existing ownership. If the property has been extended and new gas and electrical appliances installed, then permissions for these works, along with cover certificates, will also be provided.
- The Fixtures and Fittings Form will detail all the items remaining at the property once it has been vacated by the seller, e.g. washing machine, dryer, fridge and freezer if these white goods are included in the purchase. Once you own your home (within the initial days), you can use this form to check that the declared items remain in place and have not been removed from the property. The seller is legally bound to return the items to your home if they are missing. The seller is also responsible for ensuring that the property is cleared of all rubbish and left in a clean and tidy condition on completion. There should not be any changes to the condition of the property (unless agreed) from when you made your offer.

- If the property is leasehold, you will receive a Management Information Pack. This can take weeks to obtain, so the seller needs to have this request in hand well in advance. You will receive a share of freehold document if the property retains a freehold share.
- The Property Information Form will provide the details required for you to make further informed decisions on the purchase the property, including the following:
    o Boundary fences, responsibilities and information on adjacent properties.
    o Issues relating to disputes and complaints.
    o Any rights or legal restrictions to the property (e.g. public footpaths).
    o Notices and proposals from neighbours or the Council on local developments.
    o Planning and Building Regulation Consents, along with the relevant Completion Certificates, for alterations or work completed on the property.
    o An electrical certificate for any electrical work done as part of the UK national standard, BS 7671 (Building Standards Requirements for Electrical Installations). There should be an Electrical Installation Certificate or, where applicable, a Minor Electrical Installation Works Certificate that confirms the work meets this standard. There should also be a Building Regulations Compliance Certificate confirming that the work meets the Building Regulations.
    o A Building Regulations Compliance Certificate from a Gas Safe registered engineer who has installed a heat producing gas appliance in the property., e.g. gas boiler, fire or cooker or hob.
    o Certification for the replacement or installation of new windows (FENSA reports).
    o The relevant appliance guarantees and warrantees.
    o If the property is under 10 years old, a copy of your New Home Policy and Warranty documents, including the National House Building Council (NHBC) warranty or another recognised Certificate (e.g. Architect's Certificate).
    o Whether the property is a listed building or in a conservation area.
    o Details of any maintenance contracts in place, e.g. for the alarm.
    o Any Restrictive Covenant or other Indemnity policy / policies, including those for the Chancel (the cost to repair a church that some homeowners

can be required to contribute to), along with any additional insurances or fees required.
- o Services to the property and locations of gas, electricity meters and water stopcock.
- o The EPC for the property and condition of the central heating and wiring.
- o Parking facilities for the property occupants e.g. garaging or off-road parking.
- o An Environmental report including details of drainage and flooding risks.

Survey report

Once the property survey is conducted, you will receive the survey report with information on the interior and exterior of the property. This includes a report on the grounds and stability issues, as well as advice on any large trees, either on your desired property or on the neighbouring properties, which may impact the property you are looking to purchase. The insurance company will be asking about trees affecting the property when you obtain cover as land subsidence is an expensive issue to investigate, prove and resolve.

> Read the survey documents thoroughly and ask the surveyor (directly) any questions that you may have. The surveyor has inspected the property and produced the report so will have first-hand knowledge of the property, especially if there are areas of condensation, damp, leakage or infestation noted in the document. Once you have discussed the report with the surveyor, if you have any serious concerns, you may wish to instruct additional relevant companies to provide you with an investigative report and quote for repairs. Collate all the investigative reports you have obtained and feel free to discuss these with the surveyor to obtain input and advice on the next steps you need to undertake.

You can also view the property again so that you can check it against the survey report and any additional reports and quotes you have obtained for remedial works. If these repairs and / or costs are substantial (e.g. if a part of the roof needs replacing), you may wish to consider lowering your offer price after having taken these costs into account.

If you have any further queries or concerns, raise these with your solicitor for clarification. The agent, who will have direct access to the seller, many also be able to answer your questions. Ensure that you have information in writing so that you can rely on this in future.

Your mortgage application

Once you have provided all the requested information to your mortgage provider, and the surveyor has delivered the valuation report to them, a decision will be made by your mortgage provider about your mortgage application.

If your application is not successful with your initial mortgage provider, you can look for another mortgage provider. However, you will be asked if you have had loan applications rejected, and this will go against your credit rating. The loan rejection itself will not affect your credit score, but each time a loan application is made, a Hard Check is registered, and any more than one credit application every 3 months is enough to reduce your credit score. So, a large number of hard or complete credit checks in a short period of time can lower your credit score.

It is also likely to limit the mortgage products available to you from lenders who may require a higher deposit or charge increased rates of interest as your credit scores indicate that you may be a high-risk customer. While mortgage providers have differing criteria, your mortgage provider will see the Hard Checks on your credit report each time you have make a credit application as these checks are visible to all companies and can remain on your credit report for 12 months or more. Using mortgage brokers can assist with applications as they will find a suitable mortgage product for you so that you are only applying for loans you are eligible for.

You can elect to withdraw your offer to purchase the property if your mortgage application is rejected and clear your credit rating and / or obtain a larger deposit before making another application. In this case, your solicitor will bill you for the portion of the purchase process that has been undertaken.

> If you are successful in obtaining a mortgage, your mortgage provider or broker will send you a Key Facts document, with Terms and Conditions, detailing the mortgage offer. Read this document thoroughly and ask your solicitor for any clarification. Ensure that you fully understand your mortgage provider's offer, even if you have a broker who will review the information to ensure that the mortgage documents are correct and according to your needs. If any of the details are incorrect, it will make a substantial difference to your monthly mortgage repayments and once you sign the documents, you are legally committed to the repayments.

If the offer is accurate, advise your broker and solicitor that the documents are correct and according to what you expected for the amounts, terms, interest rates and repayments. This is especially important if you are obtaining more than one product, e.g. if you obtain two mortgage products which combine to provide a total mortgage liability of £300,000 as follows:

- A 3-year capital repayment tracker mortgage for £100k.
- A 5-year fixed rate interest only mortgage for £200k.

Ensure that these amounts are correctly allocated to the relevant product, i.e. that the mortgage document shows that the £100k is for the 3-year capital repayment tracker mortgage and the £200k is allocated to the 5-year fixed rate interest only loan (and not vice versa). We have experienced the situation where the details were entered incorrectly, and the monthly re-payments varied greatly from our expectations. After discussions with the bank, this was corrected by the bank, but it did impact on our time and effort and caused additional stress with the sellers, who were already difficult and unreasonable.

Check your mortgage documents and ensure that the agreed rate is applied to the products, especially if the rate for each of the products is different. Also check that the initial and subsequent rates are as you expected, e.g. the initial rate for the tracker mortgage will generally be lower than the later SVR that the mortgage will revert to (after the initial period of your mortgage) if you continue with your mortgage.

Ensure that the term of each product is what you agreed to and that the end date stated in the document is what you expected it to be.

Check that the loan to value calculation is correct and according to the Key Facts document you were provided with when you initially applied for the mortgage.

Confirm that the setup fee, administration fee, product fees and any other fees (if these are being charged) are the correct amounts as were communicated to you initially, and that these are included in the mortgage repayment, as opposed to being paid at the start of the application (or vice versa, according to what was agreed).

Examine the repayment details for each product and ensure that these amounts correlate to what you agreed with your mortgage provider or broker, and that the total amount of your monthly payment is correct and as you expected.

Gazundering, gazanging and gazumping

> There are certain practices that are legal, though unpleasant and inconvenient, whereby a seller or a buyer can undertake the following actions after an offer has been accepted:

Gazundering

When a buyer lowers their offer price prior to exchange of contracts, this is called Gazundering. This can happen for several reasons, including a survey that devalues the property or a downward market.

Gazanging

This is when the seller decides to cancel the sale. It happens usually because property prices are increasing, and they can make more money if they hold off selling until later.

Ghost gazumping

When a seller raises the agreed sale price prior to exchange, this is called Ghost Gazumping. A buyer can decide to either pay this or withdraw from the sale and seek reparation through their Home Buyers Protection Insurance (if this policy was taken out).

Gazumping

This is when a seller accepts an offer after they have already accepted an offer from another party. Gazumping can happen at any time up to exchange and a potential buyer can lose money spent on conveyancing work and survey costs. The seller may have done this if they have received a higher offer, or if someone was able to complete faster, or is in a better position to proceed. Where gazumping is concerned, there are a few things you can do to protect yourself as a buyer:

- Pay for a Home Buyers Protection Insurance, also known as Residential Abortive Transaction Insurance (RATI). If you are gazumped, you can claim back some of your expenses, e.g. conveyancing fees and survey costs.
- On acceptance of your offer by the seller, ask for the property to be taken off the market so it is less likely to attract further potential buyers.
- Ask for an exclusively period which should allow sufficient and reasonable

time to complete the activities to exchange. Your solicitor can draw up a contract between you and the seller to formalise this. This is called a Lock Out Agreement and grants you sole rights to the purchase of the property for the agreed period. To show the seriousness of your offer, you may be expected to pay a refundable holding deposit or potentially a non-refundable deposit. Obtain legal counsel from your solicitor on this as issues highlighted in a survey report might mean you do not wish to progress with the purchase of the property and you could lose your deposit.

- Agents are legally bound to advise the seller of all offers made, so ensure that you keep the activities moving quickly (e.g. the survey and mortgage application).

- Be proactive and responsive throughout this entire process so that the seller is not inclined to be tempted by other offers. Having planned well, you can quickly share the documentation and information you have already collated, e.g. details of your solicitor, your mortgage provider and the pre-qualified mortgage agreement you have obtained. Ensure that the survey is done in a timely manner and follow up with your solicitor regarding progress on searches and timely responses from the seller's solicitor. Ask the agent to keep the seller informed of your progress. If you have direct access to the seller, keep them informed and updated; follow up on anything that they address that appears to be an issue (happening now) or a risk (may or may not happen in the future).

- If you have done everything you can to progress your purchase and appeal to the seller, but you are still gazumped, you may be inclined to improve your offer. Find out from the agent what elements of your offer need to be amended - it could be more money, a shorter time to completion, or fewer conditions. Keep in mind that you may get gazumped again by this seller if they have already done this once. If you have no success, you can then claim on your Home Buyers Protection Insurance and look for another property. This is an unfortunate situation to be in, but if you have found a good property previously, have confidence that you will find another one.

When it appeared that the chain was about to break on the sale of one of our properties, we obtained the contact phone numbers and email address of the potential buyers. We texted and emailed them, advising of the risks involved. This helped all parties to build a rapport and compare scenarios, leading to issues being resolved.

Exchange of contracts

Any queries about the legal process and documentation or requests from the agent or the seller can be directed to your solicitor, who will be your advocate during the entire buying process and will guide you accordingly.

Keep in touch with your estate agent for progress updates and ensure they have all the information they require. Work with them to ensure all parties (including the rest of the chain) are fully focused on completing the sale to the agreed dates.

There are many things to consider in readiness for this stage of the purchase. Just prior to exchange of contracts, there is an increase in effort from all parties as all the exchange activities must be completed imminently. Your availability and response times will be crucial to close the incomplete activities, so think about how you can make yourself more accessible during this period.

Don't be pressured by the agent or the seller into undertaking any activities or meeting any dates or costs that you don't believe is appropriate or agreeable to you. Refer any issues or matters to your solicitor and obtain advice rather than dealing with things by yourself in isolation. Be aware that communication with your solicitor will incur cost, however dealing appropriately with other people's requests and demands is part of conveyancing, so you may need this level of assistance and support during the purchase of your home, especially if this is your first experience.

We had several particularly unpleasant experiences with the sellers of one of the properties we purchased. They were difficult to deal with from the beginning and made demands on us that were clearly unlikely to be fulfilled, including:

- Making late requests and expecting immediate turnarounds.
- Setting rigid, non-negotiable and unrealistic dates for exchange and completion (then changing these dates).
- Giving no prior warning and wanting to exchange well in advance of agreed dates.
- Not giving us access to the property before completion after agreeing that they would (even after exchange had taken place).
- Applying undue pressure on us and our solicitor.

> The agent was also bullied by the sellers and was unable to manage them and their expectations. The sellers gave us an unrealistic ultimatum to exchange within 24 hours when it had already been agreed with solicitors for both parties that the exchange date was weeks away. They also stated that if we did not meet the 24-hour exchange ultimatum, the price would increase by £20,000 (ghost gazumping). After we received these ultimatums, we decided that we would not go ahead with the purchase of this property as we were not prepared to put up with this type of unreasonable and unacceptable bullying behaviour. But within an hour of stepping away, we received a call from the agent advising that the sellers had dropped their ultimatum and that we could proceed to the agreed exchange date and without applying the £20,000 increase. We then decided to go ahead with the purchase on this basis. So, don't give in to these playground bullies - they step down when you face up to them!

Once your solicitor is satisfied that all queries have been answered by the seller's solicitors, and all searches have been completed favourably, you will be contacted to confirm a completion date before the contract can be exchanged by your solicitor. Confirm this date with the agent so that both yours and the seller's date match. Your initial offer would have provided an indication of the exchange date, but at this stage, definite exchange and completion dates are agreed.

Your deposit money needs to have been received by your solicitor and the funds cleared prior to the agreed date of exchange. Your solicitor will hold your deposit in a Client Account, ready for payment to the seller's solicitor on the exchange of contracts. If you are buying a property that is a new build, then the deposit will be paid to the developer's solicitors. In this case, your solicitor will need to obtain the National House Building Council New Build Guarantee Scheme for the property to ensure that your deposit is protected if the developer goes into liquidation.

Obtain building and contents insurance on the property prior to exchanging contracts. Ensure that you have checked that all the external door and window key locks are according to British Standard otherwise it could impact any future insurance claims you may need to make. To enable you to obtain full contents insurance, including cover for theft, the door and key locks will need to be to the required insurance approved standard (five lever mortice locks with British Standard Kite Mark BS3621, sash and deadlock mortices, multi point locking systems on uPVC doors, night latch and window locks). Discuss your requirements in detail with your insurance provider. You may even want to ask the sellers who they are insured with, so you can obtain a comparative quote using the same information they have for the property. Provide evidence of your building and contents insurance to your solicitor for your mortgage provider.

Your solicitor will contact you when the exchange documents are ready for signing. Ensure you allow for the appropriate amount of time to review the documents with your solicitor before signing them.

Check that your solicitor and the seller's solicitor have been in contact with each other to ensure that identical contracts have been signed by both parties, and that these contracts have been formally exchanged by the solicitors (this is when the purchase and sale becomes legally binding).

Once contracts have been exchanged, you and the seller are legally bound to complete the sale and purchase of the property and any changes made to the Contract can only be agreed by both parties.

Prepare for your move

Refer to the *Moving home Chapter* in this book for detailed information on preparing for your move.

Completion of contracts

There is increased activity just prior to the completion of contracts, so make yourself as available as possible for any calls or responses you are required to make. There is generally a gap of up to 28 days between exchange and completion of contracts. However, it is not uncommon for exchange and completion to happen on the same day so that deposits don't have to be paid in advance. As you would expect, this is very stressful for all parties concerned. It is advisable for you to ring your solicitor on the morning of completion to confirm that everything is in place.

Once the remaining searches and legal requirements have been completed, your solicitor will deal with the transfer of the ownership of the property. They will contact you in writing to confirm their fees and associated costs, the Stamp Duty due and the balance of the purchase price, and notify you of the date the full, final, payment needs to be made by. They will also advise you of the insurances or indemnity policies that have been put in place. If you have agreed the purchase of additional chattels from the seller, there will be a list of these with costs that you will need to review and confirm. You will also be advised by your solicitor of when you need to sign the mortgage deed and completion documents by.

Once you have made all the required payments as noted above to your solicitor (including any additional funds towards the purchase of your home), and signed the legal documents for completion, including the Mortgage and Transfer Deeds, your solicitor will communicate this to the seller's solicitor and your mortgage provider. Your solicitor will obtain the mortgage advance from your mortgage provider (24 hours before the completion date) and arrange the bank telegraphic transfer of monies to the seller's solicitor.

Once the seller's solicitor has confirmed back to your solicitor and the agent that the purchase monies have been released, the keys to the property can be formally released to you by the agent. The conveyancing is complete when you are satisfied that the property is in the condition that you expected, with fixtures, fittings and chattels remaining in the property as agreed.

Refer to the *Moving home Chapter* in this book for detailed information on checks that you are recommended to undertake when arriving at your new home.

Congratulations on the purchase of your new home! Now it's time for you to celebrate!

Moving

Refer to the *Moving home Chapter* for detailed information on moving home.

Post-completion activities

Within 30 days following completion of contracts, your solicitor will send you confirmation that your Stamp Duty has been paid. Your solicitor will register you as the new owner of the property at the Land Registry. You will also receive the registered ownership document. For freehold property, this means a confirmation that you are now the registered owner of your property. The Land Registry has largely digitised all land records, so unless your property that has not been registered previously, you will not receive any Title Deeds. For a leasehold property, you will receive a copy of the lease along with any service charge accounts.

You will also receive a copy of the following documents:

- For new build properties (or properties under 10 years old): Buildmark (NHBC), or other recognised Certificate (e.g. Architect's Certificate) or new home policy / warranty documents.
- Chancel repair indemnity insurance, any restrictive covenant indemnity insurance policy, or any other legal cover where it has been required to be put in place (as explained in your solicitor's report on the Title).

Enjoy owning your new property!

Checklist – Buying your property

The following Checklist will help you to plan and track your progress through this process.

Plan and confirm requirements

- ☐ Confirm the reason you are buying a property as this will influence your approach.
- ☐ Confirm your purchase strategy and what type of property you are looking to buy.
- ☐ Thoroughly plan and have clear and detailed requirements written for your purchase.
- ☐ Ensure you have sufficient funds for the deposit, stamp duty and solicitor's fees.
- ☐ Calculate your budget and confirm how much you can afford to spend each month.
- ☐ Ensure your credit score is healthy.
- ☐ Find the best mortgage product for your needs.
- ☐ Obtain your pre-qualified mortgage agreement from your lender

Start your property search

- ☐ Thoroughly familiarise yourself with the area local to where you are buying.
- ☐ Use local professionals, they know the local area, and can all engage with each other.
- ☐ Inform your own networks, agents, sellers, property developers you are looking to buy.
- ☐ Research chosen properties, using online resources to identify any obvious issues.
- ☐ View properties at different times and days to assess the neighbourhood and noise.

Pre-offer due diligence

- ☐ Find out everything you can about a property you are intending to offer on.
- ☐ Request from the agent comparable examples of similar properties in the area.
- ☐ Check if the property is listed or in a conservation area.
- ☐ Request evidence of any completed works done to the property.
- ☐ If it is a leasehold property you are buying, obtain details on the lease, fees and costs.
- ☐ Find out why the seller is moving, how motivated they are and type of buyer they want.

Offer and acceptance

- ☐ Make your offer only when you are certain that the property is the right one for you.
- ☐ Obtain from the agent what level of offer would need to be made to be taken seriously.
- ☐ Remind the agent if you are a first-time buyer or unencumbered, if this is the case.
- ☐ Provide the agent with your pre-qualified mortgage agreement.

- ☐ Once you offer has been accepted, advise your mortgage provider or broker.
- ☐ Notify your solicitor of the acceptance of your offer.

Plan your move

- ☐ Refer to the *Moving home Chapter* for information on planning for your move.

Prepare for exchange of contracts

- ☐ Agree regular updates with your solicitor on the progress of enquiries and searches.
- ☐ Carefully review all the legal documents and relevant information for the purchase.
- ☐ Read the survey report thoroughly and address any queries with the surveyor.
- ☐ View the property again to check it against the survey report and any additional reports.
- ☐ If successful in obtaining a mortgage, thoroughly read the Key Facts document.
- ☐ Check your mortgage documents and ensure that the document is correct.
- ☐ Protect yourself against gazundering, gazanging, ghost gazumping and gazumping.

Exchange of contracts

- ☐ Direct any queries about the legal process and documentation to your solicitor.
- ☐ Keep in touch with your agent and ensure they have all the information they require.
- ☐ Make yourself available prior to exchange of contracts.
- ☐ Pay your deposit to your solicitor with funds cleared prior to the date of exchange.
- ☐ Obtain building and contents insurance on the property prior to exchanging contracts.
- ☐ Allow time to review the documents with your solicitor before signing them.
- ☐ Check that your solicitor and the seller's solicitor have been in contact with each other.

Prepare for your move

- ☐ Refer to the *Moving home Chapter* for information to prepare you for moving home.

Completion of contracts

- ☐ Make yourself available for any calls or decisions that need to be made.
- ☐ Contact your solicitor prior to completion to confirm that everything is in place.
- ☐ The keys to the property will then be formally released upon your solicitor's advice.

Moving

- ☐ Refer to the *Moving home Chapter* for detailed information on moving home.

Post-completion activities

- ☐ Check Stamp Duty payment has been made 30 days after completion.
- ☐ Check you have received the registered ownership document or a copy of the lease.

Chapter 2

RENOVATING YOUR PROPERTY

Overview

Whenever you approach the renovation of a property, ensure you have a clear understanding of what you are going to achieve, what budget you have available, how much time you have allowed to complete your project and whether your build team is fully available when required. All these need to be realistic or you will create unnecessary stress while undertaking your project. Additionally, you will need to keep in mind who you are renovating for. Different levels of upgrade will be required depending on whether it's your own home, an investment property, or a property you will flip.

In this chapter we discuss the importance of planning, being clear about your requirements and locating the right trades and resources, as well as the importance of managing your budget, communication, and the project management of your renovation. Later in the chapter, we explain how to undertake a renovation project room by room.

Plan your renovation project

> Plan exactly what you want from your renovation, whether it is in your current house or a house that you are expecting to purchase. By planning ahead, you will save yourself time and money, as well as reduce your chances of any nasty surprises later on.
>
> One of the main rules of renovating your house is to only spend money on changes that will increase the value of your house, especially if you are looking to sell the property after the renovation has completed. You need to make the most out of your renovation budget so that you can maximise returns. Although this may limit what you choose to do to your property, it means that you are not making empty investments. This rule still applies even if you are planning to live in your house for a period of time before you eventually sell it.

If your budget is limited, make a list of the priority tasks to be completed, especially if your renovation project is to be completed over many years. Decide what the essentials are. For example, carpets can be expensive, so you may choose to live with bare wooden flooring throughout the house until you can afford to purchase carpets. Or you can put down some old rugs if you have these.

There is a logical order in which renovation works should be approached and undertaken. If you do not follow that order, you may end up having to undo or redo completed work in order to complete basic repairs and improvements.

Chapter 2. RENOVATING YOUR PROPERTY

Preparing a plan is a very useful way of listing the required works in order as well as estimating the likely cost and time required for a renovation project. Also, if funds are restricted, it will allow renovation works to be prioritised without compromising the end result or wasting money. If you do not have a proper plan and fix all the details at an early stage, including when you may require specific members of a build team, this can cause uncertainty and delay when you are in the middle of the project. If you do not have a clear idea for the whole house committed to a plan, then you risk doing work that has to be undone further down the line.

Determine if you are going to live in the house while renovating. The answer to this may also dictate the priority order in which you renovate the property. You may need to complete one area or floor first, so you can live in it while the rest of the house is developed. The deciding factors will be time and cost, which will mean either renting somewhere off-site or potentially holding up the renovation process by moving around the house as it gets completed. Also plan for how you and your family will manage during the property renovation if you are all living in the house and there are interruptions to the gas supply, electricity or water.

Decide whether you are going to hire a building firm to undertake the renovation work, or whether you are going to hire contractors independently. This may depend on what budget you are working to and the funds you have available, as well as how much control you want over the renovations. If you decide to hire the contractors independently, then it is essential that you have a plan of what needs to be done with your property. Obtain advice and input on any potential structural changes from a qualified architect, or at least a builder, during your planning phase.

When hiring the contractors independently, schedule them so that they do not all come at the same time. Create a schedule of work and plan the priority order for the work to be started and completed, and make sure that this logically runs together. As an example, do not have the electricians come after the plasterers, as they will have to work on the walls which have already been plastered.

Have the plumbing installed in the house before any of the other work gets done. Doing this will ensure that you will have a ready water supply to the property and also the contractors will have water for the work they need to undertake. Also, have any structural changes completed swiftly after the plumbing, so that the construction of the property is in place as soon as possible.

Proper planning to a detailed level means that you can also prepare a proper budget. Even for simple things such as having materials delivered, need planning. Is the road wide enough for the lorry to turn? If it cannot get into your driveway, will you need to demolish a wall, or is the distance from the road short enough for materials to be transferred by hand?

Confirm who are you renovating for

> Be clear about who you are renovating the property for, such as a residence for you to live in, an investment for you to rent out, or a property to sell on. The work you decide to undertake, and the budget that you set, will depend on this. Enlarging a two bedroom house to make it a three or four bedroom house, in the catchment area of a great school, will be a better investment than undertaking similar improvements in an area where the local school does not have a good record.

Having an avatar of a potential buyer in mind will assist with planning how you will approach your renovation project. It will help to distinguish the people who will buy in that particular neighbourhood, what they're likely to be looking for and what might put them off.

In London, expensive basement conversions are popular for adding living space, especially where the garden is small. If a basement conversion is considered unusual in your area, it might have the opposite effect and put potential purchasers off. If your garden is big enough, it would make better sense to add more living space by extending outwards.

In an area popular with families, an extra bedroom or a playroom would be a good investment, but a gym or garden pond would be less so. Replacing a bath for a shower might be a mistake as families with young children and babies usually want a bath in their home. Review your property with a degree of objectivity and a critical eye. Consider whether anything is missing that other neighbouring properties already have.

Decide what work to do

> When you are planning a large renovation project, and you have listed out all the required work, it can seem overwhelming and you may spend all your time trying to decide what to do next, rather than moving forward with it. Break down all the work into smaller sub-projects. Then put them in a priority order of importance. Do this with each activity.

Chapter 2. RENOVATING YOUR PROPERTY

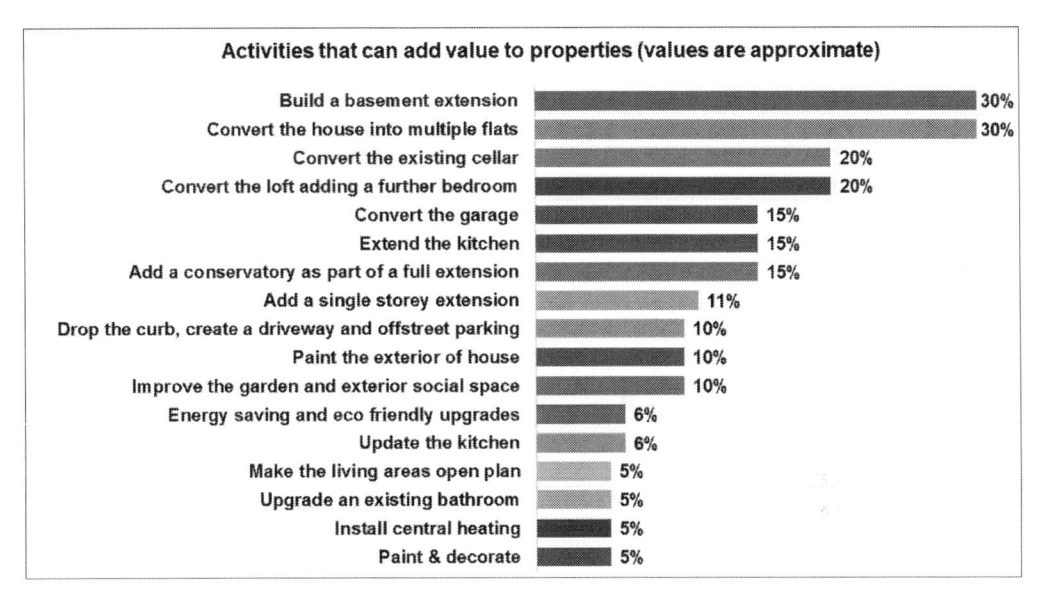

The following illustration provides an indication of property value added via activity:

Activities that can add value to properties (values are approximate)

Build a basement extension	30%
Convert the house into multiple flats	30%
Convert the existing cellar	20%
Convert the loft adding a further bedroom	20%
Convert the garage	15%
Extend the kitchen	15%
Add a conservatory as part of a full extension	15%
Add a single storey extension	11%
Drop the curb, create a driveway and offstreet parking	10%
Paint the exterior of house	10%
Improve the garden and exterior social space	10%
Energy saving and eco friendly upgrades	6%
Update the kitchen	6%
Make the living areas open plan	5%
Upgrade an existing bathroom	5%
Install central heating	5%
Paint & decorate	5%

While the value added will depend on how much you spend to achieve this uplift, the appropriate renovation activity needs to be undertaken. For instance, a basement conversion is the most complicated of all extensions as this underpins the house. You may have to deal with party wall issues, it requires site access for digging machinery, any groundwater issues and waterproofing will need to be overcome, and you will need planning permission for any structural work. Any of these could affect your time allocation and budget, as with anything unforeseen or delayed that has to do with building works.

Surveys

The first stage of any renovation project is to obtain a detailed assessment of the current condition of the property. If you are buying a property to renovate, commission a chartered surveyor to undertake a survey and provide a report identifying any essential repairs needed. The report will also provide recommendations for further investigation by specialist surveyors into any suspect areas such as infestation, subsidence or heave, damp or drainage problems. The different types of building survey are explained below.

Survey level one: RICS Home Condition Report (HCR)

The RICS Condition Report details the condition of the property, identifying any risks or potential legal issues and highlights any urgent defects. It uses simple traffic light ratings to identify the condition of the key elements of the property. This is typically the lowest priced of the surveys and is aimed at conventional properties and newer homes.

Survey level two: RICS HomeBuyer Report (HBR)

This is most suitable survey for standard properties in reasonable condition. It provides you with detailed information and a choice of either a survey, or a survey and valuation:

- The HomeBuyer Report (survey) includes all the features contained in the RICS Condition Report. It offers advice on defects that may affect the property with repairs, as well as ongoing maintenance advice.
- The HomeBuyer Report (survey and valuation) has all the features of the RICS Condition Report. It provides advice on defects that may affect the value of the property, and on any repairs and ongoing maintenance. It also includes market valuation and insurance rebuild costs.

Survey level three: RICS Building Survey

This report is essential for larger or older properties, or if you are planning major works. This is the most comprehensive report and provides you with an in-depth analysis of the property's condition. It also offers advice on defects, repairs and maintenance options.

If you are planning major works, the report will reveal the type of construction used across different areas of the house. This will affect the type and extent of any alterations that can be made, including the techniques and materials that are appropriate. Using the incorrect renovation techniques can lead to extensive damage to an old building, such as with earth construction like cob and clom or rubble stone walls, oak framing, and random slate walls.

If the building is to be extended or remodelled, it is useful to obtain an exact scale drawing of the layout of the building. This will prove to be a valuable starting point for making design decisions and is also likely to be required as part of any planning applications. The right surveyor can be found via the Royal Institute of Chartered Surveyors.

When the surveyor has completed the survey and provided their report, ask them for an indication of the likely cost and priority of any repairs they have observed that need remediating. Take the opportunity to also ask them where they think additional space can be added or optimised.

Chapter 2. RENOVATING YOUR PROPERTY

We usually contact the surveyor after we have received and read the survey report. We find that it helps us to discuss their findings directly with them. It also assists us in obtaining the clarity, input or advice necessary to making decisions on the property.

Gather your requirements

We find this stage of the property ownership process the most exciting, because it calls forward all our creativity, imagination and resourcefulness. It also challenges us to overcome issues, which we do through conversations and collaborations, building stronger relationships along the way with the people involved in our renovation. This culminates in further experience and provides for more enjoyment in the renovation process and outcome. This is a time to really enjoy crafting and refining your vision. Focus on what inspires you. While this phase can be testing, keep your eyes on the completed prize!

When we are renovating, furnishing or staging our properties, we pour through magazines and online resources such as Pinterest or Google images for ideas and inspiration. We also attend homebuilding and renovating shows to see what new ideas and trends are being presented. Holidays are a great time to gather ideas and be inspired. We take lots of photos on our travels, taking design cues from shops and restaurants in towns and villages as well as hotels and resorts, taking note of their surroundings, rooms and environments.

Think about why you are renovating as the reason will drive how you approach the design and what budget you will set. Have you already purchased the property you want to renovate, or are you in the process of identifying a property to buy? Before you buy a property, there are several things you should check so you don't get any unpleasant surprises, especially when it's too late to back out of a purchase, or when you have significantly progressed your renovations.

Check the deeds to the property to find out exactly where the boundaries lie. Do this irrespective of any intention to add extensions to the property.

Walk around the property and check:
- Any signs or musty smell of damp.
- Cracks in internal walls and gaps in the pointing between bricks on external walls.
- Age and condition of the boiler, the central heating and whether it is efficient, the state of the radiators and any signs of leaks or rust.
- Any evidence of insulation to hot water tank and lagging of pipes.

- Signs of longstanding leakages with the plumbing.
- Whether consumer units, fuse boards and circuit boards are up to date.
- Old light switches and sockets or braided flex hanging from ceiling roses.
- Double glazing with signs of condensation or moisture that might need replacing.
- Draughts through poorly insulated windows and doors.
- Cavity wall and / or loft insulation.
- Damaged or leaking guttering, evidence of blockages around external gutter drains.
- Water damage on floors and ceilings or signs of tide marks on lower walls.
- The general condition of the property, quality of the bathroom and kitchen and decor.
- Missing slates on the roof or cracked chimney stacks.
- Invasive Japanese knotweed in the garden.
- Trees which may block light and cause a nuisance, or hedges requiring maintenance.
- Well-established trees with roots close to the boundary walls.
- Any tree preservation orders and conservation area designations.

If you are looking for a property that requires a minor cosmetic upgrade, any property you view that requires a lot of work is likely to put you off. Conversely, if you are intending a major renovation, you may not be too concerned about the overall condition of the property and the amount of work to be completed as long as you can get it at a reduced price.

Write down your requirements. Be clear about your vision, what you want done during the renovation and the expectations you have of the completed project.

Take the following into account:
- Are you renovating to rent out, sell on at a profit (flip), or are you intending to stay at the property and want to create the perfect living space for you for the future?
- Do you especially want to use specific green or organic materials in your build?

Chapter 2. RENOVATING YOUR PROPERTY

- Do you want / need to use historically accurate materials for an older property?
- Are you intending to extend as well as renovate? If so, what new spaces do you need?
- How many additional bedrooms or bathrooms will the property need?
- Is the kitchen adequate or will it need improving and extending?
- Do the rooms flow? What about orientation and room positioning?
- Do the main living areas look out over the garden or have a view?
- Is the only bathroom downstairs?
- Can the external cladding be improved?
- Is there room in the loft area for conversion to living space?
- Is the garden big enough for the size of house?
- Do you need to allow for a household member who is not fully mobile or disabled?
- Have you decided the finish you want for the renovation (budget, standard or premium)?
- Have you created a mood board of the type of design style you want?
- Do you need to engage a qualified architect to make the best of the space you have?

Once your requirements are clear, start looking at what needs to be done versus what you would like to do. It may already be clear what structural repairs are necessary, but they need to be considered in the context of the whole project to avoid doing work that may have to be undone or redone later.

Go around the house looking at everything that needs attention, and at the same time think about things that you might want to change, even though they're not wrong as such. As an example, the roof might need replacing, but could you build an extra bedroom in the loft at the same time? If the windows in the lounge are damaged or rotten, would bi-fold or patio doors be a better way of linking the garden to the house rather than replacement windows? Would removing an internal wall to merge a dining room with the kitchen create a room that is better suited to modern cooking, entertaining and living?

If your property is listed, under a covenant, or in a conservation area, there may be planning restrictions in the areas that you live in, or specific to your property. If this is the case, ensure that you understand what is expected of you and who to seek out as planners can bring the full force of the law to bear if you break those rules. If the property lies in a private estate, you may need to get planning permission from the estate as well as from the local council.

If you are planning to add an extension to your current property, engage a qualified architect, as it is important to understand the detail that is necessary when considering the building of an extension. Extensions can be added to the back, side, or front of an existing property, or can even be another floor built above the existing property. There are many pitfalls than can befall you if you have not taken every possible precaution before starting a build. Local councils may also like to know that they can deal directly with the architects to obtain the required information accurately.

Also think about space as well as light. Have windows as large as possible, doors that open directly to the garden and rooflights to maximise natural light. Plan your lighting to counteract any dark area, rather than adding lamps later. An architect can help you with this and advise you on the materials needed to build your extension as well as how to enhance the look and feel of the property whilst conserving energy (heating, lighting, etc). You may also want to secure the services of an interior designer, depending on available budget. Both architects and interior designers have studied different techniques that can be applied when designing a particular type of structure or area. Select your architect and designer very carefully. You are entrusting them to act on your behalf.

List your requirements

> We use a requirements list to articulate what works we want done on a property, including who will provide the materials and when the materials will be required. The cost is broken down by room and trade. This makes it clearer for the builder to quote on.

Chapter 2. RENOVATING YOUR PROPERTY

We also create an additional requirements list for any future phases of work. We have this additional list also quoted for so that we know what our budgetary requirements are for the future. As well, we obtain an indication of how long the future phases are expected to take. This allows us to plan for time and cost. An extract of our renovation requirements list is provided below:

ITEM	DESCRIPTION	Material Supplied By (Who)	Materials Required By (Date)	QUOTE
	(CLIENT'S NAME) RENOVATION REQUIREMENTS LIST (ADDRESS OF PROPERTY & DATE)			
1	**GENERAL BUILDING, MAINTENANCE & REDECORATION**			
a	Supply skips for end to end job	Contractor		
b	Remove all wood/laminate and carpet floor coverings. Check floors, ensuring free of creaking and replacing/removing flooring as required to prepare for laying carpet and vinyl	Contractor		
c	Fit laminate flooring in kitchen/dining/lounge, hallway and foyer	Contractor		
d	Paint all walls, ceilings, doors and all other woodwork and wallpaper agreed walls	Contractor		
e	Replace the front door with a new black composite door	Contractor		
f	Maintenance checks and inspections - Electricity Test Certificate and Certificates for servicing of boiler, gas, heating and water heating. Replace & test fire and smoke alarms	Contractor		
g	Fit new radiators in foyer and kitchen and replace all other rads with new	Client		
2	**KITCHEN & UTILITY**			
a	Supply & fit new boiler to the utility room and fit new wall unit over the boiler	Contractor		
b	Remove existing kitchen and make good	Contractor		
c	Refit with complete new kitchen as per kitchen plan from supplier - kitchen delivery date XXXX	Client		
3	**MASTER BEDROOM**			
a	Demolish ensuite and rebuild new to the size and layout agreed	Contractor		
b	Alter doorways as agreed & form new doorway from ensuite through to the new master bedroom	Contractor		
c	Install wall storage recesses in ensuite shower	Contractor		
d	Ensuite - fit new suite, wall tiles, accessories, heated towel rail, mirror & storage cabinet	Client		
4	**FAMILY BATHROOM**			
a	Remove the family bathroom suite, and wall and floor tiles	Contractor		
b	Fit new wall tiles, heated towel rail, accessories, fan, shaving point, mirror and storage cabinet	Contractor		
c	Refit new bathroom suite and to agreed positions	Client		
5	**LIGHTS & SWITCHES GENERAL**			
a	Change/install motion sensor security lighting outside where agreed	Contractor		
b	Fit satin metal dimmer switches in all rooms & hallways	Contractor		
c	Replace the downlights in the kitchen with new satin fittings	Contractor		
d	Install 2 small led lights in the shower recess and double light switch outside of ensuite			
6	**BASEMENT STORAGE**			
a	Re-point damaged areas	Contractor		
b	Supply and install a new door and frame, double glazed uPVC	Contractor		
c	Prepare the walls and apply two coats of exterior white emulsion	Contractor		
7	**EXTERIOR**			
a	Re-cement loose paving stones outside the back of the top garage	Contractor		
b	Repair tiling on roof as per Survey Report	Contractor		
c	External drains to be cleaned and cleared	Contractor		
		TOTAL		
		PLUS 20% VAT		
		GRAND TOTAL		

Decide on your build team

Before taking on a property to renovate, thoroughly cost out the renovation to confirm that the project is financially viable. Once you have taken possession, properly assess the extent of the works required so that you can get a detailed financial schedule in place.

Some mortgage lenders will help fund your renovation project and also offer the money in staged payments. If this is the route you are going to follow, enquire what those stages are and work out when you will have each step of the renovation finished.

Be realistic about what work you can afford to do and when you can do it. If the property is not in a habitable state, your priority should be to make it dry and safe as well as have heating and hot water, so you can move in. This will save you the cost of living elsewhere while the renovation work progresses. Avoid moving in until the major works are completed so that you have rooms available in which to cook, wash and sleep. Then living among cosmetic alterations is not so challenging.

Check for any grants or tax concessions. These are not common but there are grants available in some instances for restoration and home improvement work, either via local councils or from National Heritage. There are also VAT concessions, such as a reduced rate for dwellings that have been empty for three years or more. To avoid the potential for disqualification, ensure you apply for grants before starting any work.

> When renovating, never take on the first builder, tradesmen, other person or company that you see. Get at least three quotes for every job and prepare a specification for them to quote against. Ask for recommendations for previous customers whose work you can inspect, then go and speak to them. Then choose the person who gives you a fair price but also, importantly, who you think you will be able to best work with.

If you are inexperienced at renovating, consider getting a project manager to look after the restoration on your behalf. This will be an extra cost, but there are likely to be savings of time and money that could have been wasted through your inexperience or indecision. Hiring a project manager also allows you to continue with your day job, and your earnings may offset the hiring cost.

You need to be comfortable with your build team, especially your main contractors, as they will be spending a lot of time in your property and you will be dealing with them frequently. Good communication and professional relationships are really important for the project to run smoothly. We have nearly always had very competent builders and other trades people working on our properties. The road to completing our renovations has at times been rocky and unnecessarily expensive, but the quality and standard of the output of our build teams has been reliably high.

Source reputable builders and trades people whenever you can. Obtain recommendations from friends, neighbours, other trade contractors and trade bodies, or online trade rating websites. See at least three different contractors and check their credentials. Avoid contractors who won't give references, and also be aware that for those that do provide them, their references are not always genuine, so contact the referees.

> It is really dangerous to use someone who does not know what they are doing, especially for anything that involves gas or electric. You should always use:
> - A registered gas engineer for any gas work and installations, such as for a boiler, heating appliance, hob or cooker.
> - A registered electrician for any electrical work and installation, such as new consumer board, rewiring, lighting, electrical sockets.
> - Someone in a competent person scheme for work that needs building regulations approval (unless you obtained approval yourself).

Even if you are considering doing the renovation work yourself, you will still need a Gas Safe Registered Engineer for any work involving gas, and a qualified electrician registered with an industry body such as NICEIC, NAPIT or ELECSA for all electrical installations. You will need to provide their safety and completion certificates when you rent or sell.

Check if the contractor you are considering is a member of an approved trader scheme. Checking out trade credentials is important but be aware that many trade associations only ask members to pay membership fees, so there's no actual assessment of the members. If you are concerned about a particular person or company, enquire with your local planning department or the trading standards authority. They may be able to point you in the direction of someone that they know by reputation.

You can source reliable trade contractors from online directories of recommended and trusted tradespeople who have been vetted and monitored and meet standards of trading. Background checks on tradespeople are made before they can become a member. Once they join, members agree for feedback from their customers to be put online for all to see. Once work has been completed, homeowners leave a review of the tradesperson, and it is this feedback that gives other homeowners peace of mind that they have found someone reliable. Companies like TrustMark (the only Government endorsed standards scheme for trades in and around the home), Which? Trusted Traders, Checkatrade, TrustATrader and RatedPeople all provide this information.

Before you meet the contractor, write down a clear and detailed description of exactly what you want done. Also collate a list of questions to help you to obtain all the information you need to compare and choose between contractors. Make sure you can communicate with them easily as this will help you sort out any problems that come up later.

> When you meet them, write down what they say they will do. If you do hire them, you will have a record of the job details from this conversation, as well as the written contract you will both need to sign before any work starts. If you are not comfortable with a particular contractor, don't hire them. Move on to the next person you have identified – you will find another contractor to do the work.

Validate what a contractor or their website tells you, especially if they have knocked on your door or telephoned you to offer their services. Request from them a business card, letterhead, or their full contact details. Then do a search on the internet for the business, find the number listed and check it's the same as what has been provided directly to you by them. Ring the business to check that it exists and that the contractor works for them. Also ask to see proof of qualifications such as an NVQ in construction for builders, or a card from the Construction Skills Certification Scheme. Find out if they have signed up to any schemes such as Competent Person Schemes. This will provide an indication of their qualifications, e.g. to sign off building works.

Check if they have a trade association membership to organisations such as FENSA or the Consumer Protection Association (CPA). Trade associations can tell you about qualifications for particular types of work and they can also confirm if a contractor is a member. Be wary if a contractor who just provides you with their mobile number as they may be difficult to contact if problems come up. Most of the contractors we have engaged have been great, but it always pays to be vigilant with your checks to put your mind at rest.

Obtain quotes

Obtain written quotes from at least 3 different contractors before you decide who you will hire. Compare all the quotes to help you decide if you are getting a fair price. Having the quote in writing allows you to check what you agreed and prove it if there's a dispute later. Once you say yes to a quote, it becomes a binding agreement between you and the contractor, whether there is a formal contract in writing or not.

> Make sure you obtain a quote, and not an estimate. A quote is a fixed price which confirms what you are getting and how much it will cost. An estimate is a rough guess and you could end up paying more. The contractor has a legal right to charge you what the price should have been. They cannot charge you more than the price on their quote unless:
> - You ask for extra work that is not included in the quote.
> - They let you know they have to do extra work and you agree to pay more for it.
> - They made a genuine mistake when calculating the price.

Be wary if a contractor won't put a quote in writing as it is an indicator that they could be unreliable. Also, be cautious if their price is a lot lower than other quotes you get as it could mean they are not quoting for exactly the same work, do not have the right skills and experience, or that they are not being honest.

> Be very clear about the work you want done as this will help you get the most accurate price and prevent misunderstandings later. Their quote should include:
> - A fixed total price and not a daily rate and if it includes VAT.
> - A breakdown of all the work to be undertaken and the materials required.
> - Separate costs for each material and part of the work it relates to.
> - How long the quote is valid for.
> - When the price can go up, e.g. only if you agree to extra work.

If you get a daily rate instead of a fixed total price, there is a risk that the contractor could elongate the work to get more money. Avoid this by getting them to put in writing how many days the work will take, how many hours of work counts as a day and when they need your go-ahead to work more days. We have had daily rate contractors who have consistently only worked partial days and weeks but creatively invoiced us for full time work. We haven't used them again.

If you are thinking of extending your home, there are many factors involved in costing an extension project, from the size of the project right down to the quality of the paint you use on the walls. For a basic breakdown of average extension costs, you can use online extension cost calculator tools. Also approach several builders and get full quotes for the proposed extension. Get them to explain the quotes until you are satisfied.

Check your contractor's insurance

Before saying yes to a quote, check the contractor has the appropriate and relevant insurance in place, such as Contractors' All-Risk Cover, Employer's Liability Insurance, Professional Indemnity Insurance and Public Liability insurance. If they are going to be undertaking 'hot works' such as welding, soldering, torch cutting, grinding and hot riveting, or are applying heat to roof coverings (replacement of felt coverings on flat roofs), they should have a relevant hot work permit or hot roofing within their public liability insurance.

These activities present a heightened fire risk by involving the use of heat, or the creation of sparks and other sources of ignition. A friend of ours was having his house built and the builder was grinding the steel frame with an angle grinder. The area around the work was not protected and the sparks damaged two of his neighbour's luxury cars and a run of uPVC windows. The damage came to around £25,000. The builder did not have the correct insurance and our friend was being pursued for the costs!

Sign a contract

Once you provide a contractor with the go-ahead, you have made a contract with them, even if it's not written down. Always try to get a contract in writing before you start the work. Consider one of the standard forms that the builders will be familiar with, such as a JCT (Joint Contracts Tribunal) Home Owner Contract. If the contractor provides you a with contract, check it covers everything that you agreed. If they do not provide you with a contract, write your own. Be wary of any contractors who will not put anything in writing.

Written contracts do not need to be in legal language, they just need to outline exactly what you are paying for (they can refer back to the quote for this) and everything you have agreed on, such as timings, tidying up, materials and payments. It can help to look at example contracts, or create a contract using a template, e.g. for home repairs or maintenance, you can download a free contract template, or for building work, you can download an example contract or buy a contract template.

Make sure the contract covers:

- Start and finish dates, the agreed rate, the number of days the work will take, working hours per day, why delays might happen and what the contractor will do about them.
- How and when the contractor will remove rubbish and clear up after themselves and who pays for delivery and collection of any skips.
- Who pays for hire materials and equipment the contractor buys, how they will provide you with invoices, receipts and paperwork, and if / when they'll use subcontractors.
- How and when you will pay. Aim to pay them by credit or debit card, and not cash. Avoid large deposits, upfront payments and contractors who only accept cash as it is a sign they could be dishonest or unreliable. Make stage payments and hold some money back, particularly if it is a big project. Agree the point or milestones in the work schedule when payments are due. Include a snagging period as it means problems can be put right before you make the final payment.

A note about paying by credit and debit cards. If you pay by credit or debit card, you may be able to get your money back through your bank if something goes wrong, such as the contractor not turning up and refusing to pay back your deposit. If this happens, contact your bank and tell them want to use the chargeback scheme. If you pay more than £100, but less than £30,000 by credit card, tell your card company that you want to make a claim under section 75 of the Consumer Credit Act. Using section 75 could help you get back the full amount of the item, the cost of repairing it, an amount to reflect that the item or service wasn't satisfactory (such as financial compensation to make up for poor quality service or goods), or compensation if the faulty item caused damage (such as a faulty washing machine damaging a floor).

Do not agree to pay everything up front in case something goes wrong or the contractor does not turn up. If they ask for a deposit to pay for materials, offer to buy them yourself instead of paying a deposit as at least you will own the materials in case of mishap.

If the work is expected to take a long duration to complete, you may not be able to avoid paying a deposit. Try to push down the amount of deposit you pay to as low as possible, and do not agree to more than 25%. Make sure you are provided with a receipt for the deposit, as well as receipts for any materials it covers. You can protect your deposit or staged payments until the work is complete with a deposit protection scheme, where your money will be stored in a secure account until you and the contractor are both happy with the work. Or you could obtain an insurance-backed warranty or guarantee to cover the cost of finishing or fixing the work if they do a bad job or go out of business.

You may be able to cancel the contract if you change your mind within 14 days of giving the go-ahead or signing a written contract. If you agreed that the work could start within the 14 days, you may be required to pay for some or all of it. This is fair because spending has occurred on your project.

Hiring trade contractors is critical to the success of any renovation project. Professional developers state that getting the right team around you is crucial and you should keep them together as much as possible. Take time to consider where you want to do the work yourself and where a professional would be a better choice. Then take your time choosing the right people as it will be well worth it in the end.

Refer to the *Stress, issues and conflict Chapter* for Q&A on obtaining resolution with trade contractors.

Organise your budget and finances

For any renovation project, the most important thing you need to take stock of is your finance. This will guide your planning and direct your renovation. Calculating how much you have to spend will influence the duration and size of the project.

You could start your renovation project with a smaller budget, and once you have re-decorated and re-carpeted, the overall improvement should allow a small re-mortgage. This could be used to upgrade or renew the new kitchen and bathroom.

It is advisable to have a contingency of 15-20% to allow for the unexpected expenses that can arise when renovating older homes. This can help with accommodation elsewhere while major work is being done, as well as cover some unforeseen issues or unplanned costs. You will also need to create a separate budget for decorating and furnishing the property once the building work is completed.

Once you have confirmed your costs and budget for your renovation project, record all your estimated costs. We use an Excel spreadsheet to manage and

Chapter 2. RENOVATING YOUR PROPERTY

track our costs. Every expense needs to be recorded, including items like skip hire (if you are paying for this separately). Also record what you yet have to pay for, when and how much. It is important to have this record to protect both you and the trades working on your property from overcharging or any misunderstandings around expected payments. Ensure you check your budget versus actual spend so you have sufficient funds to the end of the project.

Budget properly and monitor progress regularly. This is one of the most common things to get wrong. If you just guess a figure for everything, or just have a rough figure in your head for the whole renovation or restoration project, you are going to get a nasty shock when the bills come in.

To help control your costs, consider the following guide.

Do:

- Shop around to get the best prices.
- Invest in design work and detailed drawings.
- Keep the design simple.
- Ensure your design is space-efficient.
- Finalise decisions before starting.
- Schedule work so that it proceeds in the correct sequence.
- Agree labour rates and hours in writing.
- Keep a close eye on work rate.
- Encourage your contractors to keep a tidy and efficient site.
- Find sales and offers, buying in bulk where appropriate.
- Allow for wastage on materials.
- Use standard material sizes to reduce wastage.
- Buy previous year's appliance models.
- Salvage, recycle and buy reclaimed materials.
- Combine expensive quality pieces with bargain items.
- Buy seconds and end-of-line products.
- Only undertake DIY tasks that you are confident in.
- Visit the site where possible.
- Heed the adage 'Measure twice and cut once'!

Don't:

- Make unnecessary changes from what was agreed in the quote and contract as it almost always adds cost and delay.
- Hold up the project unless agreed with the main contractor.
- Make critical decisions and choices as you go along.
- Leave the kitchen design until the walls and ceiling have been plastered.
- Over-order materials.
- Run out of an end-of-line product.
- Use lots of individual bespoke materials.
- Buy 'bargains' that may never be used.
- Skimp using cheap finishes, this is false economy.
- Lose materials on an untidy site.
- Repair when replacement is beneficial and more cost-effective.
- Renovate if demolition and a new build is a cheaper and sounder option.
- Have excavated earth taken away when you could use it elsewhere.
- Agree to variations without a written quote.
- Borrow using expensive credit cards.

Insurance cover

Make sure you have the right insurance for your renovation. Most people insure their property and its contents, but many are unaware that home contents or buildings insurance may not cover them for extensive building work. If you make alterations without addressing this with your insurance company, you might find your policy is voided, so claiming against it will be impossible should anything go wrong. Standard insurance policies only cover an inhabited house; if you plan to move out while the work is carried out, make sure you have informed your insurance company.

We had a situation where one of our builders fell through the kitchen floor. We discovered a large pool of water under the floor. It was coming from an old lead waterpipe that had punctured, and bin bags had been placed over the leaking pipe to deflect the water spraying up under the kitchen floor. Our insurance company would not cover us, and we were unable to get any recourse from the survey company. As the property had been purchased

Chapter 2. RENOVATING YOUR PROPERTY

> by us only a few months previously, we were advised to pursue the claim through the seller's insurers. We did this and were compensated.

Contact your home insurance company to let them know what work you're having done, how long you expect it to take and the expected cost. They may amend your policy while the work is being carried out, or they might not be able to cover you, in which case you'll need to look for a quote elsewhere. Find a specialist renovations insurance company. The level of insurance required will depend on what works are being carried out.

You can take the following steps to protect your home and reduce the chance of a claim while renovating a property. These could help to cut the cost of your premiums:

- Increase your home security by installing alarms (burglar / security and smoke alarms).
- Install door and window key locks that meet British Standard (BS) 3621. Some insurers may reduce your premium or may make it a requirement.
- Install security lighting as this will help deter burglars because it makes them more likely to be seen. Installing motion-detecting lights will alert you if there is someone outside.
- Install a safe to keep expensive items. This can help offset the potential extra cost of insuring high-value belongings.
- Insulate water pipes as they can become damaged when they freeze and thaw. Insulating or lagging pipes can help prevent them from freezing in the first place, which reduces the risk of them bursting and flooding your home. Escape of water is one of the most common reasons for any claims on home insurance.
- Protect yourself against subsidence and heave. Your surveyor should check for signs when you buy a property, and this should be noted in your survey report. The ground under a property can be affected, causing it to sink (subsidence) or the ground to swell up (heave), especially if it's built on a clay soil. You can help protect against this by maintaining your drainage systems and pipes, and by removing trees and shrubs that are too close to the property (5-10 metres). Remember to seek professional advice before chopping any trees down.

If you have taken all the measures within your renovation project to protect your property, there is a reduced rick of claiming insurance. Some insurers offer a discount if you have not made a claim, which could help reduce your renewal insurance premium. Once the renovation is completed, check if you need to change or update your insurance.

Planning and consents

It is generally known that local council permission is required for building work or alterations to properties. However, it is not always clear how the planning and building regulations approval differ. The following are descriptions of each.

Planning

Approval for planning is necessary because local authorities guide the way that the countryside, towns and cities develop. This includes the use of land and buildings, the appearance of buildings, landscaping considerations and highway access, as well as what impact the development project will have on the general environment. Most applications for planning permission are decided within eight weeks, unless applications are unusually large or complex, in which case the time limit is extended to 13 weeks.

Building regulations

These approvals are required as local authorities have set standards for the design and construction of buildings to ensure the safety and health of people in or around the buildings. They also include requirements to ensure that fuel and power is conserved, and facilities are provided for people to access and move around inside of buildings.

Contact a Building Control Body (BCB) to check the building regulations or request approval. You can apply through local authority BCBs or a private approved inspector. You must decide on the type of application for your planned build, extension or alteration work (there are different rules in Scotland and Northern Ireland). The types of building regulations applications are:

- Full plans, which is the most thorough and involved option. Expect a decision within 5 weeks to 2 months. You will be provided with a completion certificate within 8 weeks of completion of the building works as long as it complies.
- Building notice, which is an application for smaller projects only. You can start your work 2 days after you have submitted your notice to your BCB. You are not provided with formal approval (as you will expect to with a full plans application).

- Regularisation, where you can apply for retrospective approval from a local authority BCB for work already carried out without consent. We would not recommend this approach as you can't be sure that you will definitely receive approval after the fact. We always obtain permission prior to starting our projects.

If you want to start work immediately, check with your local planning authority and take on projects that are classed as permitted development, such as converting an existing garage or roof space. If you do need to obtain statutory consents for all or part of your proposed works, factor in the amount of time that will be required to process the application.

If you are employing the services of a qualified architect for an extension, they will discuss with you what you need to do to obtain planning permission. Even if you own the property, you must seek planning permission from your local authority. Planning permission allows neighbours to object to any proposed additions to a property if they feel it may affect their view, the amount of natural light they are entitled to, or if it reduces the value of their own property at the time of sale.

If you want to make any structural changes to your home, such as putting doors in to make an ensuite, or knocking down any walls, you will need permission from your local Building Control Body. In most cases planning permission from the local council is not required for internal alterations (with some exceptions).

Make sure that you know and understand the different consents that you will need to address. Consider whether you have permission to use the building as a dwelling, or whether you will need consent for a material change of use. If it is a listed building, ascertain whether it is also in a Conservation Area. Even if you do not require planning permission, you will almost certainly have to comply with building regulations. Depending on the type of property, you may potentially require a party wall agreement with your neighbours. An architect can guide you through this minefield.

Generally speaking, unless your house is listed, you won't need planning permission for interior work or minor works outside the house. If building work takes your house nearer to its boundaries, or if it is more than a set amount in volume (there are different limits for different types of houses), then planning permission will probably be needed.

When in doubt, always check with your local planning office. Most offer a free, informal consultation with one of their planning officers before you apply. They will advise you as best they can how likely it is that you will be granted permission. We usually call our local planning office in advance to obtain initial information so that we can be prepared with the required particulars when we visit the office to discuss the details of our application.

How to apply

If you do need planning permission, you can either apply for it yourself, or ask your builder or architect to apply for it on your behalf. After contacting your local planning authority to check whether you need permission, and the type of permission you need, complete the correct form. You can submit the form online, along with all the relevant drawings, showing the plan of the site, details of your changes or additions, and any other relevant information to support your application as well as the correct application fee.

The planning authority will check your application, making sure you have submitted everything correctly, and asking for any further clarification or documents if necessary. You will receive an acknowledgement in writing that your request has been received; this is usually done within a week. They will review the plans and verify if they comply with the local plans for the area and do not infringe any other planning rules.

As your neighbours can appeal should they be adversely affected by your plans (e.g. by light being blocked through their windows or their garden overlooked). A good way to assist this process is to visit your neighbours and explain what you are doing. You can then deal with any objections they may have before the planning application is submitted. People are more likely to be put out if the first they hear of your plans is when the notice is stuck onto the lamppost outside their front door.

The planning office will put notices up in your area to let people know what you are intending to do and wait for a set amount of time (approx. 8 weeks) to see if anyone questions or objects to your plans. If there are no objections, the plans are assessed at a meeting of the planning committee, and if all goes well, planning permission will be granted to you.

There are three possible outcomes from a planning application:

- Permission is granted
- Permission is granted with conditions

- Permission is refused.

If you obtain permission, but with conditions, you must comply with those conditions when you undertake the work. If you cannot meet the stated conditions, you can re-work your project and re-submit the plans if you still wish to proceed with them.

If permission is refused, you can appeal to the Planning Inspectorate. They will review the decision and assess whether your planning committee followed the correct process. If they find that your planning committee did not follow the correct process, they may grant planning permission. It is worth trying this only if you believe that they have made a mistake, as it will be up to you to explain why they did so in your appeal documentation. If you are advised by your architect or builder that any appeal is unlikely to be successful, it is best to talk directly to the planners about the reasons for their rejection. You can then re-apply for permission with a new set of plans that have taken those objections into account.

The main thing to remember is that if you do not get planning permission, or if you go against conditions set out in your permission, the planning authorities have wide-ranging powers. They can stop your build and instruct you to demolish or correct the offending part of your project. If you do not comply in time, you will be taken to court. Again, we strongly recommend that you obtain planning permission before embarking on your project.

Conforming to building regulations

Building regulations exist to ensure our buildings are safe to live in, more energy efficient and accessible for disabled people. Many regulations been changed in recent years to ensure commonality across Europe so that materials can be traded across European borders. It is up to you or your contractor, architect or craftsman to stay up-to-date with these regulations. With a renovation project, there could potentially be a conflict of interest between modern regulations and old materials and techniques.

The enforcement of building regulations in all countries of the United Kingdom is applied by the local planning offices in the various regional councils. A private approved building control inspector only has the responsibility for checking that the building regulations are complied with during the course of your building work. This is on an advisory basis only as they do not have formal enforcement powers.

Depending on the extent of your renovation, you may or may not be visited by a building control inspector to check that you have complied. With a renovation project, you will need to know the regulations that were in force when the house was built. An architect should be able to assist with this.

Listed buildings and conservation areas

When you purchased your property, it should have been made clear to you if it was listed. If you are unsure, you need to check this as it is a criminal offence to carry out unauthorised work on a listed home. Many buildings built around 1840, or earlier, are likely to be listed. Over half a million properties in the UK are listed. Check with British Listed Buildings if it is listed, and if it is, you will need to obtain Listed Building Consent (LBC) for any alterations. Even the type of paint used needs to be authorised (painting a listed home with a plastic paint or using gypsum plasters is not permitted). Check before starting work.

The most important thing about renovating a listed building is to seek advice about what work needs to be done, and what the restrictions are, before you buy the property. This cannot be emphasised enough. The purpose of listing is to protect it for the future. If that can be better served by allowing the use of the building to be changed to suit modern living styles, then the authorities will listen to your proposals, but there are no guarantees.

If your renovation is intended to restore a property to its full glory, the local planning authority will consult with the correct authority in that country, such as English Heritage in England and Wales, Historic Scotland, or the Environment and Heritage Service in Northern Ireland. They will ensure that the renovation goes ahead in the right way and that the appropriate materials and techniques will be used to preserve the integrity of the build. If agreement can be reached by all the relevant parties, you will be given LBC and you can then proceed. Depending on the grade of your property, consent even may be necessary just for you to redecorate your property. There are several major impacts on your renovation project for a listed building. These are:

- The build will be delayed longer while these consultations are progressing.
- The cost of the build is likely to be greater than if the property was not listed, as you will be unable to use modern materials and techniques.
- You may find it more difficult to borrow money on the property to fund the work.
- You may come to a disagreement over the planner's decision, which could stop the work and involve court action. This is best avoided.

Chapter 2. RENOVATING YOUR PROPERTY

Where an extension is planned for a listed building, the idea in the past was to imitate the existing building so that they blended in. More recently, some planners have requested that the new part be completely different to provide a clearer dividing line between old and new, but to be designed so that the two complement each other. This does provide challenges for architects. In some cases, the new part will be completely different, but in the same materials. In others, it will copy the design of the old house but use materials or colours to differentiate.

> It is essential to abide by the laws for listed buildings. Making any alterations without LBC can result in fines, or even a one-year prison sentence, along with being forced to put the work right at your own expense. Doing nothing to a listed building that you own is also illegal. If you neglect it, legal action can be taken to force you to restore it.

There are bright sides to renovating a listed building, not least the pride of restoring something worth keeping. If you have LBC, you may be able to reclaim VAT from the builders and other trades that you use on the renovation. You will need expert advice to ensure the consent is applicable as it usually does not apply to repairs and maintenance.

Grants may be available to assist you with paying for some of the work. The administrative body for listed buildings (in your country) may be able to help, along with the local authority, but probably only for the top two listed building grades.

For most people renovating a listed building, they are likely to have been attracted to it due to its age, importance and architectural significance. The planning stage just needs to incorporate more time and money.

A home that is located in a conservation area has another protective status that can impact work done to it. Restrictions in conservation areas generally only affect the exterior of the property, as the intention is to preserve or enhance the character or appearance of an area. Your permitted development rights (works that you can usually do without planning permission) will be affected as you may require planning consent for works that are authorised elsewhere.

Project management

You can either hire a professional or manage the project yourself. There are a number of activities and tasks to be managed during a renovation project, so ensure you make the right decision for the long run.

Hire a professional project manager

If it's a complex renovation and needs expert knowledge, look to employ a professional project manager. For example, plumbers and electricians work almost completely independently when undertaking the first fix work (i.e. all the work required to take a building from foundation to putting plaster on the internal walls – constructing walls, floors, ceilings, inserting cables for the electrical supply and installing pipes for the water supply).

> However, two things are crucial to a trouble-free project:
> - Both trades need to know the plans for each other's work, because it will all need to work simultaneously at the end when the electrics are coupled to the plumbing.
> - They both have to lay materials through walls, roof spaces, ceilings and floors, and often need to be working in the same space at the same time, so their activities need to be coordinated to ensure that they're not in each other's way. Additionally, joiners need to know about the work of the plumber and the electrician so that they leave the required gaps for wires, pipes and so on. Plasterers also need to know what the plans are so that they can ascertain when they can come in to finish walls and ceilings. Often these craftsmen will work independently and need to have their time arranged well in advance. It's easy to see where things can start to unravel, and delays can build up.

It will cost money, but it might be cheaper than correcting mistakes that may arise from inexperience. As the work begins, an experienced project manager will prove their worth, making sure that materials and workers are where they need to be, and fewer delays occur. They will liaise with the builder and main contractor to ensure work is carried out to the correct specification.

Manage the project yourself

Seek as much advice as possible, especially from people who have done it before, if you decide to manage the project yourself. Some people are prepared to live on a building site until structural work is completed. Obtain all the quotes well in advance so you can confirm your expenditure. Be aware that timescales can shift; project completion does not usually take place within the initial scheduled plan. Be aware that purchase and delivery of materials may not correspond, and that all the activities expected from the build team during the renovation may not always go as planned.

> Make sure you record (via email or text) key communication and agreements so you have an audit trail to refer to. This will protect both parties from any potential disputes that may arise during or after the renovation process.

> Also make sure you capture and file all the paperwork, invoices, receipts, copies of contracts, guarantees, legal paperwork and permissions as you progress through the project. You will then have a complete record of expenditure and key documents on completion of the project. Having evidence to hand and being able to produce it in a timely manner will also help with swift resolution of issues.

Write a schedule of works

> Clearly write down all the steps required to renovate the property before you make a start. Prioritise any work that needs to be done, starting from stopping any decay or stabilising the building. Work being undertaken in one room may impact another (e.g. where plumbing and wiring are involved). Have a clear vision for the whole property and prepare a schedule of works, listed in order, e.g. re-wiring to be completed before the walls are plastered.

If you are adding an extension or carrying out major structural work, consult the appropriate professionals first as there may be implications you are unaware of. As an example, converting the loft might seem like an isolated job from the rest of the house, but adding an additional habitable floor carries with it building regulation demands. These may require you to fit safe doors, a sprinkler system and mains powered alarms. Be aware of these kinds of issues early on as they will affect your budget as well as the aesthetics of your property.

Be aware of how long building projects can take so that you can more accurately plan for them in your works schedule or project plan. As an example, the average timelines are:

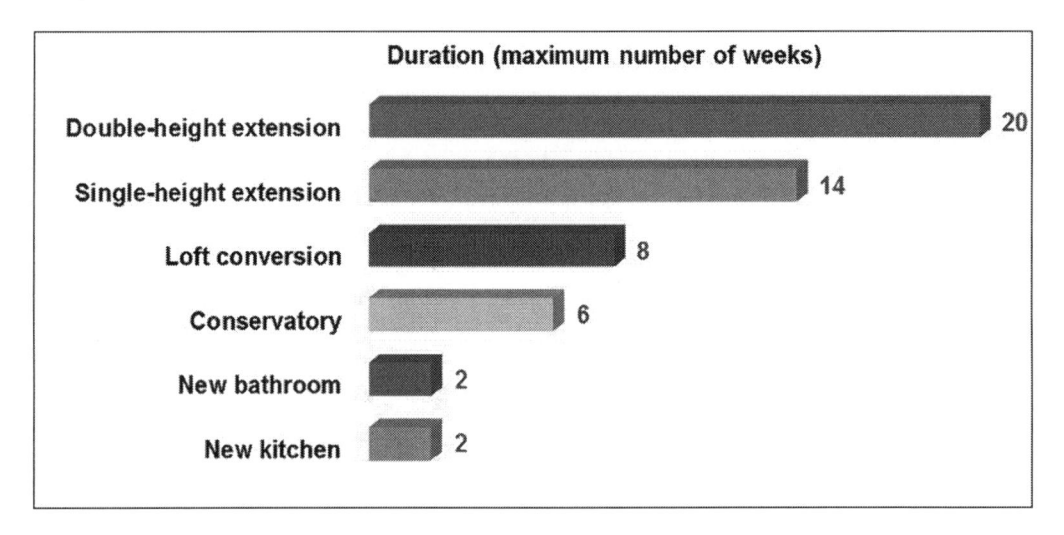

Project	Duration (maximum number of weeks)
Double-height extension	20
Single-height extension	14
Loft conversion	8
Conservatory	6
New bathroom	2
New kitchen	2

Prioritise

In terms of the priority order of a renovation, consider the following:

1. Check the gas connection to the property. If you do not have gas to the property and you need to have it installed, book the work in as early as possible as it can take weeks to obtain an installation date.

2. Have the electrics checked. If you need a new meter, or anything else, sort this out as early as possible as it can also take weeks to arrange.

3. Make the property weatherproof. Plastering, electrics and joinery all need a dry environment. If the building is not weatherproof, that is the first thing to fix. Do your walls, roof, insulation, doors and glazing as quickly as possible. Once the building is watertight the time pressure for the interior not as critical, work can continue inside the house when the weather is bad, and exterior work can be done when the sun shines.

4. Check plumbing and ensure that you have water to the property. Also check for leaks.

5. Get rid of everything that is not necessary or required, or have it repaired / modernised:

    a. Anything that you do not want, sell on eBay / Gumtree, or take to a salvage yard.

> b. Donate to the charity shop or organisations helping people furnish their homes.
>
> c. Put anything else that is not salvageable or able to be sold in a skip.
>
> 6. Begin the renovation, starting with a room to sleep in, a bathroom and the kitchen. Make sure you have one liveable room that you can escape to!

You are likely to have different things influencing your order of priorities. Time, money and available skills will all play a part in this. If you are paying money to live somewhere else while the renovation is being completed, then spending money to get things done quicker may be a good overall strategy. If you plan accordingly, you should be able to move into one part of the house when it's finished (while the rest is being completed).

Identify and plan dependencies

> Two things will come out of this process – a list of tasks that depend on each other, and another list of jobs that may be related, but can be done at any time without affecting the remaining work. Armed with these lists, you have an overall picture of the project that will be of great use for you.

If the jobs you are working on come to a halt for reasons that you cannot control (e.g. because of the weather or late delivery of some materials), you can select jobs that can be done from your independent list to ensure work continues and you are not maintaining workers who are inactive. For example, you might be stumped on a delivery of new bricks for your house, which means your bricklayers can't work without these, but at least they can rebuild the wall that you had to knock down to let in that big lorry last week!

Phase the work

If you know that you won't have enough money to complete the whole job in one go, consider how you can break it up into phases so that you have work that can be left until later. With major works, try and get it all done in one go as it will be a lot more expensive to get builders back on site to undertake a second phase of key activities. Once completed, you can concentrate on getting all the inside work done on one floor, then move in and complete the rest as and when you have time and money.

There are certain jobs that will be a lot more expensive if they are done in two chunks, such as initial wiring and plumbing, while the second fix stage is able to be delayed without significantly increasing the cost. Second fix refers to all the work after the plastering of a finished house, e.g. electrical fixtures are connected to the cables, sinks and baths are connected to the pipes and doors fitted into doorframes, and these require a neater finish than the first fix.

Ensure you're not buying a money pit. In an older property be prepared for anything, right down to half the wall staying on the wallpaper when stripping it off, or holes behind the panelling that were not evident until the panelling was removed. Bring in the trades as many times as you need to in order to know the magnitude of the work to be completed.

The amount of work required will be different for each property. Just be careful not to bite off more than you can chew. If you are new to renovating, look to do up a dated property rather than a wreck. A new kitchen, bathroom, central heating, carpets and re-decoration will miraculously transform something dark and decrepit into a desirable property.

You can always leave projects that require architects, specialists and the planning department to another time when confidence and funds are more plentiful.

Weekly project meetings and slippage

> Plan to visit the site as much as possible while you have contractors working on your property. This may be a challenge if you are working, but use your lunch break, or come home early from work on some days to connect with the contractors on site. Discuss with them the progress of the work against the plan and any issues that require your input. Make any required decisions while there. If you cannot physically get to the property during working hours, agree with the main builder or contractor to be provided with a daily update, via the phone or text. This will enable you to be appraised on progress, issues, delays on deliveries, or any decisions they need from you.

If there is going to be slippage, the faster you know about it, the easier it is to make contingency plans to deal with it. It's important to know about slippage and address it as swiftly as possible. The project plan will have to be updated accordingly. Some tasks might be completed in a shorter time than expected, and others (probably many more) will take longer than anticipated. When that happens, updating the plan will make you aware of what other activities may have to be shifted. You may also obtain a view on how to claw back the time by re-arranging other tasks.

Re-planning many not be sufficient. The plan is at the core of the project but it's not the project. If the plan is being updated (e.g. the window supplier is going to deliver three weeks later than initially planned), then the contractor relying on the windows will have to be told and re-scheduled. For the three-week delay not to be significant, perhaps the plasterers will have to be told not to come until the windows have been delivered, unless there are enough other jobs that need to be done before they come in (e.g. fitting central heating pipes and laying electrical wires through the walls). Updating the plan will show you whether or not you need to postpone certain contractors (in this case, the plasterers).

> Keep communicating with your trades throughout the project. Make yourself available to respond to queries and ask for updates as your home improvements progress. If problems or holdups arise, ask what the impact is and how they will be resolved. Communicate regularly with the main contractor.

Make sure you record, via email or text, key communication and agreements made to ensure you have an audit trail to refer to protect both parties from any potential disputes that may arise during the renovation process.

Payment schedule

> Knowing when and how to pay your contractors can be daunting. With the exception of a small deposit, no monies should be exchanged until a key milestone in the project has been reached. The milestones need to be agreed between the two of you, and you both need to sign off on them as part of the contract. Setting up a payment schedule is a fair way to keep all parties satisfied. It ensures you both know where you stand.

On a typical extension or self-build, the builder cannot continue past the foundation excavation until it has been passed by a building inspector, which needs to occur prior to concreting. This can be used as a key milestone. In most extensions, this work is completed in a week. After the inspection has been undertaken, it is safe to make a stage or milestone payment. The same approach can be followed (where applicable) for the drainage, ground floor slab, electrical first fix, structural steelwork and completion stages. All these elements require a building inspection and can form the agreed payment milestones. If you're unsure of inspection stages, contact your local council.

There may be instances where large deposits or payments are required for specialist items, such as timber frame or made-to-measure items. To ensure there is a need for the payment, insist the builder provides a copy of the manufacturer's terms and conditions.

Don't be pressured into making payments before agreed stages of work have been completed. We always make payments after the week's work is done, and not in advance, and disbursements depend on agreed milestones. If there are particular materials that are required for our renovations, we usually pay for them directly to the supplier over the phone when the builder is at the specific store. Or if we have been provided with a copy of a receipt, we check the items that have been purchased and pay the supplier or builder. We use trade accounts with a large number of our suppliers, so we are also able to put items on our accounts and check these directly before making payment.

> It is also good practice to retain 5% of the contract value, and release half of this retention at practical completion. To motivate your builder to return to fix any issues that may arise, make a snagging list of any defects five months after practical completion, and send it to the builder. Give them a month to rectify the defects. If the builder fails to return, they are no longer entitled to the final retention payment.

One of our builders provided us with a receipt for his whole month's purchase, rather than for our particular renovation, and we only knew what we were being asked to pay for because we checked the purchase dates on the invoice (which started well before our project) and the items on the bill (which included a 3-piece bathroom set which wasn't our requested suite). So always ask for receipts and keep them. Check the dates and items before you make these payments. While it's not always possible to know what every single item is on the invoice, if there is a significant payment expected, you can either ask your builder or Google the particular item to identify where it fits in with your renovation. You can also call the suppliers and ask them (refer to their details on the invoice).

Work out a payment schedule with your builder or main contractor. Establish an agreement to make staged payments based on approved milestones. This will form part of your contract.

Engage with suppliers

> With suppliers, phone them regularly to check that your delivery will be on time. If there is going to be a delay, they are unlikely to let you know in advance as they are always hoping that they will make the date. In most cases, the first time you hear that they are not going to deliver perhaps is a day or two before the scheduled date. By then it is usually too late to put in place a contingency plan to obtain replacements based on the same schedule.

Keep on top of all inter-dependencies and the separate tasks, as well as the different tradesmen, taking care of them. If one person cannot come in and do their work because someone else hasn't finished, or suppliers have not delivered, it's not their fault, but you will be expected to pay for their time. If you have agreed with your contractor that you will be in charge of obtaining materials for all the jobs, then it is up to you to plan, coordinate and chase the suppliers to ensure the delivery arrives on time and in readiness for the different trades that will need them, otherwise you could delay the project and incur costs.

> We have experienced delays several times. For one project, we were informed by the reseller several times that our chosen tiles were on their way, even after the delivery date was delayed. When we turned up at the reseller's store to discuss this directly with a member of their management team, we were advised that their supplier was no longer producing these tiles. We left the store and sourced other tiles elsewhere. This caused us delays, cost us considerably more than we expected and caused a lot of stress. So, keep up regular communications with your suppliers and re-confirm deliveries.

The renovation project

How you approach a renovation project will depend on your budget, whether you are intending to live in the property, whether you are doing it up to sell on quickly (flip) or are upgrading it as a buy-to-let investment. These are all different motivations and depending on what the renovation is looking to achieve, you will need to consider various options with varying priorities. If you are intending to live in the property, you are likely to inject more of your personality into it and invest in a more premium finish, compared to a property you are flipping.

> Refer to the *Interior design and decorating Chapter* for detailed information and ideas.

General renovation

Start your project by getting rid of everything you will not keep. This includes carpets, curtains, outdated or damaged fitted furniture, and as much junk and debris as possible. Strip off old wallpaper and repair any holes or cracks in the walls, sanding and filling to a smooth finish so they are ready for painting. If the walls are in very poor condition, they can be reskimmed with a finishing coat of plaster, creating walls that are as a good as new. You can then choose to either personalise or repaint the walls in a light neutral shade, such as an off-white, with the same colour on the ceilings, which will reflect light and making the property feel more spacious. Repaint the woodwork, including the skirting, architrave and doors, in a complementary neutral colour, or in a dark contrasting colour to make a bold statement.

If ceilings are in bad shape, opt for pulling them down and replacing them with new plasterboard. Do the she same with damaged skirtings. Repairing these can be quite involved and time consuming, so in most cases, it is better to just start again. Sand, stain or paint the floorboards if they are in good condition, or you can lay wooden laminate flooring. Replace damaged or outdated light fittings and shades with new. If the kitchen and bathroom are out of date, update them or replace them with new.

If anyone in your house is an asthma or allergy sufferer, this is likely to influence your choice of paints, flooring and soft furnishings. Think this through and obtain the appropriate input to make the right decisions about the materials you will use.

Electrics and lighting

Have all the electrics in the property inspected to ensure they are fit for purpose, including the consumer unit / fuse board, ensuring it will meet your current needs. Make sure all the electrical plug sockets are working properly and install additional sockets for your new requirements, such as for computers, the home office, the entertainment / home cinema systems.

Have the light switches, dimmers and timers inspected to ensure they are working properly. Confirm whether the existing light fixtures and fittings need replacing (either for practical or aesthetic reasons). Install additional lights as required (e.g. kitchen spotlights, bathroom lights, office or study, outdoor security lights). Also fit new sockets, switches and dimmers for a more contemporary look (satin chrome is a good option). Look to provide further illumination to dark areas in the house.

Assess whether you need any rewiring undertaken for additional requirements, e.g. if you are installing a security light outside on your porch. Upgrade your smoke and fire detectors, as well as your house alarm (change the security code). Install other electrical components such as smart meters, underfloor heating or solar power panels as required. Positioning of the controllers for meters, electric heating and solar power installations will need to be discussed with your electrician. One of our contractors advised that we should have a thermostat in the middle of the largest wall in the dining room because it was the required midpoint, but we convinced him that the side of the wall would be more convenient as we intended to place furniture and artworks on the main wall. So, have a say in the details and agree a compromise.

If you have invested in an electric vehicle (EV), or intend to, consider in your electrical requirements whether you will install a Wallbox chargepoint as it can also be attractive to future property buyers or renters. The chargepoint can reduce the charging time for your vehicle from around 25 hours to approx. 5-8 hours. The government currently offers grants to support the use of electric and hybrid vehicles through the Office of Low Emission Vehicles (OLEV). The Electric Vehicle Homecharge Scheme (EVHS) is providing grants up to 75% of the cost of installing chargepoints for electric vehicle at domestic properties across the UK. Refer to the government website for updates and further information.

Make sure you are provided with an electrical certificate for any electrical work done as part of the UK national standard, BS 7671 (Building Standards Requirements for Electrical Installations). There should be an Electrical Installation Certificate or, where applicable, a Minor Electrical Installation Works Certificate that confirms the work meets this standard, along with a Building Regulations Compliance Certificate confirming that the work meets the required Building Regulations.

Plumbing and heating

Upgrade your plumbing during a home renovation project, particularly if it involves the bathroom, kitchen or laundry room. Replace any older, galvanised pipes with new copper piping. Have old sewer pipes checked as they can get obstructed over the years, eventually backing up into the shower, bath or toilet. They need to be cleaned out or may need to be replaced. Replace any outdated plumbing fixtures with those more efficient.

To cater for the plumbing and heating consumption requirements of the inhabitants of the property, decide on what type of hot water and central heating system you will install. The types of hot water systems vary, but the main systems used in the UK are:

Combination or Combi boiler
A high efficiency water heater and central heating boiler in a compact unit. It heats water directly from the mains when you turn on a tap. A hot water storage cylinder is not required, nor is a cold water storage tank in the roof. Perfect for smaller properties where there is little or no loft space, no hot water cylinder allows increased living space. No cold water storage tank enables for loft for conversion, no risk of loft pipework freezing, less pipework makes installation cheaper. **Cost to install: from £1,000.**
Regular, Traditional, Conventional, Heat only boiler
For homes already with a heating and hot water system with a separate hot water cylinder. A cold water storage tank is required in the loft for the hot water cylinder and a tank that maintains the water level of the central heating system. A good option if the property has an older radiator system, as it might not be able to cope with the higher water pressure from a system or combi boiler. Also, good for homes where a lot of hot water is used at the same time, where there are two or more bathrooms and where water pressure is low. Compatible with solar water heating systems for a lower carbon footprint and lower costs. **Cost to install: from £1,500.**
System boiler
Requires a cylinder for storing hot water with the main heating and hot water system components built into the boiler. No need for a tank in the loft, so no worries of leaks or frost damage. A good option for a home with little or no loft space or where the space is planned for a conversion. Compatible with solar water heating systems. Ideal for homes with more than one bathroom, it supplies constant hot water to a number of taps at the same time and is economical to run. Built-in components make installation quicker and neater. **Cost to install: from £2,000.**
Heat pump
Heat pumps extract heat from the ground outside or air for use in space or water heating. They work best with large storage tanks which do not need to be heated to such high temperatures. **Cost to install: from £6,000 (air system) to £9,000 (ground system).**

Your local water supplier can test your property's water pressure and flow rate. The water pressure test provides an indication of how high in the air the water can reach. The flow rate is the maximum volume of water that can flow into the property, typically measured in litres per minute. If the mains supply pipe work is unable to provide for peak water requirements, then there are options you can discuss with your plumber, including pumps, boosters or an upgrade of the mains supply pipe.

Confirm the heating system you will install for all the rooms in the property, including underfloor heating (water or electric). Replace old radiators with those that are more efficient. We have always done this in all our properties to ensure maximum efficiencies. As well, this has given us the opportunity to install some designer radiators for features and focal points. For your fireplace, consider whether you will opt for a wood and solid fuel fire, wood burning stove, gel or bioethanol, gas or electric fire. The type of fire you install will depend on whether there is a working chimney or not.

Make sure that you obtain a Building Regulations Compliance Certificate from a Gas Safe registered engineer for the installation of a heat producing gas appliances in the property, e.g. gas boiler, fire, cooker or hob.

Accommodate space saving appliances such as a combined washing machine and tumble dryer if you have any space restrictions.

Energy efficiency

Another key area to focus on is energy efficiency. With rising energy bills, people want cost-effective homes when it comes to energy use, rather than a house filled with ancient appliances, poor insulation and a lack of eco-friendly touches. Switch over any old energy-draining appliances to efficient models.

Check to make sure your home is well insulated with cavity wall and loft insulation and invest in the best U-value rating. The U-value measures how well an element of a building, such as a window or door, will transfer heat. The lower the U value, the better the thermal performance of the product. Invest in the best windows and doors you can afford. If your house has old, single-pane windows, replace them with double or triple glazing units to boost energy efficiency. All these modifications to your property will ensure a better EPC rating, creating a home that is more comfortable and has lower running costs. This will also be more attractive to future buyers.

Layout of the property

For your home renovation, you may decide you need more space in general. Older houses tend to have more rooms that are partitioned from each other, while the modern trend is for an open layout.

If you need to increase space, investigate the most cost-effective means of doing this:

- If you're considering removing walls to connect different rooms and expand specific areas, this can be costly. Any structural work requires consultation with a professional. Layout changes may require a foundation upgrade. Bear this in mind before proceeding.
- Converting your attic or basement to living areas can be a more cost-effective way of increasing your space, rather than making drastic layout changes.

- Many people build an extension, such as a conservatory or ground-floor extension, to open up their kitchen for a more social and entertaining space. This is a very good way to renovate your home but be mindful that planning permission is needed for certain types of extension. You are recommended to engage an architect or structural engineer.

Kitchen

A lot of attention is paid to kitchens. Some reports suggest a new kitchen can add up to 6% to the value of your home. If your kitchen is looking tired, you don't have to spend a fortune to give it a fresh new look. All it takes is a little time, effort and creativity to improve the heart of your home. Browse magazines, view online, visit high street and design stores for great ideas on where you can get good free advice. Also attend home shows and view renovated properties for sale. Friends and family can also be a good source for ideas because they know your property and (most probably) your affordability.

Update your kitchen on a budget

Existing kitchen cabinets can be painted inside and out, along with drawer fronts. Invest in a high-quality paint to ensure a durable finish. Update the existing cupboard and drawer handles with a high-end option to provide a more contemporary look.

If you like the existing layout and storage space your kitchen already offers, another option for a fresh look is to replace the doors, drawer fronts, handles, worktops, sink, taps and splashbacks while keeping the carcasses. For a standard £3,500 kitchen (with handles, but excluding appliances and worktops), around £2,200 is for the carcasses. Replacement doors start from around £20-50 per door. You can save on the cost of the cabinets and labour, as well as reduce stress and disruption. Many online companies provide replacement kitchen cabinet doors and drawer fronts. If you do want to invest in a run of carcasses, companies like Ikea stock standard carcasses onto which different styles of door can be fitted and interchanged.

You can also completely change the look of your kitchen by replacing your existing worktops. Although new worktops can be costly, changing just this can make it look as though you've had your whole kitchen renovated. Laminate is the most cost-effective to purchase, but there is a vast range of options for all budgets, including wood, granite, quartz, ceramic, glass, Corian and stainless steel. If you have spare budget, consider extras, such as heat rods that can be fitted into the surface for a permanent pan stand.

Chapter 2. RENOVATING YOUR PROPERTY

Splash backs are perfect for protecting kitchen walls and can be made from a variety of materials, e.g. tiles, toughened and mirrored glass, acrylic or laminate, stone, granite, marble, pressed metal and stainless steel. Glass and stainless steel can be expensive options, but they make a statement. Laminate and tiles are good budget buys and a great opportunity to add colour and pattern. With tiles, grouting needs to be regularly cleaned to prevent mould and mildew. Choose standard size tiles (mosaic or brick) from a selection of materials, including ceramic, glass and stone.

If you are purchasing new kitchen appliances, search online. Your local high street stores can also have good deals. Buy these goods when the big sales are on. If you are not concerned about having the latest models, there may be deals being offered on older stocks to make way for the new models. However, make sure that whatever you buy is a reliable brand and has the highest energy saving rating (A+ to A+++). Buy from reputable dealers and stores, especially if you can get a free period of warranty as part of the purchase. Some online dealers offer lower prices, while other stores advertise price matches. You can use the lower offer to purchase through a price matching supplier.

We have had good experiences with John Lewis as noted below:

> We purchased a Smeg retro fridge from John Lewis for one of our properties, which came with a free 2-year John Lewis warrantee. It was a stunning bright red (we had waited for its arrival to colour-match our kitchen wall) and we had specially requested a left-hand opening door to work efficiently in the kitchen we had designed. While it looked gorgeous, we didn't feel it was working properly from Day 1, and we addressed it several times directly with the local John Lewis store that we had ordered it through.
>
> There were various people sent to fix it over a period of several months, both from John Lewis and from Smeg. In the end, we told the store that we wanted to return the fridge and obtain a full refund as the issues had been over such a prolonged period of time. John Lewis offered us a replacement, which we declined because we were so fed up by then, so we were provided with a full refund.
>
> We have always found John Lewis easy to deal with, and this is the reason why we continue to buy our appliances and household items through them. When there have been issues, the staff have been efficient and courteous. We also like the fact that they price match; this has been particularly useful for us when undertaking renovation projects.

It's a luxury to buy the appliances that you want, but it's not always possible when facing the realities of the expense of each of the white goods (with the related cost for long term energy efficiency) and availability of space when you are taking on a renovation project. A combined washing machine and tumble dryer can be a good option for a space saver. But they tend not to be as energy efficient and do have smaller capacity. Tumble dryers with heat pump technology are more energy efficient as 50% less electricity is used (this is because warm air is being recirculated in the dryer). Some tumble dryers use technology that monitors and selects the correct drying cycle for each load.

If you are on a tighter budget, keep your existing appliances if they are still modern and in good condition. If they do need replacing, consider buying used or refurbished appliances, as these are not necessarily of low quality. There are second-hand or refurbished items that are still in excellent condition, but you may have to search to find them – try bargain shops, used appliance stores, or garage sales.

Redesign and replace your kitchen

There is a lot to consider when completely redesigning your kitchen, from the layout and how it will best function to the final design. Take your time to decide what you want in the new design. Here are some guidelines based on our experience with designing new kitchens, which we have done with all our properties.

Get ideas

Bring together a collection of images that you have seen. These could be online images, from magazines and brochures, or photos taken in kitchen showrooms. Create a mood board to help you to identify styles, colours, materials, textures and accessories.

Consider your requirements

Assess your existing kitchen and list what you like and dislike about it. Think about how you want to use the space, whether it is just a place to prepare meals, or if it is to be a more multifunctional area where you are able to socialise with family and entertain friends. Consider also how you cook, what you cook, as well as who you cook for, as this will influence your kitchen design.

Consider whether the current space works or if it needs reconfiguring, opening up or extending. A popular option is to remove the existing wall between the kitchen and dining rooms to provide an open plan space.

Chapter 2. RENOVATING YOUR PROPERTY

The layout of the kitchen should be designed to perfectly fit your lifestyle. To best plan the preparation and cooking space, use the design concept of the working triangle of the kitchen. This is where the three outer points are the fridge, sink and cooking hob, with imaginary lines between these forming the triangular shape. The three points of the triangle should be near enough to each other to make meal preparation efficient, but each work area should be not be cramped.

Think about what your must-haves are. These may include sleek modern worktops, a statement island, lots of storage cupboards, or specific appliances that will make your life in the kitchen much easier. Write down your kitchen requirements as it will enable your discussions with a kitchen specialist to be far more focused.

Make sure the style of kitchen you choose is timeless, stylish and unlikely to date quickly. Otherwise, you may have to renovate the kitchen again if you decide to sell your house in the next few years. If you are intending to flip your property, the kitchen needs to have a wide-reaching appeal and avoid fads.

Consider the following in your new kitchen design:
- How you move around your kitchen, and therefore the best location and layout.
- The number of electrical plug sockets you will need, and their location. With how we cook these days, we want tablets to display recipes, TVs to watch and music to listen to. Build in plenty of electrical and USB sockets as well as TV ports.
- Lighting required for the kitchen as well as for social or entertaining spaces.
- The size, positioning and type of hob (induction, gas, ceramic or solid plate).
- The type of cooker hood or extractor you need. You have a lot of choices, including ceiling, canopy, chimney or wall-mounted, island, pendant and downdraft.
- The type of oven and its positioning in the kitchen layout. Your choice of oven includes single, double, double built-under, compact or freestanding.
- How much of social space do you want to have for entertaining or engaging with family and friends while you cook.
- Whether you would have a table or a breakfast bar, and the placement of these.

- Whether the food preparation area is to be located next to the hob and oven, and the refrigerator in proximity to the cooking area.
- Whether there is space for large appliances, e.g. an American style fridge freezer.
- The amount of storage you need, and the type of storage required.
- The location of utensils, dinnerware and small kitchen appliances.
- The amount of worktop, number of display units and shelves required for kitchen gadgets, appliances, iPod or music docks.

Kitchen plumbing and heating

Consider whether you will be using existing plumbing for sinks and appliances or whether you will require additional pipe work. Wherever you decide to locate your sink, install your dishwasher as close to it as possible to keep the plumbing simple.

If you are planning to include a kitchen island that houses a sink or other appliances, you will need to ensure that plumbing and electricity supplies are in place for them before any flooring is laid. Include in the design the locations of all the appliances to ensure that there are sufficient electrical sockets and they are where you need them to be.

If you don't have a separate utility area, you may also wish to have your washing machine located in the kitchen. This would be best placed near the dishwasher so that plumbing remains uncomplicated.

Underfloor heating has become a popular replacement for radiators in kitchens as it does not take up any valuable wall space. If you decide to install underfloor heating, this will also need to be installed before laying the kitchen floor.

Kitchen lighting

When planning lighting for the kitchen, it is a good idea to make it as flexible as possible so that you can regulate areas of your kitchen independently. We use spotlights above cooking, preparation and washing areas for focused lighting in these work areas, whereas cabinet underlights and plinth lights help to set a social mood in the kitchen.

Use a kitchen designer

> Always try to visit a company that has a showroom where you can inspect the quality of the company's product, along with the standard of their installation. Also, do some research and find out who the recommended retail members are. Which? provides impartial consumer advice on retailers, combining it with track records for product, service and installation, so you can check online.

To ensure great design and innovative ideas for your kitchen, secure input from a professional kitchen designer. They will make sure that your new kitchen works as efficiently as possible and will illustrate this to you in a 3D rendering of your kitchen layout and design. They will also have the latest knowledge of products, fittings and fixtures, and will be able to source everything required for you. When we have used kitchen designers, they have worked hard to make use of every square inch of available space for us. As we are very detail orientated, they have often made numerous 3D renderings for us until we have agreed the final layout and design.

Our kitchen designers have always started with a site visit to see the layout, take measurements and assess any challenging obstacles or unusual features that they will need to work around in their design and better quote for the job (e.g. a chimney breast or an odd shaped wall). Our recommendation is to only agree the quote for the design and installation of a kitchen once the designer has looked at the space.

When designing a new kitchen, people generally believe that an island will easily fit in the design with accompanied seating. If you are including an island in your new kitchen, make sure enough space has been allowed in the design for seating. You will need a walk space gap around the island of a minimum of 800mm. A 1000mm gap would be more comfortable and will allow for 2 people to pass each other, or an oven door to be open at the same time. It is also important to consider the correct clearance or space needed for individual seats or bar stools.

Once the design has been completed, ensure you are provided with a written quotation and full breakdown of every aspect of the entire job, with all the components of the kitchen, including the cabinetry, worktops, splashbacks, accessories and installation as well as flooring and any structural alterations. Check what has been included in the cost and whether the company will also be overseeing the project from start to finish.

Don't sign the agreement unless you are prepared to honour your side of the contract. Some terms and conditions have expensive cancellation clauses. Pay no more than 25% of the total contract value until you have received full delivery of the goods, then pay the balance once you have checked over the delivered items. If components of the kitchen are missing, you will have some level of recourse if you haven't paid for the entire delivery.

Confirm your budget

Be clear with your kitchen designer about your budget so they can help you decide where to save and where best to invest your money. Using open shelving is less expensive than closed cupboards and using roomy low-level, pull-out storage may mean you need fewer wall units, which saves on cost. Only invest in what you think you will use, rather than the appliances on display (with far more programmes than you are likely to use). Budget an additional 10% for contingency against unplanned or unexpected costs.

Here are some ideas for where to spend and save money when choosing your kitchen:

- Buy the best worktops you can afford as they are one of the most hardworking elements of any kitchen. Composite, granite, and solid surfaces are all great investments as they are durable, tough and will provide a luxurious finish to your kitchen.
- Make sure your kitchen cabinets are good quality. Don't be tempted to skimp on thin carcasses as they won't last very long. Choose carcasses that have a minimum thickness of 15mm all round, or more.
- You can save from your choice of cabinet doors by recreating the rich wood veneer finish using laminate or PVC foil finishes. Hi-gloss doors also come in different price brackets, depending on whether they are lacquered or laminated; a lacquered kitchen can cost a lot more than a laminate equivalent.
- Buy the best oven and hob you can afford.
- Spend less money on the laundry appliance, but still purchase a reliable brand.
- Spend your money on things that matter to you; you can always add small luxury appliances and accessories in the future.

Chapter 2. RENOVATING YOUR PROPERTY

Employ professionals

The way your kitchen is installed is very important. It can make all the difference when you are using it daily. A bad kitchen fitter can make any kitchen look terrible, but a good fitter will ensure that even cheaper units look great and fit well. Ask for recommendations, go through a registered trade association (e.g. Federation of Master Builders), or search online on trade rating websites such as RatedPeople, Checkatrade and TrustATrader.

If your kitchen makeover is a simple refresh, you will only have the kitchen supplier and fitter to co-ordinate. However, if it is a larger project, there may be builders, electricians and plumbers involved. Consider engaging a project manager. Your kitchen supplier or qualified architect (if you're on a very large or complicated renovation) should have the knowledge and skills to project manage this. Delays and mistakes in kitchen planning can be costly, and there is a need for a plan to be in place, with an updated schedule of works, so that everyone is clear about what needs to be done, when and who by.

If you are planning to make structural changes to your kitchen, such as knocking down internal walls between your kitchen and dining room, installing rooflights or bi-fold doors, planning permission is not usually required as this is typically covered by permitted development. Most single-storey extensions are covered by permitted development, however certain exclusions and criteria apply. Even if you don't need planning permission, it is still worth applying to your local planning authority for a lawful development certificate. The certificate is also useful when you decide to sell. If you are planning to make structural changes, ensure you use the services of an approved structural engineer. If you are preparing for a larger refit or build, always check with your local planning authority if you need planning permission or building regulations approval. Use the planning portal to obtain information but don't start work until you have spoken with them.

Many bespoke companies will not undertake first-fit electrics or plumbing so you may need to co-ordinate these activities yourself. Some of the higher-end bespoke companies do offer a full service where they will co-ordinate all the building electrical and plumbing work but be prepared to pay a premium for this service.

Finishing touches

Make your kitchen feel more connected and coherent by linking finishes, e.g. upholstering bar stools with fabric that ties in with the splashback, or pair a wooden breakfast bar with wooden stools. Small details, such as cabinet handles and knobs, can make a big difference and transform a simple scheme. Also, rather than buying everything from the same supplier, source accessories and furnishings from a variety of places, using a mix of items and accessories to create your own individual look. Adding soft furnishings, artwork and shelving displays make open-plan schemes warm and inviting. They are easy to replace and update, either seasonally or when you feel like an upgrade is required.

Consider selling items being removed from the property on sites such as eBay or Gumtree. Your old kitchen, bathroom, heating system, curtains and blinds will be of interest to someone. This can assist with both the disposal of the items and generate much needed additional cash. One of our builders was very decent about selling our disposable items and sharing proceeds. He sold the kitchen, kitchen range, and all the radiators in the property (which were unusable because they were engrained with unremovable animal hair – not a healthy option for an asthmatic!).

Living or family room

The living room is usually the first area that is seen as you enter a house. If you are updating and designing a living room from scratch, do some homework first. You can do the design yourself by just being imaginative and following your creative instincts. Before you start moving things around, visualise how you want your living room to appear. Browse online or go through home improvement magazines for a style that appeals to you. You need not have all the decor and furniture exactly as in the images, just collect the inspirational ideas. You can also ask for advice from someone you know, or a recommended professional designer and decorator.

The money involved in redecorating your living room is a major factor to consider. Furniture and decor of good quality can be expensive, especially if you are considering hiring an interior designer to do the job for you. If you are on a tight budget, there are several ways this can be done.

Make use of the existing furniture and fixtures. You may just need to clean them to make them look new. If necessary, reposition your living room and place these pieces of furniture in their new location. Older furniture that you've had for quite some time may require repairs to make sure they are still sturdy.

Some old things that you thought you would never use again might just find their perfect place in your updated living room. Make sure that the room does not look cluttered or too heavy. Ensure the room appears comfortable and relaxing as well as pleasing to the eyes.

You can make a fireplace the focal point of the room and arrange the sofa, chairs and conversational areas around it. Transform the rooms with clever use of paint colour, wallpaper, fabrics, mouldings, window treatments, rugs and lighting.

Bedrooms

People can always spruce up an old bedroom by using a little bit of ingenuity, creativity and vision. Renovating can make an old bedroom look as good as new, or even better. There are many ways you can redecorate a bedroom and you don't have to spend a lot of money to create a new look. Lots of ideas can be obtained by watching property shows on television, talking to friends, reading magazines, searching online and visiting showrooms.

Repaint the walls and create a feature wall with beautiful wallpapers to provide your bedroom walls with an instant facelift. This will lighten it up and completely renew the look. Re-upholster old furniture as it makes a difference in the overall look of a bedroom. Add art work, upcycled furniture, decorative lamps and antique mirrors for a whole new look. Complement the new style of your room with new bedspreads and cushions. Pay a visit to the linen department of any major discount store or look online for well-priced items. Invest in new curtains and blinds to compliment your design style and colours.

Bathrooms

As with kitchens, a lot of attention is paid to bathrooms. They need to be well laid out, clean and hygienic. There is a currently a trend for bathrooms to resemble an upmarket hotel spa. People are wanting to create the feeling of total peace and relaxation, like that of a retreat, with large jacuzzi baths that you can have a long soak in. You can have similar colours tiles, earthy tones and minimalist accents to reproduce this effect.

When you are upgrading or replacing your bathroom, consider the practicalities, such as whether you want to have a shower or a bath, or both. If you are planning to sell the house once you have renovated it, or sometime in the future, the type of bathroom you install could greatly affect the desirability and value of your property.

Having an ensuite to the master bedroom is a must-have for many as it improves privacy and solves the morning queue for the bathroom in larger households. Creating the space required to accommodate an ensuite can be found by:

- Subdividing one end of a large bedroom using a metal or timber framed stud wall.
- Dividing off a section of an adjacent bedroom using a stud wall.
- Forming a small shower room from an old airing cupboard or storage area.
- Dividing part of a first-floor landing area in a larger property.
- Converting an existing smaller bedroom into a larger shower or wet room.

A simple shower room can be built for approximately £3,000 to £4,000, including stud or metal framing, basin and taps, enclosed cistern WC, shower mixer and arm, shower tray, door and basic white tiles. Luxury touches and convenient features make a big impression. Think about what type of flooring you will install (e.g. tile, wood, vinyl, concrete), and whether a hot water or an electric underfloor heating system will be included in the design.

Consider also how you will finish the walls, whether with paint or tiles. If you are going to use tiles for the walls, decide if you will partly or fully tile up to the ceiling.

Take into consideration the storage you require for toiletries and how you want to display these for use in a shower or bath. We always install a recess within a shower and beside the bath and install LED lighting in the space. This is lovely to look at and functional as well because it accommodates our shower and bath products.

Change old-fashioned ceiling light fixtures and switches for modern ones. Ensure that you select lights for the bathroom that are rated for bathroom use. Consider installing illuminated mirrored shelving over the basin for your daily rituals as well as for providing additional storage. Large mirrors, strategically placed, provide a function and accentuate space by reflecting light into the room.

An essential for your bathroom is an extractor fan to ventilate the area well. This is especially important of you don't have any windows in your bathroom. Install an extractor fan that is both quiet and efficient at removing condensation.

Home office

Many people are now working from home or have a home office. Ideally, this is a separate workspace where they can be comfortable and have privacy to adequately conduct their business. Where possible, a separate room in the house, away from congestion and noise, is the best place for a home office. Setting up a functional and comfortable home office will require some furniture, at least a desk, a supportive and comfortable chair and desk lamp.

If you are creating a home office, ensure there is very good lighting and ventilation in the room. Invest in office equipment, storage cabinets and a wire management system for your computer and printers. Install additional electrical sockets, or invest in a multi plug extension socket, with USB charging ports. Ensure your electrical equipment has a surge protector. Also invest in a good wireless hub and a separate phone line (if you are conference calling and video conferencing).

The colour scheme of a home office should not be distracting. This means bright pastels, shocking pink and neon green will usually not be appropriate. If you have clients and hold business meetings in your home office, be careful when it comes to choosing your decorating colours. Neutral colours are best since they are not distracting but consider using contrasting colours to add accents and interest, or for accessories.

> Setting up a home office is serious business. The right environment should be attractive and conducive to a good working atmosphere. Anyone considering setting up a home office should pay careful attention to detail when creating their office since they will be spending many hours working in it. Take the time to make your home office a comfortable and pleasant place to work.

Loft and basement areas

Each of these spaces have distinctive requirements when renovating.

Loft for storage

Ensure your loft has no damp or condensation problems and assess the space for insulation. Fit new insulation between the joists. You can do this yourself, have it done by someone who is competent in DIY or use a professional installer. If access is easy and your loft joists are regular, use rolls of mineral wool insulation. If you plan to use the loft for storage, lay boards over the joists. Depending on how much storage area you need, you may decide to board either half the loft space or the whole area.

Insulating between the joists of your loft will keep your house warmer but this will make the roof space colder. Insulate the pipes and water tanks in the loft space as they are more likely to freeze. The cooler air in your insulated loft may allow cold draughts through the loft hatch. To prevent this, fit strips of draught-excluding material around the hatch.

Install any electrical sockets you might need and good lighting; long LED battens provide great light for the loft space.

Make sure you install a good loft ladder. We have installed a solid wood loft ladder in our properties with a loft surround, insulated trapdoor and spring-assisted storage as a kit from Screwfix for around £130. This fits a loft hatch diameter of approximately 1.15m x 0.57m, which allows for most bulky boxes and items in and out of the loft easily. It also allows for more space to comfortably get into, and out of the loft. Kits like these are also available at most building supplies stores or online.

We have previously boarded our loft space for storage, and set it up with shelving and closed, dust free wardrobes to swap over seasonal clothing and store books and DVDs.

Loft for living space

Loft conversions can be a cost-effective way to add living space and value and to your home. The cost of a loft extension depends on the type of conversion you opt for, where you live in the country, and whether you need planning permission.

> A 4mx5m loft conversion with 2 roof lights will start at approximately £20,000, including materials and labour. Larger conversions with dormers and rooflights will cost approximately £60,000, which includes the clearing of materials from the loft, relocating water tanks, insulating the walls and ceiling, fitting wood framing, plaster boarding the walls and ceiling, fitting a straight flight of stairs, installing new electrics and heating. To have a bathroom installed and have the space painted and decorated will cost extra.

There are factors to consider which can drive the overall cost up or down, such as fixtures and fittings. Cut costs by purchasing your own fixtures and fittings online or on eBay.

If any of the work you do affects the adjoining wall between your house and your neighbour's, you will need to serve your neighbours with a Party Wall Notice outlining the work you are proposing, including detailed plans. If your neighbours are concerned, they are within their rights to appoint a surveyor to view the plans and you will have to cover the costs. Try to agree on party wall issues with your neighbours early on as it takes time and is expensive to engage surveyors, especially if you need more than one.

Most loft conversions are able to be carried out without requiring planning permission. If you do need it, you will have to pay for the application, which could cost up to £1,000. As always, check with your local planning office first.

You will need to obtain Building Regulations Approval regardless of whether your project requires planning permission or not. A building control inspector will check your work at various stages, before issuing you with a completion certificate on final inspection.

Do your planning thoroughly and employ a professional architect, a specialist building firm or loft conversion company through referral or via online trade rating portals such as Which? Trusted Trader, Checkatrade, RatedPeople. Obtain 3 quotes, understand fully what you are buying, and be aware of the small pint in the terms and conditions before signing a contract.

If you are managing the project yourself, you should arrange conversion insurance to cover the new works and the existing structure. This will cover you for loss or damage whilst the property is undergoing alteration or renovation. Renovation insurance should be in place for when work starts on your property and should continue until the end of project.

Convert your basement

Having extra space is always a bonus, and basement conversions have become very popular. Many houses have cellars that have been neglected and are dark and damp. Without spending a lot of money, you can convert an unused room into a living space.

With rising property prices, children are living at home much longer to save for their own property purchase. Basement conversions are an ideal solution, providing separate living spaces, and are also great for storage, freeing up valuable space above ground. More people are building home gyms or home offices in basements.

The time to complete a basement conversion will depend on what you want to achieve and the size of your basement space. Converting a simple single-room cellar using a waterproof membrane can take just two or three weeks. More comprehensive conversions can take several months. Plan to do any basement conversion work in the summer.

> The approximate cost to renovate or create a new basement are:
> - Turning an existing basement into habitable space by tanking and insulating the walls will cost from £700 to £1,800 per square metre.
> - Constructing a new basement under an existing house and underpinning the walls will cost from £1,900 to £2,600 per square metre.
> - For whichever option you decide, installing a lightwell or new external access door will cost from £5,500 to £9,500.

If other properties join yours and you share walls that will be affected by the conversion, you must consider the Party Wall Act 1996. Speak with the owners and leaseholders of the adjoining property. If you get your neighbours on side, they may consent to the work without there being any fees involved, but you'll need to get this in writing. Otherwise, you will need to instruct a surveyor, and this can cost approximately £700 to £900 / neighbour.

If you are using a specialist basement contractor to design, build and manage your basement project, they will usually deal with required planning applications, Building Regulations approval and Party Wall Agreements (if required).

Before progressing with a basement conversion, check with your local authority whether or not planning permission is required. In most cases, planning permission is not needed when converting an existing basement or cellar but contact your local planning office and obtain their response formally in writing that you can go ahead with the work. Whether planning was required or not, you will have this in writing when you sell your property.

If you are converting a basement into a habitable space, you will require Building Regulations approval even if it only involves a change of use of an existing cellar. Building Regulations will ensure your newly converted basement is safe and energy efficient and will also cover areas such as fire escape routes, ventilation, ceiling height, damp proofing, electrical wiring and water supplies. The renovation of an existing habitable basement or the repair of a cellar that does change its use is excluded from Building Regulations.

A well-lit, welcoming and waterproof basement living space will add value as the extra habitable space that a basement creates is a big selling point.

In one of our properties, we converted the basement, fitting a new external door, new lighting and flooring. We had it painted and fully redecorated, transforming it into an attractive useable space as a gym, with the required equipment and storage.

Chapter 2. RENOVATING YOUR PROPERTY

Flooring

> Before you fit any flooring in your property, go around your house (or have your builder do this) and check for any squeaking steps on the stairs, floor boards or flooring areas. Repair any annoying squeaks as these are likely to continue to be noticeable after the flooring has been fitted.

If you are not replacing any flooring for budgetary or other reason, have your carpets professionally cleaned. Or you can strip any covering and sand, stain, varnish or paint your floorboards. Re-grout tiled floors to bring them back to life.

If you are replacing your flooring, decide what you want to install to modernise the property and provide it with a uniform and fresh look. You have a lot of choices, including polished floorboards, polished concrete, new timber, laminate, carpet, tiles and vinyl. Try switching from your traditional rolled vinyl or linoleum flooring to a more resilient, timeless material such as wood, tile, or stone. These materials will last longer and will also boost the desirability and value of your home. More recently, ceramic tiles that mimic the look of hardwood have become popular, as have travertine and slate. We installed travertine in a conservatory with underfloor heating, and it was a deliciously cosy room to be in during winter. The neighbour's cat thought so too!

If you are looking for a luxury flooring look, consider encaustic tiles. These are porcelain and ceramic tiles that create a striking pattern. They are frequently used in historic buildings and were popular in the Victorian era. Use these types of colourful tiles to create an eye-catching statement floor in a kitchen, bathroom, hallway or living area.

Decide if your flooring needs to be non-slip, child or pet friendly and low maintenance. Does the floor need to be low cost, or can it be more premium? If you are installing underfloor heating, confirm if there are any restrictions to flooring you wish to use.

To enhance the flow and feeling of space in the property, fit the same flooring throughout or ensure any change in flooring blends seamlessly and attractively. A cost saving tip for kitchens is to run your new flooring to just underneath the plinths, instead of wall-to-wall. Then less flooring product is used, and consequently you spend less money.

Home exterior and garden

> Assess the exterior of your house to make sure it is in a state of good repair. This should be high on your house renovation priority and order of works. There is no point making aesthetic changes to the interior if structural work needs to be undertaken outside.

Engage a professional to inspect your roof, including the gutters, flashing and downspouts. If your roof has been in place for more than 20 years, it may require repairs, or it could be reaching the end of its lifespan. A roofing expert will be able to determine whether it requires repairs or replacement. If the roof is covered in moss, clean this off with a pressure washer, being careful not to cause any damage to the tiles or slates.

If your home's exterior is looking characterless or tired, you can do a lot to improve its kerb appeal and add value. Clean and repaint the windows, doors, frames, garage door and any external joinery such as bargeboards, fascia and soffits.

Removing tired or unsightly features such as cheap stone cladding can restore a property's value by broadening its appeal, as can reinstating period features. Adding a well-chosen porch or canopy in a style appropriate to the existing house can do a lot to provide a focal point and character for your front door, along with shelter.

Make repairs to any cracks or damage to the house, or to its boundary walls, in the same render, brick or stonework, and repaint as necessary. If the exterior walls of your house are patchy, or the house has been repaired, altered or extended using different mismatching materials, consider painting it with masonry paint. If the surfaces are covered with imperfections or major flaws, it may be better to apply a textured masonry paint; this has aggregate added and can be applied as a lighter textured finish or a heavy-bodied paint with a deeper texture. An alternative to repainting a patchy or unsightly area would be to plant a climbing plant which would do a great job of screening areas such as this.

If you do not have private off-street parking, but have the space to create it, this will be of benefit to your comfort and peace of mind while living in the property. It will add value to your property and may even lower the cost of your vehicle insurance. A further benefit is that it will be attractive for future buyers, so it is a worthy investment. Check with your local council or authority before starting any work. Find out if you need planning permission before adding vehicle access so that you don't waste your money.

Chapter 2. RENOVATING YOUR PROPERTY

If you can add a conservatory, it will provide you with additional living space, and a reasonable return on investment, potentially increasing the value of your property by 5%.

If you are renovating to sell, an attractive, tidy and well-designed garden will add value and make a property far more desirable and saleable. Carry out the basics by cleaning up, clearing rubbish and dead plants, weeding, repairing and cutting the lawn, cutting cut back overgrown trees and shrubs and adding colour and interest with planting. Add decking to provide more entertaining space and reduce the amount of grass you need to maintain.

As with the advice in the Staging Chapter, if you have dead patches of grass from a dry summer, burns from pet urine or other damage, consider using a natural and non-toxic green grass repair colourant. This is applied from a spray bottle and will instantly turn any brown grass or spots green again. Choose a spray that is biodegradable, non-toxic, non-hazardous, and safe for children and pets.

If the lawn is too damaged, look at re-turfing it. Laying new turf is more expensive but it provides an instant, lush looking lawn as soon as you have finished. Laying artificial grass is also a good option if you want a low maintenance lawn. It provides a real grass look but offers greater wear as well as weather resistance. It is ideal for urban and small gardens because there's no need to water it in dry weather and the turf is porous, so there won't be any puddles when it rains.

If your garden is overgrown, consider employing the services of professional gardeners to get in under control. They can also provide maintenance service on a regular basis.

Final project review

> Ensure that you undertake a final project review at the completion of the agreed works and hold back final payment until the snagging issues have been resolved.

Small problems will inevitably crop up over the ensuing months after the renovation has been completed. It is best to fix these problems as they arise. If you employed trades for the renovation work, ask them to return and remediate the issues. If there are any defects that are not their fault, such as plaster cracks, expect to have to pay them for the work. If you used a main contractor, the final payment of 2.5 to 5% you held back can be released once they have resolved any defects to your satisfaction. File all paperwork e.g. copies of contracts, guarantees, legal paperwork, permissions and certificates.

All the best with your renovation project and celebrate your success!

Our renovation project photos

Below are some photos from one of our projects:

Chapter 2. RENOVATING YOUR PROPERTY 133

For more photos in our portfolio, please visit our website on www.gsansellproperty.com.

Checklist – Renovating your property

The following Checklist will help you to plan and track your progress through this process.

Plan your renovation project

- ☐ Confirm and list your requirements.
- ☐ Engage a chartered property surveyor and discuss any issues and space requirements.
- ☐ Obtain all the inputs in order to plan for how long the project will take.
- ☐ Plan how to manage if there are interruptions to the gas, electricity or water supply.

Gather your requirements

- ☐ Be clear what you want done, your vision and expectations of the completed project.
- ☐ Determine why you are renovating and who you are renovating for.
- ☐ Confirm the finish you can have for your budget (budget, standard or premium).
- ☐ Engage a qualified architect if required.

Decide on your build team

- ☐ Plan ahead when booking trades people.
- ☐ Obtain 3 quotes, choose your preferred contractor and sign a contract.
- ☐ Request all invoices and receipts as the work progresses on your property.
- ☐ Agree weekly site inspections with the main contractor to view and discuss progress.

Organise your budget and finances

- ☐ Confirm a budget for your project and organise any additional funding you might need.
- ☐ Record all your estimated costs, including 10-20% contingency.
- ☐ Closely monitor and manage your budget versus actual spend.
- ☐ Be aware of your dos and don'ts to control costs.
- ☐ Inform your home insurance company of the work for any policy amendments.
- ☐ On completion of the work, check if your home and contents insurance needs updating.

Planning and consents

- ☐ Confirm with your local planning authority if consents are required.
- ☐ If building near a boundary, check whether your work is affected by the Party Wall Act.

Chapter 2. RENOVATING YOUR PROPERTY

Project management
- [ ] Decide if you will pay for a professional or manage the renovation project yourself.
- [ ] Create a schedule of works in priority order, with dependencies, start and end dates.
- [ ] Agree with your main contractor the project milestones and payment schedule.
- [ ] Undertake weekly progress meetings and site inspections with the main contractor.
- [ ] Record key communication and agreements.
- [ ] Contact your suppliers to ensure timely deliveries and early warnings of non-delivery

The renovation project

General renovation
- [ ] Determine if there is budget to hire an interior designer
- [ ] Set a high priority on damp or structural repairs over any other requirements.
- [ ] Replace, repair and update as necessary.

Electrics and lighting
- [ ] Have electrics inspected and upgrades, rewire if required.
- [ ] Upgrade smoke and fire detectors and house alarm.
- [ ] Decide if you will install smart meters, solar power panels and / or underfloor heating.
- [ ] Obtain an electrical certificate for any electrical work undertaken on the property.

Plumbing and heating
- [ ] Upgrade the plumbing and heating system if required.
- [ ] Install the required capacity water tank and system for your kitchen and bathroom.

Energy efficiency
- [ ] Insulate the cavity walls and loft. Invest in good U-value windows and doors.

Layout of the property
- [ ] Consult a structural engineer if changing the layout, extending or removing walls.
- [ ] Consider converting your loft or basement rather than making costly layout changes.
- [ ] Confirm if planning permission is required when building an extension or conservatory.

Kitchen
- [ ] Upgrade according to your budget.
- [ ] Consult a structural engineer if you are changing the layout or extending your kitchen.
- [ ] Be thorough and detailed in your requirements for your new kitchen.

Living or family room

- ☐ Visualise how you want your living room to appear and confirm your design style.
- ☐ Create a focal point in a room and arrange conversation areas around it.
- ☐ Transform the rooms with paint colour, wallpaper, fabrics, curtains and lighting.

Bedrooms

- ☐ Redecorate and accessorise according to your chosen design theme
- ☐ Upgrade the lighting for more contemporary look.

Bathrooms

- ☐ Confirm your requirements. Decide if the space needs to be enlarged or relocated.
- ☐ Ensure there is adequate ventilation and install a quiet extractor fan.
- ☐ Replace old light fixtures for modern energy efficient and rated ones for bathroom use.
- ☐ Decide on décor and flooring; consider the storage and display requirements.

Home office

- ☐ Create a separate workspace away from congestion and noise.
- ☐ Redecorate in neutral colours and invest in good office furniture and storage.
- ☐ Ensure there are plenty of power sockets, good lighting and ventilation.

Loft and basement areas

- ☐ Ensure your loft is dry; fit insulation, flooring, good lighting and a sturdy loft ladder.
- ☐ Employ an architect or specialist company and obtain permissions for conversions.

Flooring

- ☐ Confirm what flooring you want to install, including underfloor heating systems.
- ☐ Fit the same flooring or blend throughout the property to enhance flow.

Home exterior and garden

- ☐ Make any required exterior works high priority and undertake any structural work first.
- ☐ Engage a professional to inspect your roof as it may require repairs or replacing.
- ☐ Clean, make repairs and repaint as necessary.

Final project review

- ☐ Perform a final project review at the completion of the agreed works.
- ☐ Hold back final payment until snagging issues have been resolved to your satisfaction.
- ☐ Capture all the paperwork from the renovation for tax claims or for your property sale.
- ☐ Make sure you celebrate the completion of your renovation project!

Chapter 3

INTERIOR DESIGN AND DECORATING

Overview

Interior design is about understanding requirements, creating well performing and functional spaces within buildings and delivering according to what has been agreed with the client. It could be considered a science as well as an art.

The furnishing and enhancing of a space are incredibly important, combining colour and adornments to create the beauty within the space. This is not about delivering what the interior decorator wants to create, but rather what the client believes will provide them with the level of comfort and ornamentation they can live with because it impacts them daily. An interior designer or decorator should also guide the client through the choices available. Sometimes what the client wants isn't always feasible, allowed, practical or there is another way of it being done cheaper, faster or more environmentally friendly.

Interior design and decorating are more accessible with cost-effective designs and easy visibility of trends online, coupled with expertise delivered by professional service providers and communities built around interest in exchanging views.

Celebrity opinions also generate interest. Luxury living has become a combination of traditional, eclectic and unique styles, with an inspirational and contemporary look. Even antiques can be transformed and upcycled into vital accessories for today's modern home, adding distinction and originality. Interior decorating is very much a matter of personal choice and style as what appeals to one person may not always appeal to another.

> The interior design and decorative scheme chosen for a property usually depends on whether the house is a forever home, a project to flip immediately, a house to be sold in a few years, or an investment property to hold on to. To make informed decisions on any type of project to do with design and decorating, it's important to understand the transformative nature of the elements, principles, styles and themes, as well as colours and textures provided through different mediums.

Interior design elements

There is a degree of science involved with interior design, a set of informal rules based on specific interior design elements and principles.

> There are 7 elements that are used in all aspects of interior design and decorating. If most of these elements are correctly incorporated, you will create attractive as well as functional spaces. These elements include space, line, forms, light, colour, pattern and texture. They are the building blocks of any interior design. Keeping these elements balanced is the key to creating an aesthetically pleasing design.

In addition to enhancing the appearance of a room, having these elements work together in harmony will also bring increased functionality. Start by assessing the room according to these interior design elements, and then use them to disguise or enhance the various features and flaws of the space. They can be used to create an overall design that satisfies the function of a space.

Space

Understanding the concept of space will ensure that you are well equipped to take advantage of this. Space is split into two categories:

- Positive space, which contains objects.
- Negative space, which is the open or empty space (including space between objects).

Striking a balance between negative and positive spaces in a room is essential to avoiding sparseness or overcrowding. This balance is influenced by the needs of a specific area or room and its required functionality (e.g. if negative space is required for traffic walkways).

It is also important to consider the scale and size of the furniture and objects placed in a room, as this can be used to make the space appear larger or smaller compared to the desired outcome. A tall object, such as a bookcase, can provide the illusion of height.

Line

Horizontal, vertical and dynamic lines help to both shape a room and guide the eye. Creating lines using the room's furnishings and structural design can provide harmony, unity and contrast. The following are different types of lines used in interior design:

- Horizontal lines are created by tables and other surfaces and provide a sense of stability, formality and efficiency. They can make a room appear wider and longer, as well as draw the eye to a focal point.
- Vertical lines are created by features such as windows and doorways and evoke feelings of freedom and strength. On a functional level, accentuating vertical lines can provide the illusion of a room being taller. They are often suited to dining rooms, entranceways and offices.
- Dynamic lines are diagonal, zigzag or curved. They provide energy and movement, such as on stairs. Stimulating to the eye, dynamic lines capture our attention for longer. However, too many dynamic lines in one room can be distracting and can end up overpowering horizontal or vertical lines.

Form

Form is the shape of the room, as well as any objects within the room, that are of physical form and three dimensional. Forms are generally described as being either geometric or natural. Geometric refers to hard lines and square edges, often looking man-made, while natural relates to more organic forms that appear to be created by nature. With form, take into consideration the proportions and scale of a room compared to the objects placed within it. Adding forms of similar shapes can create harmony and balance, while adding too many differing shapes can produce a confusing effect.

Light

Natural or man-made light is a critical aspect for any space as without it, all of the other elements would not be able to shine to their full potential. Beyond its functional purpose, light has the ability to set the atmosphere and mood of a space while also defining colour, line and texture. Also, lighting fixtures are a visual feature in themselves, and these can add the right touch to any design. Categories of light are described below:

- Task lighting has a defined purpose.
- Accent lighting emphasises objects.
- Mood lighting adds ambience.

Chapter 3. INTERIOR DESIGN AND DECORATING

When you are contemplating lighting requirements, consider the activities that will be undertaken in the space. Natural lighting should always be taken into consideration and can be manipulated through the clever placement of doors, windows and mirrors. Dimmer switches are able to make a space much more versatile.

Colour

Colour is a science all on its own. It has the ability to define unity, create mood and alter the perception of how large or small a space is. Colour can stir emotions and evoke memories, stimulating a physical and psychological response in our bodies. When you are considering the colour of a room:

- Think about what the room will be used for and all the activities that will occur in it.
- Study how both natural and artificial lighting will affect your selected colour right across the day and night. This is because light can alter our colour perception.
- Consider the size of the space and incorporate lighter or brighter colours in smaller spaces to provide the illusion of more space. Use darker colours to add a powerful dimension to a larger space.

Pattern

Combined with colour, pattern offers a similar use to texture in that it can add appeal to a room. A pattern is created by the use of a repetitive design that can be found in wallpapers, soft furnishings, rugs and fabrics. Patterns come in various types, such as stripes, geometric, pictorial, motif, organic and animal prints.

When using pattern, consider the size and style of a room. If you introduce pattern into a small room, this should be done sparingly to avoid overwhelming the space. However, patterns that create horizontal or vertical lines can be used to provide a heightened sense of space. Complex patterns made up of contrasting colours and lines can be used to liven up a room, but they are best used as a feature wall. Large scale patterns can work well in a big space and become a prominent focal point for the room.

It is important to know what category the pattern falls into, in order to ensure that the essence of the room is maintained. For traditionally styled rooms, you can use organic, floral prints. For a contemporary look, experiment with geometric and abstract prints.

Texture

Texture refers to the tactile surface of an object or of a particular finish. As an element, it can really bring a unique dimension to a room. Mix the textures within a space for a subtle sense of depth, such as glossy, coarse and smooth. From furniture to accessories to fabric, texture has the ability to add interest and detail, making it visually pleasing to the eye and providing a room with feeling. Texture comes in two forms:

- Visual texture is perceived by the eye from viewing an object. The effect is usually found in the form of pattern.
- Actual texture refers to tactile textures that can be seen or felt. It has 3D characteristics, such as a fluffy, colourful cushion. It can be appreciated with touch and with the eye.

Interior design principles

The principles of interior design are time-tested and provide guidelines on how to use the interior design elements, or building blocks, for successful creation.

Balance

The principle of balance is concerned with keeping the user's brain in equilibrium. The balance of a space can be attained by the use of any of the following three methods:

- Symmetrical balance, where the whole space is divided into two halves by a central line. The objects are placed in similar positions on both sides of the line, with each side a mirror of the other.
- Asymmetrical balance, which occurs when an odd number of elements are used. An imaginary central line is assumed, with the most visually attractive elements placed nearest to the central line, and other objects placed further away.
- Radial balance refers to a central point around which the objects are arranged around it in a circular manner.

Emphasis

Emphasis implies that the central point of a space should be more attractive, and that all other elements of that space should emerge from that focal point. So, the focal point should be carefully designed with impressive colour, texture, size and shape.

Contrast

The principle of contrast refers to the change in the colour or luminance of objects. One object may be bright in colour and the object next to it may be lighter. Likewise, contrast can be achieved using form and space. Contrast makes muted objects more beautiful by placing them next to brighter objects.

Scale and proportion

Scale and proportion relate to the relationship between two different objects, or two parts of an object. Scale denotes size; proportion refers to magnitude, quality and colour.

Rhythm

Rhythm is the arrangement of elements of interior design in a space. It means the arrangement should create a rhythm in your mind while you are looking at it. The following three methods used to achieve rhythm:

- Repetition, where elements of the same size, colour and shape are used repeatedly.
- Alteration, which occurs when two or more elements are arranged alternatively.
- Progression, where elements are arranged in such a way that the size or colour gradient of the elements are gradually increasing or decreasing.

Unity and variety

Unity should be maintained in such a way that the eye of an observer will move smoothly from one shape or object to another. At the same time, the observer should not feel any monotony. Variety should be shown in the form of textures, colours, shapes or sizes.

Interior design styles and themes

> Take your time to perfect the design you want and ensure the finished property will meet your needs. Think about what interior design style you like, instead of letting the architecture of your property constrain you. Make the design your own, but plan carefully, so that the final result is cohesive and intentional. Blend elements thoughtfully with a specific, unified vision in mind from start to finish.

The easiest way to find your design style is to start collecting ideas. Look through decorating magazines and home improvement websites, as well as Pinterest and Google. Cut out or print out images and pictures of things that catch your eye, like a particular sofa style, a cool lamp, a wall colour, window treatments or a fabric. Or it might just be the feeling that a room gives you. You may have taken photos in your travels, including those of the stunning hotels you have stayed in. Create a scrapbook of the images you like and use a mood board to centralise your ideas for each room. This will help you to get an idea of how each room will look and feel.

Collect samples of existing fabrics or colours that are going to stay in the room. For instance, you may decide to keep the carpet and you want to keep your grandmother's chair. See if you can clip a small piece of extra fabric off the chair where you won't see it. Clip a small square of the carpeting out of a closet area. If it's a painted piece, you can use a paint sample from your local paint store to match it as closely as possible. Keep these items with you while you are out and about so that you can match it to anything else you find interesting which may be appropriate to your project.

> We use a floor plan to guide our colour scheme and feature walls, as well as the purchase and placement of furniture and fittings. Doing this ensures us of the entire property having a cohesive flow. It also guarantees that no areas are missed.

If you don't have an existing floor plan, take measurements of the room, and of any furniture and fittings that are staying in that particular room, and create a simple floor plan to scale. Take photos of the entire room, along with all the pieces you are retaining. As you collect all these samples and notes, organise them in a way that makes sense for you, either by room, or by concept, such as furniture ideas, lighting, colours, fabrics and window treatments. You will then begin to see a pattern or similarity in what you like. This will lead you to styles you prefer, and the names of these styles, enabling you to investigate further should you wish to do so. The floor plan will provide you with a point of reference which you can also use to mark placements and colour schemes.

Chapter 3. INTERIOR DESIGN AND DECORATING

> If you are not comfortable with drawing a floor plan, there is software available, as well as online apps that provide services for free such as Floor Plan Creator, Room Sketcher, iHome Registry. They provide a very professional-looking solution.

While you don't want to be constrained by existing architecture and style of your property, if you want to copy a style that you have seen, be certain that it will work in your house.

The following are the main styles that are defined in interior design today:

Modern

The modern design style was created between the 1920s and 1950s. It typically refers to a home with clean, simple, crisp lines, a simple colour palette and materials that include metal, glass and steel. It is sleek, with minimal use of accessories.

Mid-century modern

Mid-century modern is a design style of the 1950s and 1960s. There is a presence of retro nostalgia, as well as some elements of minimalism. It is characterised by clean, simple lines, hints of blues and greens, and plenty of wood and rusty metals.

Contemporary

Contemporary describes design based on the here and now, with clean, unadorned spaces. Metal and glass are popular materials and intricate details are kept to a minimum. To create a sense of space, furniture tends to show exposed legs.

Minimalist

Minimalist design works on the principle that 'less is more'. Interiors are stripped down to their essential elements and empty space is left to make the design statement. Black, white and primary colours are often regarded as best for a minimalist space, with simple, streamlined furnishings. Minimalism is defined by functionality and ultra-clean lines.

Industrial

Industrial style draws inspiration from a warehouse or an urban loft, typically with high ceilings, old timber, stripped floorboards and dangling metal light fixtures with sparse functional furniture. Several pieces of abstract art or photography add a dash of colour to an otherwise neutral colour scheme derived from primary materials like wood and metals.

Scandinavian, scandi luxe & hygge

Scandinavian design brings simplicity with mostly all-white colours and natural form-pressed wood, bright plastics, enamelled aluminium, steel and wide plank flooring. Colour comes from art works, natural fibre throws, or a single piece of furniture. Scandi luxe uses Scandinavian design with a touch of luxury, where white, pastel and blonde wood meet brass, copper and marble. Danish hygge is gaining popularity with interiors incorporating design for mood, peacefulness and well-being. It's based on increasing enjoyment in life.

Traditional

Traditional design style is about classic details, an abundance of accessories and sumptuous furnishings. Traditional homes often feature rich colour palettes, dark finished wood and a variety of textures and curved lines. Furnishings have elaborate and ornate details and fabrics, such as velvet, silk and brocade, which may include a variety of patterns and textures.

Transitional

Transitional borrows from both traditional and modern design. It incorporates modern materials, such as steel and glass, and unites them with plush furnishings. Transitional design also includes relatively neutral colour palettes, creating a relaxed and calming space that feels stylish and sleek, as well as warm and inviting.

French country

Architectural features include irregular pale plaster walls and distressed ceiling beams and timbers, often using dark rough raw wood. There is rustic flooring, with the use of stone, clay, brick or old wooden boards. Rustic furniture and hand-carved decorations are utilised. Armoires are used for pots, pans, clothing, tableware and bed or bath linens. Large dining tables have a dull waxed or low-sheen finish and chairs have ladder-backs or vertical slats, often with rush seating. Colourful Provençal printed fabrics of greens, lavenders and bright orange are displayed, with designs including sunflowers, olives, roosters, grapes, lavender, and beetles. Baskets, an old jug or copper pot, or clear glass vases hold flowers. The focus is on old and charming.

Rustic

Rustic design uses unfinished and raw elements, including stone and wood. It incorporates accessories from the outdoors. Warmth emulates from the design and architectural details, for example, vaulted ceilings that are adorned with wood beams or reclaimed wooden floors. Many designs now integrate rustic design with modern accessories and furnishings.

Coastal

Coastal style originates from the iconic U.S. beachside area, with light, airy colour palettes and cool neutral shades of blues and greens. Natural materials, plenty of glass, breezy white draperies, blue and white striped patterns for pillows, large windows, white plush sofas, and painted white wood are also common fixtures of the classic coastal style.

Bohemian

Bohemian design reflects a carefree lifestyle with few rules. Bohemian homes include displays of collections, globally inspired textiles and rugs, vintage furniture and light fixtures. Items can be found in a variety of sources, including flea markets. This eclectic style incorporates a glamourous chandelier with a mid-century chair and well-worn rug.

Hollywood glam

Hollywood glam is a design style that is over-the-top, opulent and luxurious. It is dramatic and perfect for making a statement. This design style can incorporate some features of Victorian design, including antiques and plush, velvet furnishings. The colour palettes are particularly bold including purples, reds and turquoise.

Shabby chic

Shabby chic is inspired by vintage, but compared to Bohemian and other styles, tends to be more soft, delicate and feminine. Furnishings are often distressed or have antique-style finishes. Its colour palettes include white, cream and pastels. Light fixtures and wall hangings may be ornate and continue the feminine vibe of shabby chic design.

Vintage

Far from being old-fashioned, vintage interior styling can be incredibly versatile. The best vintage interiors keep clutter to a minimum. There is use of either a vintage cabinet (or similar storage unit) used to update an interior in a stylish yet practical way, or open shelves displaying books, trinkets or vintage accessories.

Casual

With people enjoying more relaxed lifestyles, many homes today are decorated using elements of the casual style. Casual rooms have simple details, textured elements in fabrics and accessories, restful horizontal lines, soft upholstery, low-lustre surfaces, and arrangements that avoid perfect symmetry. Furniture is often long, large and horizontal, rather than vertical and tall or petite. Large and chunky tables give a feeling of comfort while providing space to spread out.

Eclectic

Eclectic interiors bring ideas from a range of different periods, trends and styles. The best eclectic interiors are a cohesive blend of old and new uniting texture, colour and pattern.

Paris apartment

The Paris apartment decorating style ranges through many decorating periods, including Neoclassical, Baroque and Rococo. Contemporary Parisian apartments incorporate Mediterranean, Old World, Art Deco and Cabaret influences. Rich jewel colours like crimson, emerald green and royal blues are accented with black, gold and white. Furniture and accessories have a time-worn elegance and vintage look. Chairs, tables and armoires are painted in black or cream, with gold accents, blending beautifully with dark, carved wood. Rich silks, luxurious brocades and velvets enhance upscale interiors. Accessories include vintage posters of French nightspots and signs, large train station clocks, black wrought iron tables and shelving, as well as scenes of France, Paris, or the Eiffel Tower.

Tropical chic

Tropical chic includes comfort, warmth and a touch of the exotic, using jungle themes, restful earthy colours and natural elements. It mixes a lot of texture and intricate pattern with simple details and a few large accessories. Designs include palm trees, large-leafed banana plants, animal prints, rattan, leather and grass cloth. This look is mostly used in living rooms and family rooms but can be adapted for master suites and bathrooms as well. Colours include ivory, beige, camel, tan, deep brown, soft gold, pale yellow and greens of light sage to darkest green, with accents of dark brown, black or muted reds.

Global themes

Country and culture-based themes from across the globe are applied to the above styles, with development continuing as people travel across the world regularly. Indian themes, along with inspirations provided by Bollywood, show an appreciation of rich colours and elaborate designs. Thai, Chinese and Mediterranean themes inspire with intense shades, as does Morocco with its African and Spanish influences. The Japanese theme offers serenity that embodies practicality and relaxation. The renown Arabian Nights tales feature themes of luxury and mystique with Sheherazade's stories. All countries offer impactful constructs into the world's melting pot of creations, influencing fashion as much as interior design and decoration.

Colour theory

The colour wheel is a circular illustrative organisation of colour hues. It displays the relationships between primary, secondary and tertiary colours and is based around:

- Primary colours: red, yellow and blue. They are termed 'primary' because they cannot be made by mixing any other colours, though all other colours are derived from these.

- Secondary colours: green, orange and purple. Primary colours are mixed to produce these colours.

- Tertiary colours: yellow-orange, red-orange, red-purple, blue-purple, blue-green and yellow-green are made by mixing a primary and a secondary colour. The name is of the colour is hyphenated, with the dominant hue named first.

Colour theory advocates the use of a maximum of 3 colours together for a logical structure. However, it depends on what combination creates colour harmony and balance in your visual experience and satisfies your personal colour association.

Influence of fashion designers

Our inspiration comes from seasonal changes and keeping up to date with in-trend fashion colours. It's no longer possible to remain unaffected by international influences. Decorative interior colours and patterns shown by retailers are intimately linked with seasonal changes and portray inextricable connection with fashion as colours and design configurations are revealed each season by the fashion houses with their vogue styles.

The on-trend offerings from our high street home stores means we are provided with a range of fashionable seasonal coloured fixtures, fittings, accessories and decorations. Utilising these little luxuries in time-appropriate seasonal colours is a great way to bring these colours into your home and update your interior space without undertaking a major seasonal refurbishment project.

For Spring and Summer 2017, yellow was the mode and our fashion maestros and maestre covered the catwalks in all its various shades. For Autumn Winter 2018 and 2019, head to toe animal prints grace worldwide walkways and storefronts.

The Pantone Fashion Colour Trend Report for Autumn Winter 2018 informed us of what is being presented by designers at New York Fashion Week by featuring rich autumnal hues combined with a classic colour palette. The Pantone Trend Report for Spring Summer 2019, based on London Fashion Week, depicts rich vibrant colours, with centre stage being held by red, orange, pink and green.

To obtain an early view of in-trend colours, styles and designs, the Pantoneview home + interiors book is useful for inspiration on seasonal changes relating to fashionable colours and home applications.

The colour wheel and use of colours

Careful consideration needs to be given to mixing paint colours otherwise you can end up with shades that look muddied. A colour wheel can help you to become familiar with where different colours fit in, as well as make you aware of the colours which sit next to each other, along with those which are directly opposite your chosen colour.

We keep a colour wheel on hand whilst decorating or staging a property. It helps us to identify colours which will be appropriate for use, as well as the associated tones and shades that can increase our colour palette for the particular property.

Chapter 3. INTERIOR DESIGN AND DECORATING

The overall interior design and the colours you use can make or break the image you are attempting to portray with your property. We are providing detailed information on paint and wallpaper colours here because it is so important to get this right to create the appropriate image.

Consider what the in-trend colours are for the season or the year. While magnolia paint may be widely used all year around, it's exciting to use up-to-date colours. These can also provide talking points for your visitors. A few years ago, hues of orange and pink were the in-trend colour combinations used across the fashion industry, from clothing and shoes to soft furnishings.

Your choice of colour will also depend on the purpose of your renovation: whether you are painting your property to sell, rent out or live in. Pale neutral colours are best when you are selling as this creates a light environment which can be accented with any other colours the buyers will introduce.

Slightly darker neutral walls (combined with dark carpets) are popular for rentals so that wear and tear is less conspicuous. When you are painting your home to live in, along with any family members, try to obtain a consensus (where possible) to ensure everyone is happy living with the colours that have been chosen for your home.

The purpose and location of the room should be top of mind when deciding on which colours you choose. Deciding who will use the room, what will it be used for, and when is it likely to be used, can influence the colour and shade. Ascertaining were the room is located in the house and the direction it faces, whether the room gets a lot of sun or is dark, if it's large with high ceilings and filled with natural light or small and compact, will children or adults use it, and if it's for use all day or just in the evenings, will help to develop your senses for the habitat and purpose of the room, leading you to colours and combinations that would be best suited.

If you are renovating a room you will use as a study every day to develop new food ideas, you will be looking for stimulating colours to inspire you, whereas a small child's or elderly relative's bedroom will suit soft and calm colours to encourage a restful night's sleep. In the properties we have renovated, even though open-plan living has become popular in the UK, we tend to paint adjacent rooms in different colours to delineate and separate the rooms so that it's use is clearly defined.

You can paint, wallpaper or put a mural on a wall in any or each of the rooms in your home to create a feature walls and give each room a uniqueness. We like to have bold colours and bright wallpaper on bedroom walls that the headboard is placed against so that we can see the wall when we enter the room, but the remaining walls are painted in light or dark neutral, or calm colours, so that sleep is undisturbed.

Each colour is not just that in its entirety, it has different tones, tints and hues that you can use. Blue can go from a soft baby blue to a heavyweight dark navy, with several other shades in between. Look around at the colours of the items in your home and to help you to select the right colours and tones that you would like your walls painted in. Dulux offers a paint matching service whereby you can scan any item and the Dulux app will match the shade, so you can then buy that specific paint colour for use in your home.

We use test pots and paint a square foot of cardboard or heavy paper and move it around to different walls in the room and house at different times of the day and in different lights as well. Later, when we are shortlisting our choices, we paint the test pot colour directly on the different walls to make sure we absolutely love it before making a final decision. In our first property we used 24 test pots, all in different shades of cream, before concluding that the initial test pot we purchased was our first choice!

> If you think a colour is too bold for your walls but want to use it, apply accent colours to the walls and match articles in the room in that colour, e.g. soft furnishings such as cushion covers, quilts, curtains and rugs, or paintings, objects d'art or a platter on a coffee table.

Natural and artificial lighting will alter the colour you see, so look at your experimental test pot painted walls at different times of the day and night before you finalise your choice of colour. Matt paint absorbs light, whereas gloss paint reflects light and illuminates the space around it. We had a large purpose-built bookshelf along an entire wall, where we painted the back wall in a velvet touch burgundy and the shelves in white. The room looked luxurious and moody, turning it into a space where people said they felt cocooned.

> Always use colours and shades that you can relate to personally and directly. This means using colours which make you feel positive and happy, showing you have a connection and a good gut feel about them. These colours, with your sense of belonging and feelings of comfort, will pre-pave your experience in your home in the same way. Using colours that you already love means you will then be happy coming home and living 'in' those shades.

Chapter 3. INTERIOR DESIGN AND DECORATING

If you are using wooden or wood-coloured flooring (whether it's laminate, vinyl, hardwood or tiles), use your colour wheel and a swatch of the flooring colour to match it to your choice of wall colour

We used real wood flooring in a property and due to our painter's time constraints, we had the walls painted before the floor was installed. To show both the floor and the warm, cream-toned walls at their best, it took us seventeen different coats of wood stain to get the flooring to the colour that we were happy with. We absolutely loved the floor and the colour we ended up with and understand that, to this day, it's still going strong with the current owners.

Monochromes

The use of monochromatic colour schemes has always been popular. Using one colour for the entire room don't need to end up looking tame, boring or lacklustre. Monochromatic schemes can be brought to life by adding different tints, shades and hues of the same colour, along with the addition of different textures.

Use metallic accents, small furniture and soft furnishings to liven up monochrome rooms.

Black

Black remains an in-trend colour. It looks expensive and luxurious and can be combined with any other colours easily. We had a stunning wallpaper in our hallway which was a combination of matt black and lustrous gold. It became the talking point for visitors. Black requires a certain boldness and combination to make it work. People believe that black can get lost in a small room because it absorbs light, but the right combination of colours and accents, along with soft furnishings, can bring sophistication to a room.

White

White also works with all other colours. To stop white looking too clinical, mix it with different shades of white and soft cream. Or combine it with other colours, whether they are warm, cool, neutral or bright colours. Depending on your colour scheme, you could have bright colour pops or subtle blending. Black and white tiles have always been popular in hallways, kitchens and bathrooms. White walls in a study help to clear the mind and leave it uncluttered for sharp thinking but still have accents for stimulation. Feng Shui teachings espouse the combination of a gentle shade of blue and crisp white as one of the best calming colours.

Yellow

This can range from the softest creams to sharpest yellow. Using the traffic light system, amber yellow heralds warning, or in another shade it can be cheerful and stimulating. Using the right shade of yellow for yourself is quite an art because some shades can leave you feeling happy while others don't help when you are anxious. In a lot of our properties we have used a different shade of yellow, from buttery golds to creamy whites, because it looks so cheerful and sunny.

Green

Green is associated with optimism and growth. People like using green as it brings the garden into their homes and makes them feel close to nature. Along with being a calm colour, green also feels fresh and nourishing. It must be good for you because green vegetables are! Greens range from jewelled jade to pale asparagus and are appropriate for any room. Look at gardens and forests for inspiration while combining greens. If you don't like green, add leafy plants to your home to purify the air you breathe. Just be aware that plants expel carbon dioxide at night, so don't have them in your bedroom.

Blue

Blues are known as cool colours but can certainly be warmed up. Light blue is used for creating a calm and relaxing environment. We have used pale blue silk saris interwoven with gold and white flowers for curtains in guest bedrooms. Sapphire blue is stunning when used as an accent colour on feature walls. And when combined with silver, it is luxurious and stylish. We have navy and bright orange sheets which make the bedroom look exotic.

Indigo

Indigo is the colour between purple and blue. It is also known as royal blue and is associated with the Divine and intuition, being the colour of the third-eye chakra.

Indigo indicates sophistication. It is a strong and moody colour which looks great in big rooms with high ceilings. We painted a kitchen in indigo in a previous property. It was coupled with sparkling cream bench tops and large windows providing lots of light and reflection. And while not everyone can live with such strong colours, that's what we had the most positive comments about during our viewings, with potential buyers saying the kitchen looked stunning. We have also seen small rooms look very elegant and moody in dark navy and indigo combinations.

Purple

Purple is made up of red and blue, shown on most colour wheels as violet, and is also known to be a royal colour. Usually accents of this paint colour on one wall, along with items in varying shades of purple, are used for effect (e.g. deep purple velvet cushions). We used purple and gold silk curtains in our bedroom in a previous property and our property buyers purchased these from us because they complemented the rooms beautifully when coupled with the black and gold wallpaper on the feature wall behind the bedhead. Use this colour if you are feeling bold and adventurous; if it's not for you in the long term, you can always cover it with a coat of paint or wallpaper over it!

Pink

Pink remains in-trend with fashion designers. It is a calm colour and is often associated with romance and love. Think of rose quartz, which is associated with the heart. It can range from soft pink to fuchsia. Light pink is a good colour to use if you have an office in your home where you are seeing anxious clients (e.g. a psychotherapist). Use of pale pink furnishings can be soothing and relaxing in the bedroom. Bold pinks add energy and you can either use these bright hues on a feature wall or for accents with painted furniture or furnishings. We have a deep pink antique chair which sits beside a bright white glass-topped contemporary vanity unit in the guest room and the combination of these colours, along with their opposing design period styles, brightens an otherwise dark room.

Orange

Orange is warm, happy and inviting, without being in-your-face like a flamboyant red. It is too stimulating for bedrooms but can used for an accent wall or as soft furnishings in the brightest orange. If this is your favourite colour and you want to use it as a wall paint, consider using a soft tint of orange on your walls, rather than a vivid orange; you will then be able to live in it every day instead of it becoming an eyesore very quickly. Blue is on the opposite side of orange on the colour chart, so you can have complementary shades of both these colours in your room.

Red

Red is hot, bold, inciting and exciting. According to Feng Shui principles, red is used to stimulate, so it's not used in a dining room because it encourages eating, talking and moving very quickly.

In one of the initial properties we renovated, we wanted to use red for the feature wall in our kitchen. We were particularly attracted to the shade of red that the BBC uses and managed, with great difficulty, to obtain the code for the colour, China Red. Delighted with our achievement, we didn't bother with doing a test piece with a sample pot, but (unadvisedly!) proceeded with having all the kitchen walls painted with 4 coats of this colour of red. Over the next few months, we got used to all the kitchen walls being painted bright red. The room had large windows, floor-to-ceiling French doors, black benchtops and maple kitchen units, so it looked contemporary. The property was re-sold recently, and we noticed that the same colour is still on the walls.

If you are using red paint, make sure you do several coats because it shows up all the imperfections on the wall underneath, especially if the wall is not plastered well. And unlike us, use a test pot first!

Retro colours

Retro colours have been in-trend for ages. Pastel shades of pink, green, blue, yellow, cream and others in the scheme provide a range of classic looks from the 1920s vintage era. Sharp orange and bright red colour pops remind you of the 1950s American diners. While it's largely used in restaurants, retro colours look fun if you have a kitchen diner, especially if you can have retro-styled seating arranged in the room as well. A retro corner in the kitchen works well for easy catch-ups over coffee and impromptu family meals.

Metallics

Metallic and shimmer paints on your walls can look glamorous. Gold, bronze, brass, silver and steel accents can work with most colours. You can start with using the hue that is reflected in the metal. Gold and bronze go well with warm or hot colours like red, silver thrives with cool colours like blue and indigo is very in-trend with brass. Several different shades of green work well with all metallic colours. Sequinned throws, scarves or bedspreads and crystallised cushions add opulence and luxury to a bedroom.

Mediums to transform your walls

Paints

Paint is a very powerful tool in decorating and design, whether you are decorating an object or a whole building or designing the walls and floors of your house. Paint has the capability of making things look totally different. A once gloomy room can be brightened up by painting the walls with light colours.

With the right choice of colours, designers and decorators are able to achieve solutions that create a mood, camouflage flaws and enhance appearance. To set the right mood for a space, they will determine the purpose of the area first. A bedroom requires a different colour choice than a work area.

> While it's preferable to use one colour for the entire structure, the pairing of bold and contrasting colours makes for visual interest, encouraging conversation. But the colour palette you choose depends on the purpose of your property. If it's for investment only, rather than one you will live in, then it's likely that less time, effort and money will go into investigating the various colours, combinations and types of paints because you want the property completed and rented out as soon as practicable.

Flaws in properties are always present; they often cannot be avoided, but we can do something to hide them. This is when paint as camouflage can be used. If the ceiling of a room is too high, a darker paint will make it appear lower, or if you want to create the illusion of a larger space in a small room, paint the walls in lighter colours. For large cold rooms, paint them with warm colours like orange, red or pink.

If a wooden floor is damaged, paint it with a colour that matches or contrasts with the wall colour. If the pieces of furniture for a dining set do not match, paint the table and chairs with a single cohesive colour to create a unified effect. For tables and chairs in an art room, you can paint them in different colours to create a fun space. Old art frames can be painted a colour that blends or contrasts with the colour of the wall where they will be hung on. Classic wood furniture can look new again by applying a paint colour that matches the shade of the room, or one that is close to the tint of the original material.

Don't be afraid to try new, innovative ways of using paint. Add visual interest with geometric patterns or flowing ribbons using bold, contrasting colours for striking impact.

There are also many paint finishes available for different applications:

Matt

Matt emulsion is most commonly used on walls and ceilings and where the surface is uneven. It is a flat finish with a sheen level less than 10% and is non-reflective in appearance. It is less washable and can be subject to scuff marks when used in high traffic areas e.g. hallways. Durable matt options, available in most ranges, are designed to resist marking.

Chalky

Chalky matt is one of the most popular finishes when upcycling furniture. The finish is completely flat and creates a chalky or distressed appearance. Its sheen level is around 2% and it can be over-coated with a sealer or wax.

Eggshell, satin, silk, soft sheen

Each of these finishes is visibly shinier with a sheen level at varying degrees of around 20% or more.

Eggshell and *satin* finishes are used for trim as a modern alternative to gloss. They have a dull shine and are used for skirtings, window surrounds, sills and frames. It is a more durable finish than matt, with a better wash ability and a smoother appearance. Eggshell finish is suitable for decorating larger areas such as walls and ceilings. Acrylic eggshell paints are recommended due to lower VOC (volatile organic compounds) content.

Silk and *soft sheen* finishes are used for walls in high traffic areas, like kitchens and hallways, due to their more wipeable properties and greater resistance to steam. Higher sheen finishes highlight imperfections in walls.

Gloss

Gloss is available for interior as well as exterior decorating. The sheen level is high, at around 90%, making it highly reflective and washable. Water-based and acrylic glosses will have less sheen than solvent-based glosses. Commonly used on trim, gloss will provide a beautiful mirrored effect. In commercial kitchens, special gloss finishes are available for walls for hygienic washable food preparation area.

Masonry

Masonry paints are available in smooth and textured finishes. When choosing masonry paint, weather durability is a key factor. Differences are:

Smooth – the finish is matt, smooth to the touch and easier to keep clean.

Textured – the aggregate added to this paint gives a lightly textured finish, ideal for covering imperfections on exterior walls. Heavier versions give a much deeper texture and are suited to walls with large flaws or where a deep texture is required. A textured finish will need cleaning more often.

Wallpapers

One of the biggest problems in presenting properties is large blank walls that create a feeling of emptiness, not fulfilling their potential for visual impact in a room. Wallpapers provide a great opportunity for design ingenuity and creativity, lending versatility to a room. They can be relatively inexpensive but can greatly enhance the design of a room. An entire room's design can be built around wallpaper. They are an effective and popular way to decorate walls and bring them to life. Wallpapers also provide an opportunity for colours and patterns to be incorporated into a design.

A large wall can benefit from using wallpaper with patterns or stripes. Additionally, it can be used to create a statement, interest and focal point. Vertical stripes add height to a room, while horizontal strips create the illusion of a wider space. Another option for creating interest is to incorporate a dual design by using a striped pattern on the upper half of the wall, and a solid or floral print on the lower part. Borders near the ceiling create visual interest and give the illusion of height to the room, as it calls attention to the ceiling.

> When using wallpaper in more than one room, you can create fluidity between two rooms without having to use the same wallpaper. This fluidity can be achieved by using different tones of the same colours, contrasting colours, or similar patterns.

Murals

Answers for what to do with a wall are available to consumers by ready-made design solutions. However, these design solutions do not always fulfil our expectations. Sometimes, the greatest fulfilment comes from exploring our own creative tendencies in order to manifest what we like.

Walls are one of the biggest challenges when designing a room. You can present a work of art on your wall that is both beautiful and reflective of who you are. Use murals created manually by hand (using stencils or in freehand) or an inspiring wallpaper mural (sold per square metre). These are great ways of adding a real wow factor to your wall. Take into consideration the room you are going to put the mural in, as well as the person or persons who will be the primary users of the room. This will help you visualise the saturation of colours that can be used as well as the freedom of design.

Faux finishes

In many countries, faux finishes have become very popular. These are finishes that are so artistic, they do not look like wallpaper or paint. The faux finish can be applied to any type of surface, including walls, metal, glass, ceramic and wood. A faux finish lasts longer than wallpaper. Since it is not paper-based, it will never peel off. It can be coated with polyurethane (available in satin, matte, or semi-gloss finish) for a longer lasting appeal. With the different techniques possible with faux finishes, a small room can appear larger and more spacious, or a larger room can seem cosier.

Faux finishes include different shades of a base colour shaped as big blocks, marble effect, variations and shades of one colour for a soft effect, striped tone-on-tone, terracotta tile effect, mottled or parchment fresco look, copper patina and golden glaze. The faux effects are obtained by applying primer, glaze and coating before using brushes, rollers, sponges, feathers and wood-graining tools to obtain the effect you want.

Mouldings or covings

Some of the more versatile items to consider in your interior design effort are mouldings or covings and decorative trims. These can be made out of wood, metal or plastic. Adding these to your decor can increase the perceived value of the property.

Mouldings can be used in many different places and ways, including:

- Skirting boards, chair rails and around windows.
- Door trims. Add an additional decorative moulding to an existing single architrave for a different look.
- Crown mouldings. Place at the top of the wall as a transition to the ceiling.
- Stair railings. Handrails can be used in your stairwell for elegance and safety.
- Wainscot capping. Utilise moulding to cap off wooden panelling on the lower part of the walls of a room for a finished look.
- Framing on a wall as a design statement. Add a contrasting paint, wallpaper or finish to the area inside of the moulding frame.

Utilise fabrics and soft furnishings

People are often faced with the dilemma of changing the look of an entire room without spending all their budget. When major changes in furniture, structural renovations to the home and any other major overhauls are out of the question, the capacity of fabric in various textures and colours should be considered for transforming a room and bringing it to life. When incorporated appropriately, fabric can exhibit the theme of the season, or the mood of the room, and can direct interest to the dullest spaces.

> Depending on how they are used, fabrics can bring a unique mood to a room. Heavy, richly coloured and textured fabrics usually bring a more formal, ornate feel. Sheer fabrics used in window treatments, hanging on bare walls, or even just thrown over the back of a couch or an ottoman can bring a more fun, airy and flirty feel to a room. Used properly, fabrics achieve design changes at a relatively low cost and with much less effort. They can take the place of accessories and furniture and can create as much impact as a new coat of paint or wallpaper. Fabrics allow for versatility of design by mixing and matching, with temporary solutions such as slipcovers created at a fraction of the cost of more permanent alterations. Keep an eye on in-trend designs and colours depicting seasonal changes so that you end up with an updated look.

In the living room and the dining area, seating comprises much of the space. To have visual impact, most of the design incorporated into the room must come from the seating area. Fabrics are the best solution for providing temporary or permanent overhauls for your sofa or couch. Sofas that are badly stained or worn can be re-upholstered. When looking at fabrics for re-upholstering, choose one that will blend in with various colour schemes as re-upholstery is permanent in nature. Slipcovers are a good option for allowing seasonal colour changes in the room and are available ready-made online, or on the high street. They are also good for mixing and matching the sofa with other pieces of furniture or accessories, fitting in with the decor and mood of the room more quickly, easily and economically. For the dining area, the dining chairs or stools may be fitted with covers and skirts for a more decorative effect or to provide a seasonal colour scheme in the room.

Windows create a dramatic architectural impact whether inside or outside the home. However, inside the home, many windows end up as nothing but arbitrary openings in the wall or ceiling space, not maximizing their potential to become focal points or contribute to the design for a room. Have curtains and blinds custom-made to your fabric choice and specification or purchase more cost-effective ready-made curtains and blinds online. They may not be made of the highest quality fabrics, but we have found them to be perfectly adequate. Used appropriately, they can look impressive and have a remarkable effect.

Choose works of art

Selecting art for your home should be pleasurable as it will be a source of enjoyment for you for many years. The key is to work out what kind of art you like, how it will fit in with the rest of your interior design plans, and how to exhibit the piece to its best effect in your home. You may already have a good idea of what art you like. If not, there are many opportunities to browse through works of art within your community at local exhibitions, galleries and art fairs. Neighbouring restaurants or cafés may also exhibit the work of local artists. The internet provides the largest variety and depth of art available worldwide. One of the advantages of online searches is that you can look for the specific kind of art you are interested in e.g. photography, impressionism, sculpture and abstract painting.

Style is another consideration when selecting art for a room. If your house is furnished with antiques, you are most likely to use antique-style frames around the paintings you hang. If you have contemporary furniture in large rooms with high ceilings, you are apt to display larger and more contemporary pieces. When selecting a painting, select one or two of the boldest colours in your room and look for pieces of art that have those colours in it. You're not looking for an exact match. Picking up one or two of the same colours conveys that the painting belongs in that environment. But there are no absolute rules. Any design strategies should be considered guidelines only, so experiment until you are happy with it. An eclectic mix of artwork can work. Just ensure that your display is cohesive.

> Paintings should always be hung so that the centre of the painting is at eye level. A sculpture could sit on the floor, on a table, or on a pedestal, depending on the design. Put up ceiling spotlights that can be adjusted to focus on your artworks or use individual lighting for each piece.

Chapter 3. INTERIOR DESIGN AND DECORATING

Design and decorate in a day

Great designing and decorating do not have to cost a lot of money or take a significant amount of time. You can create a lovely home using elements in unexpected ways.

If necessary, disregard the original purpose of a room, re-define it and use it in a way that works best for your lifestyle. In separate instances, we have previously used an ensuite bedroom, a dining room and a lounge as study rooms because they fitted the purpose. Think outside the box and have fun while you are designing and decorating your home!

It's important to plan ahead and be prepared for the day. In advance, empty out a room and think of it as a blank canvas. See what utilisation ideas you can come up with, even though it may take several tries before you achieve what you want. Creating a space that is multi-functional as well as interesting can be easily achieved by dividing the space into several smaller areas. The living or family rooms are usually the rooms where maximum usage is most desirable. Think of the style you would like to display, and the theme suited for the space. Keep in mind your larger pieces of furniture, furnishings, accessories and artworks. Confirm you colour scheme and purchase all your materials in advance so that you can start your project as soon as possible on the day.

As an idea, bring your china cabinet into the living room, remove the doors and place books, accessories and family photos in it. This will create an interesting focal point in a room that is missing architectural central points. Add elements of comfort to your room because it is important that a room feels cosy as well as looks good. Place an ottoman where you might place a conventional coffee table. Putting a circular glass top onto a bird bath can create an attractive side table, or stack old suitcases to create an instant table for an ornamental lamp. Use old golf clubs, copper plumbing, or PVC pipe, painted with a faux finish, for curtain rods. Put up large, decorative mirrors or lean them against the wall. These are swift change options for completing you project within a day.

Design and decorate the room using your choice of style, colours and mediums after confirming your focal point. Don't neglect the ceilings in your home. You can adorn them by painting and adding embellishments like crystals or elaborate wood mouldings. Mirrors or murals on bedroom ceilings can also be fun!

Design and decorate on a budget

> Decide on a budget ahead of time, pace your decorating and include money for accessories. Decide on one room at a time and assign a priority within your room. Have a plan (which includes a target date for completion). Confirm your style, theme and colour choices around your focal point, keeping in mind your larger pieces of furniture, furnishings, accessories and artworks.

Measure your room to scale and draw a floor plan, showing windows and doors. Decide on a focal point. Measure your furniture, rugs and any other large items for that room, draw these to scale (in relation to your floor plan) and cut out the drawings. Place these drawings on your floor plan and move them around until you arrive at an arrangement that you like. This is much easier as you are not having to physically move heavy pieces of furniture around the room. This process will also help you to decide if the items are proportionately correct for your room. Think too about ceiling height and traffic flow.

For the chosen colours in your scheme, repeat these on your walls at eye level, mid-level, and floor level to achieve good visual balance. View colours and patterns during daylight and twilight hours before making a purchase. Repeat any pattern or textures in a room at least twice. Paint and wallpaper are great for updating and freshening a room and generally cost very little. If you do not plan to be living in your home for a long period, invest in accessories like artwork, cushions and rugs that could be used in another home.

There are many ways that you can stretch your decorating budget and find bargains on quality furnishings that will bring years of beauty and style to your home.

Look for ideas that are low-cost or even at no-cost. Study displays in furniture stores and design centres. You can go online and view properties for sale that have been newly renovated or newly built. Pay attention to the colours and materials you encounter in restaurants, banks, and clothing stores. Fashion and interior design are inseparably linked, so if you are wearing it, think about the wider application of using it in your home as well. Often, the smartest buy is knowledge. Buying a few hours of an interior designer's time could help you decide where best to spend your limited resources and may keep you from making costly mistakes you'll have to live with for a long time.

Chapter 3. INTERIOR DESIGN AND DECORATING

Look to source furnishings and furniture from the following places:

- Show home sales. These can be a source of attractive furniture and furnishings and they are unlikely to be overused. The sales office will be able to advise if and when the items may be available for sale.

- Furniture or department store clearance sales. With new furniture ranges arriving, stores may need to sell off the old stock. Scratched and dented items will also be available for sale at big discounts.

- Trade with a friend. If you have a sofa that's too big and your friend has a more suitable armchair, arrange to swap either temporarily or on a permanent basis.

- Design Centres have sales for discontinued items that have been used as showroom samples. Call a design centre convenient for you to visit or check local newspaper ads.

- Auction houses are a good source of quality one-of-a-kind furniture, furnishings and accessories. Read up on auctions before you go and take advantage of the preview days to examine any pieces you may want to bid on. Many pieces that are not classified as antiques can be extremely reasonable.

- Flea markets, car boot sales and garage sales. These are cheap sources for lots of furniture and accessories and the items will generally be inexpensive, though they may exhibit a great deal of wear. Negotiation is expected, so bring cash and bargain hard.

- Salvage yards. Look for wood, excess metal and other rejected items of furniture and other items. These may be used as materials for projects like tables, stools and window treatments; many of these items may be free or purchased for a minimal price.

- Charity or second-hand stores. If you have the time and the patience, this can be an inexpensive source of great individual pieces.

- Free items. Look out for discarded furnishings found in skips (ask the owners first for sake of politeness), left on the street, or marked 'free' at a garage sale. These can often be turned into something beautiful if you can invest some time and creative vision.

- Recycling centres. Buy with the intention to upcycle. Look at furniture with an eye for its scale, lines and details. A dark wooden desk may be repainted and updated with new hardware, or an old chair seat recovered with new fabric. A sturdy wooden door in a rich colour could work well as a coffee table or desk in your home. Be realistic as to what you can accomplish as a chest with a missing drawer and a damaged top may be too much to fix if you don't have the time, tools, space and skills to repair it.

- Online: FreeCycle (items being given away for free, listed by area), Shpock, Gumtree or even eBay have amazing finds.

The principles of home decorating are more to do with expressing your personality through your own sense of style rather than with spending large amounts of money to make your home look like a picture in a glossy magazine. Don't be afraid to express your personality and don't be shy about looking in unusual places for decorating ideas.

Summary of dos and don'ts

When designing and decorating, be aware of what you can do, what you cannot do and what to look out for when creating a cohesive flow. Use the guidance below to assist you.

Do:

- Discover your personal style by reading magazines, attending home shows, browsing online and looking in stores. Take photos of interiors in hotels when you travel so that you can learn what styles and colours appeal to you.
- Consider the location of your house and its architectural style when planning.
- Plan your project in as much detail as you can.
- Draw your floor plan. Add the room dimensions, window sizes and locations. Include special features and electrical sockets that you will need to work with or around.
- Consider the function and uses of the room before deciding on furnishings and arrangements, e.g. if your dining room will double as your study, you will need room for a desk, books, lights and files, as well as the dining room table and chairs.
- Allow for natural walkways in the room (such as from the door to the closet). Later, you will need to arrange furniture with these walkways in mind.
- Ensure lights are appropriate for the task as well as for general use or dramatic displays. Use a mix of light fixtures on dimmers for maximum control.
- Decide on an overall design style and colour scheme for your project.

- Identify the focal point of the room, such as a fireplace, bed, armoire, or the view. If there is no focal point in a room, create one. Hang a piece of art or place a large piece of furniture in the room (a display cabinet or a large leaning mirror can work). You can also creatively display accessories on a bookshelf. Or use pattern and scale to construct an interesting focal point. Emphasise the more important and attractive elements of a room, rather than working through mundane components.

- Pick a signature piece you would like to accentuate so that this can aid your decorating decisions, such as a beautiful fabric, a rug or a picture. The item should embody both the colour scheme of the room as well as the style and mood you want.

- Purchase any required large items first (rugs, drapes and upholstered furniture) and then use the exact colours and style of those major pieces to coordinate all other elements. Purchase the best quality furniture you can afford. Buy quality construction that you can upcycle or adapt to make it a better buy in the long run.

- Reinforce the style and theme of the room with appropriate accessories and details. Note the specifics of your style and colour, detailing as much as possible on the room's style, such as 'French Country with a rooster motif' or 'a colour scheme that includes black and gold". Install more details in a plain and small room, considering crown moulding, wainscoting and other applications to add interest and character.

- Plan how the rooms will be decorated, including:
  o The type of medium you will apply.
  o The feature walls and what material you will use to create these.
  o Specific fittings you wish to utilise, down to door and window fixtures.
  o Any particular furniture and furnishings you want to include.

- Use the principle of repetition when planning shapes, colours, fabrics and patterns. One red accent in a room may look like an afterthought, whereas several red accents will contribute to the colour scheme. You can use a mix of patterns when coordinating the room, choosing small and large scales, stripes, checks, geometrics and plain. Ensure you end up with a cohesive scheme.

- Coordinate fabric and flooring choices before making any major purchases or choosing exact paint colours.

- Employ a variety of textures, such as shiny, dull, rough and smooth when you want to add interest to a room.

- Utilise unifying elements such as trim colour, wood tone, flooring, fabrics and motifs create a cohesive space.
- Use lines to emphasise a room's style. Horizontal lines will accentuate length and provide for a calm mood, vertical lines will emphasise height and diagonal lines will emphasise space, providing a dynamic and exciting feel.
- Use contrast to add some interest to a space. If you place furniture and accessories against a contrasting background, it will highlight each piece.
- Balance a room's furnishings by paying attention to visual weight and scale. Balance a sizeable fireplace with a substantial sofa or an antique armoire placed opposite it.
- Arrange conversational areas so that they are within 2.5 to 4.5 metres square.
- Place side tables and lamps next to seating in conversation areas so there is space to set drinks and books as well as adequate light for reading.
- Anchor spaces with rugs and furniture groupings in open plan areas to define the space.
- Link your rooms by repeating colours, fabrics and themes in varying combinations.
- Use symmetrical arrangements in formal rooms, utilising pairs of items to emphasise symmetry and balance. Use asymmetrical arrangements of furniture and accessories in casual rooms. Apply odd numbers of items, such as groups of 3, 5, and 7 when grouping accents for table displays. For interest, place items high, medium or low within an imaginary triangle.

Don't:

- Paint your walls first and then go looking for matching fabrics. Paint can be mixed to any colour, so select the shades after upholstery, carpeting, and curtain fabrics are chosen.
- Paint a room without trying a sample of the colour in the room. Tiny paint samples can be deceiving as to tone and depth of colour. Always paint a larger test area or test board to confirm your colour choice. Test colours in different rooms at various times.
- Ignore the focal point of a room by arranging furniture away from it.
- Place furniture where it will obstruct doorways, cabinet doors, natural traffic patterns, or other daily activities.

Chapter 3. INTERIOR DESIGN AND DECORATING 169

- Display all your furniture around the walls (except in the smallest rooms). Pull items into groupings in the centre of the room. This adds warmth and is inviting to guests.
- Try to construct a colour scheme from wildly disparate objects. Instead, find a print, fabric or rug with all of the colours you want to use, then edit out, repaint, or recover items that don't fit with the plan.
- Clutter up a room with copious collectables unless you're in love with that look. Most of your visitors will feel crowded in.
- Decorate around an item that isn't to your taste. If your new home came with gold shag carpeting that is not your style, you will never love that carpet. Get rid of it.
- Keep what you dislike. If it is a large item like a piece of sofa, place a slip cover over it, recover or remove it completely. You will be happier.
- Forget the details. If your chosen theme is Mediterranean, look for weathered iron drawer pulls, iron lamp bases and tile tables.
- Fall in love with cheap furniture just because it has an appealing colour or exciting fabric. Look for quality construction, good lines and elegant details first, and then cover those pieces in a fabric or finish that you love.
- Spend your entire budget on something that isn't functional, classic, or long-lasting, unless you can't live without it. Start with the basics and build from there.
- Choose colours standing in a store. Take samples with you and look at them in daylight and at night so you can make an informed decision. You can do this with paint, wallpaper, fabrics, floor coverings and some larger items. Stores will allow you to return these items, especially when you explain what you're trying to achieve.
- Spend a lot of money on expensive and transient or trendy restyling. Experiment first with accessories and colours for that trend to see how you live with them daily.
- Live with a lot of mismatched furniture that does not go well together. Unite pieces with colour either by painting everything in one colour (e.g. white, pale gold, or black) or by re-covering the items using identical or a mix of coordinating fabrics. Accessorise them with cushions to bring out the colours you love.
- Choose everything beige if you really love colour. Have the courage to use colour!

- Disregard the undertones of a colour. Every colour can be either light or dark, cool or warm, clear or muddy. Look for these colour cues when choosing a colour. Ask for help from an instore colour specialist if you're unsure.
- Ignore the mood effects of colour. Choose colour schemes that underscore the feeling you want to create in your home. Colours known for influencing mood are:
    o Red – exciting.
    o Pale blue – soothing.
    o Green – calming.
    o Yellow – happy.

For design and decorating photos, please visit our website on www.gsansellproperty.com.

Checklist – Interior design and decorating

The following Checklist will help you through this process.

Interior design elements and principles

- ☐ Incorporate design elements and principles in your scheme.
- ☐ Highlight architectural features and focal points; create one as required.
- ☐ Decide on a design style, design scheme and colour palette for your project.
- ☐ Decide fabric / flooring choices before buying major items and choosing paint colours.
- ☐ Buy large elements first using their colours and style, then coordinate other choices.
- ☐ Choose accessories that reinforce the colour and style theme of a room.
- ☐ Paint a larger test area and view it during the day and night to confirm your choice.
- ☐ Link your rooms by repeating colours, fabrics, and themes in varying combinations.

Interior design styles and themes

- ☐ When planning interiors, consider the location of your home and its architectural style.
- ☐ Educate yourself on the different interior design styles and themes.
- ☐ Determine your own style by collating a scrapbook of the images you like.
- ☐ Create a mood board for each room.
- ☐ Create a floor plan for a point of reference, marking placements and colour schemes.
- ☐ Use floor plan software and online apps that provide services for free.

Colour theory and transformational mediums

- ☐ Buy a colour wheel and familiarise yourself the primary, secondary and tertiary colours.
- ☐ Be aware of seasonal trends and fashion influences.
- ☐ Choose your colours based on who you are painting a room for – live in, sell, rent out.
- ☐ Consider the purpose and location of the room when deciding colours.
- ☐ Consider the mediums you will use to add visual interest (e.g. paint, wallpaper, murals).

Utilise fabrics and soft furnishings

- ☐ Decide on what mood you would like to create before committing to a particular fabric.
- ☐ Use fabrics to transform a room if major changes are not in the budget.
- ☐ Keep an eye on in-trend designs and colours depicting seasonal changes.
- ☐ Update your colour scheme with slipcovers for relevant furniture and furnishings.

Choose works of art

- ☐ Select the boldest colours in your room and look for art works with those colours in it.
- ☐ Short list the items to harmonise with your interior design scheme.
- ☐ Install adjustable spotlights to focus on your artworks.

Design and decorate in a day

- ☐ Plan how the room will be designed and decorated using simple change options.
- ☐ Confirm your style, theme and colour choices around your focal point.
- ☐ Clear out the room and purchase your materials in advance.
- ☐ Decorate the room, including the ceiling.

Design and decorate on a budget

- ☐ Buy an interior designer's time to confirm where best to spend your limited resources.
- ☐ Investigate where you can purchase inexpensive furniture, furnishings and accessories.
- ☐ Decide on a budget, pace your decorating and include money for accessories.
- ☐ Have a plan, including a target date for completion.
- ☐ Decide on one room at a time and assign a priority within the room.
- ☐ Draw a floor plan for each room with dimensions, features and focal points.
- ☐ Confirm your style, theme and colour choices around your focal point.
- ☐ Test your chosen paint or wallpaper samples at eye level, mid-level, and floor level.
- ☐ Complete the design and decoration of each room as budget allows.

Summary of dos and don'ts

- ☐ Be alert to the dos and don'ts for your interior design and decorating approach.

Chapter 4

STAGING YOUR PROPERTY

Overview

You can improve a property's appeal by transforming it into an attractive and welcoming home. Presenting a property in a neutral palate, de-personalising it and creating the appropriate focus, room-by-room, has proven to be effective in accelerating sales.

> Home staging is the process of preparing a property for sale to make a home appealing to the highest number of potential buyers, enabling a quicker sale for a higher price. Staging makes a house look bigger, brighter, cleaner and warmer, and potential home buyers are more likely to remember it. Staging also aims to help viewers envision themselves living at the specific property and embracing that particular lifestyle.

It is not only homeowners who are staging their homes. Private landlords are also staging their rental properties to achieve the best rental return and to let out their properties quickly. Professional investors and developers believe that properly staged properties get more viewings than those homes which have not been staged. These professionals also believe that staged homes sell faster than non-staged ones.

There are three primary factors that influence what a buyer will offer on a property – the location, the price and the condition. As location cannot be changed for a specific property, and if a seller stands firm on the price, that leaves condition as the most important variable. Most homeowners probably wouldn't show their property without at least tidying it up, but staging a home involves other, more subtle improvements that can make a home even more attractive to potential buyers. A seller needs to think about their property as a financial asset, as a commodity they are going to sell, and present it accordingly.

Preparing a property for sale does not cost much money if you are prepared to invest your time into it, thoroughly cleaning and de-cluttering, as well as removing unwanted items. But it can involve some financial investment such as painting, improving the landscaping and adding furniture and plants to give prospective purchasers an idea of what their new home could look like.

To compete in the property market these days, homeowners need to undertake particular action to complete the sale of their property. Home staging has become valuable for sellers wanting to make a good impression, thereby increasing a property's selling price and decreasing the selling time. There are many actions that you can take to increase interest in your property, and in turn, speed up the selling process.

Chapter 4. STAGING YOUR PROPERTY

In a recent report, Home Staging Profile – Latest Information on the Industry in the UK – 2018, commissioned by the Home Staging Association UK (HSAUK), the following data confirms the importance of staging properties:

- 62% of property professionals cited that home staging has great effect on the buyers' view of the property, followed by 33% that cited it has some effect, and 5% that cited that it does not have much effect.
- 95% of interviewed samples cited that staged homes sell faster than non-staged ones.
- 100% of real estate agents and property developers cited that home staging makes it easier for a buyer to visualise the property as their future home.
- 67% of real estate agents cited that the reception room is the most important room to be staged for sale, followed by 14% that cited it to be the kitchen, and 14% the master bedroom.
- 23% of the properties that were sold had the reception room staged, followed by 22% of properties that had the master bedroom staged.
- 35% of estate agents cited that staging increased the offer value up to 3%, followed by 35% who cited the increase to have been from 4-6%.
- 46% of property developers cited that staging increased the offer value above 10%, followed by 56% that cited it increased the offer value between 1-3%.
- 76% of interviewed samples cited that the seller pays for the staging before listing the property.
- 67% of interviewed samples cited that the seller hires a staging company to stage a property. The seller can be either a home owner or a property developer. 19% cited that the estate agency hires a staging company / professional.
- De-cluttering, professional photography and entire house cleaning are the most recommended services to help sell, being cited by 18%, 16% and 15% respectively.
- 100% of interviewed professionals have cited that properties with professional photography get more viewings than the ones with low-quality images.

Information courtesy of the Home Staging Association UK (HSAUK).

While having quality brochures, professional photography, advertising online and in local and national publications are necessary, your home also needs to look its best when viewings take place. Professional home stagers are experts in interior design and decoration, with specialist knowledge of how to present a house to appeal to buyers. They also have access to trade discounts and also know trades people who can help if any work requires their skills.

Preparations for staging your property should start as soon as you have made the decision to sell. Most homeowners are not objective about their properties as they are too personally connected. Whether or not you are confident about what you think you need to do to prepare your home for sale, request feedback from friends, family and local estate agents. As well, arrange a consultation with a professional home stager and ask them to provide you with a report outlining what needs to be done to present your property for sale so you could use it to stage your home, or they can do the staging with you, or even for you. Prospective buyers will establish an opinion of your property within the first 10 seconds of walking through the front door, so appealing to them and making an excellent first impression is vital when you're intending to sell your home.

> According to some professionals, a staged home can bring in up to 8% percent more than the same home without staging. In a declining market, however, the goal may be to retain as much of the original price as possible. If you want (or need) to sell your property quickly, you might have to lower the asking price. Home staging could help you avoid that.

Staging your property for sale is one of the most effective ways to enable you to sell it. However, if potential buyers are not viewing your property, discuss the issue with your agent; it may be that you will need to reassess your property or the asking price. Conversely, if a lot of people are viewing but not making offers, this is where staging can help. Buyers need an incentive when viewing, and if they notice and recall a well-presented property, this can influence their decision. Consequently, it can also justify your asking price. Remember: Staging is always cheaper than the first price reduction!

Chapter 4. STAGING YOUR PROPERTY

Key activities that help sell your property

Any activity you can take to improve the look of your property in advance of marketing it for sale is beneficial. The following list of key activities will help you to determine where to apply your money, time and effort:

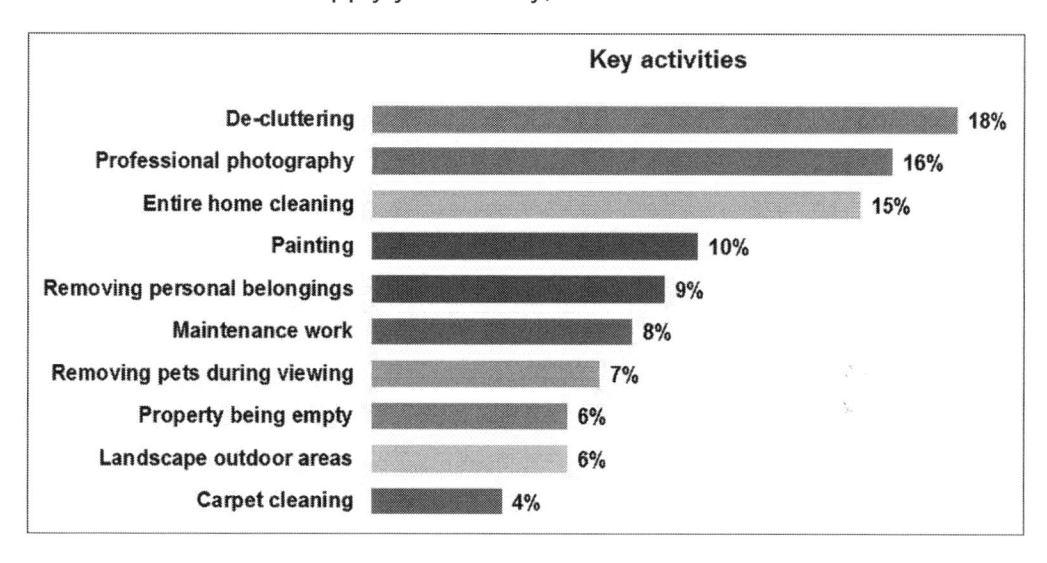

Key activities

Activity	Percentage
De-cluttering	18%
Professional photography	16%
Entire home cleaning	15%
Painting	10%
Removing personal belongings	9%
Maintenance work	8%
Removing pets during viewing	7%
Property being empty	6%
Landscape outdoor areas	6%
Carpet cleaning	4%

Information courtesy of the Home Staging Association UK (HSAUK). Data taken from a research study (December 2017 to March 2018) by the Home Staging Association UK (HSAUK) using an online survey to a random sample of 400 property professionals across the United Kingdom, including real estate agents, property developers and property managers.

> We always complete the staging process before inviting agents to provide valuations because the property is already prepared for sale and relatable valuations can be obtained. Then, once valuations and contracts have been provided, discussed, assessed and signed, this allows the photography and marketing process to be underway swiftly.

If you are still unsure of what you need to do to prepare your home for sale, speak with trusted local estate agents and ask for their advice on what improvements need to be made advice and how best to present your home.

Plan your home staging

Determine which rooms to stage

Research has shown that there are specific rooms that, once staged, benefit the sale of a property. These are shown below:

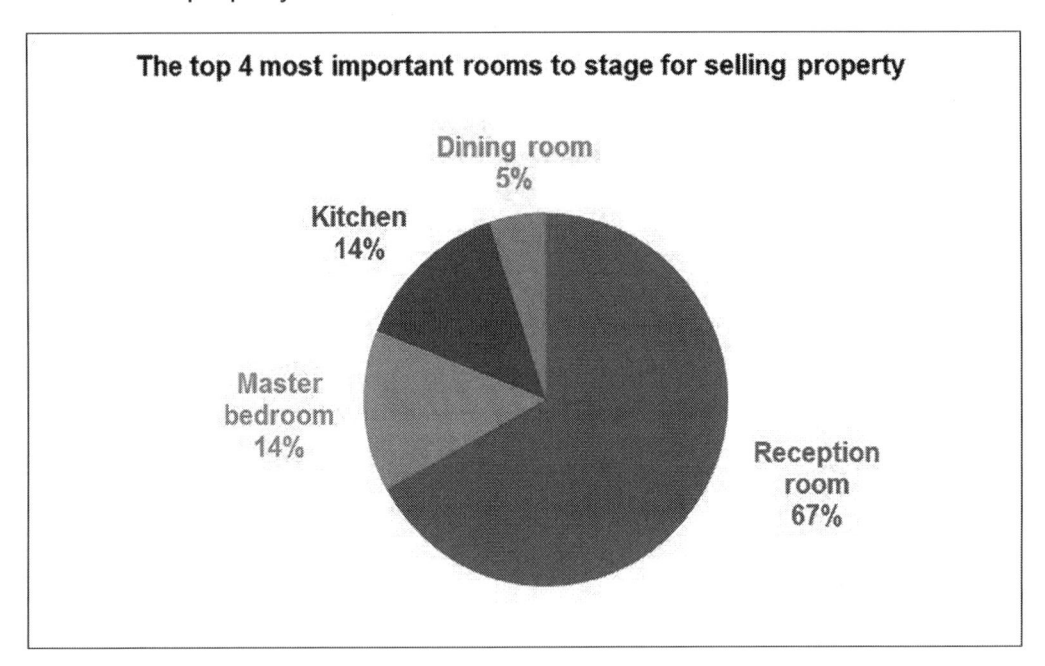

The top 4 most important rooms to stage for selling property

- Dining room 5%
- Kitchen 14%
- Master bedroom 14%
- Reception room 67%

Information courtesy of the Home Staging Association UK (HSAUK).

The reception room is shown to be the most important room to be staged for sale, followed by the kitchen and the master bedroom. But you need not spend a lot of money on an expensive kitchen and bathroom – it is the style and scheme of a property that is much more important than installing high-end fixtures and fittings.

Staging these areas appropriately will make a significant impact on how a potential buyer responds to your property. Get inspiration from sites such as Pinterest for design ideas or engage an interior designer. Then you can undertake the work yourself, work with the interior designer, or obtain a quote for the designer to upgrade the room for you. Home staging professionals can provide a full report, highlighting what needs to be done. The homeowner simply needs to follow the instructions.

Stage for your target market

In readiness for selling a specific property, we define the type of buyer we are targeting and create an avatar (a fictional character that represents your ideal buyer) according to their demographics and psychographics, so we can more easily relate to them. This means we determine who our buyer is likely to be, including their age, income level and lifestyle, and whether they are young singles or families. Then we stage our properties accordingly to maximise selling potential to the target market. It also helps them to see themselves living there.

Assess your property

In preparation for staging, we start the assessment process by reviewing each room in our property. We take notes and photos of the areas that need attention. Also, we keep a record of the features we like to highlight. We sell our properties after having completed renovations, so repairs are unlikely, however, small works may need to be undertake, e.g. painting the ceiling in a basement. In our last property, the agent advised us to have the exterior of our property painted because it looked slightly dated compared to the rest of the property, which had been completely refurbished. We weren't sure about having this work done as we didn't think the property looked in need of paint outside, but we took his advice. While the work cost more than we expected, we were pleasantly surprised at the big difference it made.

> Having defined the style of our target buyer, we prepare and maintain a styling plan, ensuring it is cohesive. We take into consideration each room's purpose, focal point and traffic flow, while maintaining a consistent colour scheme and style throughout. We also bring some of the Feng Shui and Vastu Vidya practices and rituals into play so that the energy in each of the rooms flows correctly. Staging should bring positive feelings to buyers, so we help them to experience this, as well as envision what it would be like living in our property.

Set a realistic budget

> Consider how much you are willing to spend on the staging as it can be easy to get carried away when a property is not selling. It's important to always weigh up the cost of work against the opportunity of selling your property.

If there are any obvious conversions, such as adapting the garage into extra rooms, or converting the loft, and you have the budget and appetite for it, take advantage of this opportunity. You can usually recoup the money spent on conversions. If you are unable to undertake the conversion, consider getting planning permission for it anyway. This will be attractive to potential buyers who are likely to pay extra for having the plans and the permission on hand.

If you decide that replacing certain items in your property isn't cost effective, it is often worth painting cupboards and tiles in a neutral tone to create an airier space. Similarly, if floorboards are in reasonable condition and therefore don't need to be replaced, clean and varnish or paint them, e.g. white floorboards can look fresh and clean in a dark bedroom. Investigate where you can purchase inexpensive furniture, furnishings and accessories

Obtain quotes from the specific trades for any work you cannot tackle yourself. You may have unfinished DIY jobs that need that final push to complete.

Professional versus DIY home staging

Review all the activities you need to undertake during your property sale. Decide if you need a home staging professional to help you with this part of the pre-sale activities, or if you have sufficient knowledge, time and energy to complete this process yourself.

Hiring a professional home stager

> Professional home staging is not a new idea but is now being more widely embraced throughout the world. The benefit of engaging home stagers or interior designers before putting your house on the market is that they will provide you with objective insight and an unbiased opinion as they walk around your property. They will give you a new perspective as they know how best to get viewers through the front door. In many cases, they can also hire out to you any required furniture, rugs, lamps, art and more, and this reduces the time and money you spend looking for appropriate items to stage your property.

Some home staging professionals offer a free initial meeting, then discuss options suitable for you before providing a quote, while others charge for the preliminary meeting. Both methods of quoting are reasonable. There are a number of reasons why someone would charge to provide a quote, the simplest of these being due to the amount of work to be done or the location of the property.

You may decide to have a consultation and implement the recommendations yourself. Or if you decide to pay a home staging professional to undertake

Chapter 4. STAGING YOUR PROPERTY

the work with, or for you, it's likely to be on an hourly rate, with the total cost dependant on the home being staged.

Residential and investment properties can be staged as follows:

- For residential properties:
  - Staging services can be provided using the client's photos, with consultation taking place via the telephone, on Skype, or during a home visit.
  - While dependant on the location and condition of the property, it's likely to be a fixed price consultation lasting a few hours, with a report and quotation provided.
  - A home stager can advise on storage solutions and offer professional decluttering services for every room in the house, including living room, bedrooms, bathrooms, office, study, kitchen and conservatory or orangery.
  - For any improvements required for the home, a home stager may be in a position to recommend trade contractors, e.g. to carry out repairs, painting, decorating, gardening and cleaning.
  - Some stagers are able to offer a service whether they can manage the entire project, including the work undertaken by the trades.
  - The level of service quoted for will depend on a number of things, e.g. the budget, size of project, availability of the client and the home stager.
- For dressing a property for sale, professional home stagers work with developers, builders and investors to stage their properties as show homes to improve lifestyle appeal for buyers and maximise property sales potential. Services offered can include:
  - Design and styling to suit the property.
  - Providing the appropriate quality of furniture, soft furnishings, accessories and window treatments (i.e. curtains and blinds).
  - Providing furniture hire or purchase options for different design styles.
  - The project can be quoted off the plan, or the home stager will visit the site, take the measurements, discuss the requirements and provide a quote.

Professional home stagers' services may extend to interior design services. They can design a stylish scheme, and include costs for furniture, flooring, curtains, wallpaper, bedding, towels, art work, lighting, mirrors and accessories for the design scheme.

Many sellers end up lowering their price to attract an offer. Paying for professional home staging can improve the seller's chances of obtaining close to asking price or shorten the time to first offer. Home-staging professionals can be found through real-estate agents or via the Internet. Ensure they can supply credentials, qualifications and testimonials.

There are also specialist companies who can stage your property virtually by digitally inserting designer furniture, flowers, and more into photos of your home. This works well for empty properties as the enhanced photos give the viewer a deeper connection with the house and a vision of how the property could look in the future.

Doing your own home staging

If you decide to stage your own home, some things to keep top of mind are:

- If you're selling a multi-million-pound property, outdated furniture will need to be replaced. Rather than buying replacement items, rent some appropriate pieces of furniture for a few months until you get to exchange of contracts on your property sale.

- If the appliances are old and completely out of date, they will affect the value of the property. Replace them, if possible, with free-standing appliances, which you can take with you when you move. Or rent the appliances you need to replace. Don't get top-end items; they just need to look current and be in good working condition.

- Prospective buyers will have a difficult time imagining themselves living in a property if there are multiple and conflicting brightly coloured carpets, walls, worktops and furniture. These are all likely to cause distractions by polarising rooms. You will need to redecorate in neutral paint and replace damaged or unsightly furniture with less eye-catching pieces. You will also need soft furnishings and accessories to dress the property suitably. Make sure that each room has a balanced and integrated look.

De-clutter

> De-cluttering your property does not just clear your physical environment, it also clears your mental space, so you no longer have to use up good energy thinking about these possessions. Additionally, it creates more space in the house as well as better flow.

You need to distance yourself from your property and look at it objectively, through a potential buyer's eyes, evaluating every aspect of each room in your house. But it can be difficult deciding what to keep and what to remove.

Selling a property is a very good time to review what belongings you have and to get rid of all the excess items that have accumulated over time. Start in one room at a time, beginning with the easiest room so it's not so daunting (e.g. a bathroom or hallway). If it's still too much to take on a room, then make a start with items you enjoy working with, e.g. makeup drawers, handbags, newspapers, books, magazines, CDs or DVDs. Call it an achievement even if this is all you have cleared up in an evening.

It's a great feeling of lightness when you have off-loaded belongings you no longer need, and it will motivate you to do more de-cluttering. It also leads to rediscovery of things that you love and have forgotten about. Be careful not to remove all traces of your home's character as this is what made you fall in love with your home when you originally bought it. Potential buyers could be looking for this as well.

To maximise the use of space, less is more when presenting a property. Too much furniture, or very large pieces, can have a polarising effect as well as make a room look small. Too many pictures or bookcases spilling over with books and collectables over can make a room look enclosed. Remove any bulky furniture that makes a room feel small (look to store this off site if you have an excess) and replace it with smaller furniture if necessary. This makes a property lighter and brighter.

But just removing furniture is not sufficient; pay attention to the entire room. If there is too much furniture or decor on one side of the room, it can feel lopsided. Look to group them in objects of three at varying heights to make them pleasing to the eye rather than distracting. Arrange furniture so that it is easy for potential buyers to navigate a room.

Dated homes, however large, can be off-putting to affluent young families seeking lifestyle appeal. If you want to sell at a premium to this audience, consider storing larger items and renting a few contemporary pieces to instantly transform the look and feel of your home. Buyers need to be able to imagine what the property would look like if they were living there. Make it easy for them to see all the living space available. Potential purchasers are often buying into a lifestyle as much as a property. The right presentation, along with small stylistic changes, can highlight positive aspects of a property and minimise negatives.

To prevent people from being distracted, remove all collectables and memorabilia from your home. This includes family photos, ornaments, oversized or polarising items which may distract viewers, children toys, pets' belongings and other possessions inside and outside the property.

Rather than storing belongings you don't need or use, you can pass these on to your family and friends, or donate them to charities, so that other people can have use of these items in a more meaningful way. Alternatively, you may decide to auction these items or sell them on eBay, Gumtree or via other online portals. You will not have to subsequently pack or move these items, enabling you to save space in your new property. If you really can't bear to get rid of them, then put them in storage or ask family or friends to hold them for you but do remove them from your property.

> Our de-cluttering time is also kept at a minimum because we move so often. Prior to each move, we hire a small skip and throw out everything we don't want to carry to our next property. This is done after donating usable items and leaving behind those that would be useful to new owners, e.g. tiles, carpet offcuts and flooring. In the past we have given away belongings like clothes, tables, exercise bikes and other gym equipment to neighbours, cleaners, removal teams or others because we have not used these sufficiently to warrant keeping. We have auctioned some larger pieces of furniture we bought specifically for a Victorian property that we refurbished. The remainder of the items go to charities like 9 Lives Furniture, who have collected the items, which is really helpful at such a busy time.

Similarly, we continue with all the rooms in the house until it's cleared and cleaned from top to bottom. We have found that while lofts are great for storage, they can allow space for a lot of unused belongings and detritus as well, so having a skip available is very useful, as are large rubbish bags for items designated for donation or going to charity. We try not to overthink when we are de-cluttering; this stops us wasting time reviewing all our possessions slowly, having endless discussions on when we last used them, how we felt and what someone else thought of them – it's time to either love it or leave it!

You may also want to buy some of the furniture and fittings, along with the chattels, that could be on offer at your new property, so you will need to make space for these.

Obtain external storage space

When selling your property, consider renting or having access to offsite storage space. Rather than having your property bulging at the seams, move your spare furniture and other items to free up space. Buyers will then be able to see the space available and plan how their own furniture and furnishing will fit into the area. A storage space can also be a safe place for your important documents and valuables so that they are out of sight on the days you have viewings at your property or when you are in the process of moving.

If you don't have a lot to store, and unlikely to need frequent access to your stored items, consider asking your family and friends if they will allow you to borrow some space in their spare room, loft, garage, shed or outbuildings. This will be a cheaper alternative for you.

> Only store those items that you can't bear to dispose of, otherwise your new property will be full of the same old possessions that you will need to sort through another day.

Repair and redecorate

During this stage, check that everything in the property is fit for purpose. Bring in trades if you are unable to complete the work yourself.

- Fix dripping taps.
- Check remote controls for garage doors to ensure they work smoothly.
- Check for cracked or broken glass and condition of putty on older single-pane windows.
- Repair cracks and holes in walls, ceilings and all woodwork.
- If possible, repaint ceilings and woodwork to freshen these up.
- Complete other repairs, e.g. broken or loose door knobs, handles and hinges.
- Put away belongings.
- Replace threadbare carpets.

- If the loft has a pull-down ladder, make sure it is sturdy and works well in case buyers wish to go into the loft to view the potential of the space.
- Ensure all rooms, internally and externally, have doors that can be unlocked and opened. Repair or replace any broken locks, handles and hinges.
- All areas should be accessible, including lofts, basements, sheds and outbuildings.

Consider what impression the existing decor is giving. Harmonising and neutralising colour schemes appeal to the majority of viewers. Use neutral colours to paint the interior walls. This will freshen up the property, making it appear lighter and bigger. You may also choose to apply wallpaper to create feature walls, providing interest and a focal point.

Use wall and floor mirrors to provide a sense of space and light, especially in smaller rooms. We fitted a long mirror to one of the hallway walls to reflect light into the area and provide a sense of space. Put up tasteful prints and artworks on a selection of walls but be careful not to over-personalise and add clutter.

Use soft furnishings to refashion the rooms appropriately. Accent pillows and cushions (e.g. in silk or velvet, or embellished with sequins, beads and crystals) are a quick way to update a sofa, bed or chair and provide interest, colour and a sumptuous feeling. It's a good idea to use a splash of colour to bring the design of a room together, and a bright coloured cushion or throw can work well to do this. Similarly, you can use these to tone down a room if the other colours are too vivid.

Accessories can have a significant impact on making a house feel like a home. It's worth investing in a few healthy plants, new towels and bed linen to give the impression of a loved and cared for home. Neat displays of pictures and ornaments will make the property look attractive, while injecting a little creativity will stop it from looking stark.

Make sure windows are dressed with curtains or blinds. Without any form of cover, windows can make a room feel impersonal and cool (unless it's used to frame a lovely garden or vista). Update curtains by removing heavy window dressings for simpler blinds, or curtains and poles. To maximise natural light during viewings, keep window dressings open unless it's to the detriment of the room and an eyesore. In this case, patterned bright white voiles or sheer panels can help to brighten a room. You can commission these and have custom-made curtains and blinds or buy ready-made ones online. At stores such as

Chapter 4. STAGING YOUR PROPERTY

John Lewis, you will find them to be affordable, on-trend and well-made. If you're on a tight budget, B&Q have a good range of seasonal furnishings and accessories.

Plants and flowers bring colour, life and light to a room and can also smell great. A large display of flowers in a room creates a luxurious feel, hinting at a deluxe lifestyle. Professional home stagers choose faux flowers 99% of the time as fresh flowers and plants can turn out to be expensive and require regular maintenance or replacing.

Make sure the entranceway to the property is bright and well-lit. Place a clean or new doormat in the doorway rather than having an old bedraggled one there that will cause dirt to be dragged through the property. We usually have one doormat outside and a long one on the inside of the door. Carpet specialists say that the first three steps from outside carry the most amount of dirt into a home.

Many prospective purchasers just want to buy a property and move in without having to update it or make changes. If you present your house in a way that shows you have cared for it, potential buyers will feel more comfortable about buying the property, knowing it is ready to move into and only awaiting their own personal touches. As a result, it is easier for them to imagine themselves living there.

> In one property, we used the basement as a gym room, where we had a treadmill, other gym equipment, storage cabinets and medium-sized plants in vibrantly coloured pots. We leaned a large decorative mirror against the longest wall to give the impression of a corporate gym and a larger space. We had the room painted in bright white (both the floor and the ceiling), and new lights and carpet fitted so that it looked fresh and inviting. We also laid small white pebbles all around the doorway into the gym and placed a brightly potted climbing rose and a peaceful Buddha statue there to create a welcoming entranceway. Our buyers were thrilled with the room and they bought our gym equipment as well, saying that they would let go of their gym memberships as they had such a great space to do their training.

Plumbing and heating

Ensure the boiler, radiators in all the rooms and the central heating system are all working properly. Check the water output and install a pump if there isn't insufficient pressure. Showers and taps need to be functioning well.

If buyers are going to be viewing your property during the colder months, fireplaces need to be cleaned up beforehand and fires, whether gas or electric, need to be operating well as buyers may want a demonstration. Likewise, if the fire is a log fire, have it lit in the cold months to create warmth and a welcoming feeling. In one of the lounges in a previous property, we created a focal point with a retro-look wall-mounted Smeg electric fireplace, and viewers commented that they found the ember flame effects and warmth welcoming.

> If you are selling in the winter, you will want you want your heating and hot water coming on at the correct time of the day for a warm and comfortable viewing.

Lighting and electrics

Make sure all non-functioning light bulbs are replaced and all lights are working, including ceiling, wall, kitchen under lighters and kitchen extractor lights and fans. If you have any electrical controllers, these should be working properly and correctly programmed. Ensure all electrical sockets are functioning, as a real estate agent or buyer may decide to turn on a freestanding appliance or lamp and you want to make certain these are working. Program security lighting to come on when you have viewings and check that it works.

> Check if there are any dark areas in the house that could benefit from additional lighting. If there is lighting in the loft, ensure this is working. If there is no lighting in the loft, look to install some basic lighting. A buyer is likely to want to view the loft space for storage or for the potential to convert it into living space.

Replace any fluorescent strip lights with LED spotlights where appropriate.

Flooring

Repair any annoying squeaks on the stairs or on any of the flooring. Replace or upgrade the flooring (tiles, laminate, vinyl, carpets or rugs) if it is looking outdated, tired, stained, damaged, ingrained with dirt or if it smells of animals or cigarette smoke. Wooden floors may benefit from sanding and painting or varnishing.

> If heavy furniture has been moved and the legs have left indentations in the carpet, try to return the carpet back to its original state. Dents in natural-fibre carpets (wool, sisal, and cotton) are best removed with steam from a steam iron and a hair dryer, or an iron on top of a damp tea towel. When dry, use your fingers, a brush or a spoon, to fluff up the fibres. Dents in synthetic carpets (nylon and polyester) can be removed by placing ice cubes on the dents and leaving them there for 6 hours. Use just enough ice on each indent to cover it as you do not want to risk damaging the floor underneath. Afterward, use a sponge to soak up the excess water and use your fingers, a brush or a spoon to fluff up the fibres.

Try these methods first on a dent that is in an inconspicuous area to test the carpet for colour fastness and ensure you won't damage it any further.

Clean, clean, clean

> Consider paying for a professional cleaning company to clean your property top to bottom, including steam cleaning carpets and cleaning all appliances, irrespective of whether they are included in the sale or not. They will have specialised equipment and materials, as well as trained people, to remove all manner of stains, stubborn grease, dirt and smells.

If you can't afford professional cleaners, clean the entire property. It needs to look and feel like a show home. You need to take steps to ensure that positive energy is flowing, throughout the house. This cleaning should include the loft, shed, basement and outbuildings. Even when the interior of a house looks reasonable, do not underestimate the importance of a thoroughly cleaned property. An immaculate home also portrays a well-maintained house, and this will encourage buyers to make an offer on the property.

A thorough cleanse includes cleaning under the worktops and the grout between tiles, steam-cleaning the carpets, dusting the crown moulding and ceiling fans, cleaning the windows (inside and out) and window sills, polishing all fixtures and shining all window and door fittings. Clean all appliances thoroughly, inside and outside. Clean cupboard interiors are just as important as clean switches, lights and light fittings, especially if you have crystal shades in the property – these should be ready to catch any light and sparkle brilliantly. Clean off any mildew from damp areas. Remove all dust, grime, grease and cobwebs. Remove any stains and limescale from the kitchen sink, hand basins, toilets, shower tray, shower screen and bath, as well as in any other visible places. Clean and replace tile grout with new.

Clean furniture covers and use cushions or throws to help brighten up sofas and help to hide marks or damage. Remove furniture that is embedded with cigarette smoke. If you do smoke, put small bowls of vinegar around the house and leave them out for three days prior to any viewings. The smell of vinegar and cigarette smell will dissipate once you open the windows. Make sure the fireplace has been cleaned, along with all the floors. Steam clean carpets and curtains.

Make sure that when all windows and ledges are cleaned inside and outside, check for any cracked or broken glass and condition of putty / glazing compound on older single-pane windows. Contact a glazing company to assess, repair and replace any damaged or missing putty and broken glass.

> Before we moved into a previous property, we had the interior and exterior of the windows, guttering, downpipes, fascias and soffits cleaned professionally because they looked like they hadn't been attended to for years, and we also had a sizeable renovation completed so they were covered with dust. The cleaners did a tremendous job, even using razor blades to remove the ingrained dirt, and everything looked brand new afterwards. When the time came for us to sell the property, we were asked by the buyer's surveyor to provide FENSA reports for all the windows because they thought we had replaced them!

One of the biggest turn-offs for prospective buyers is bad smells. Fix the source of any smells – clean the kitchen and all appliances thoroughly (inside and out), wash the bins in the kitchen and outside (e.g. green and brown bins), and clear any blocked sinks and drains. Remove cooking smells from the kitchen by removing grease and dirt from all surfaces and cleaning or replacing the cooker hood filters. If your waste disposal unit smells, even after you've cleaned it, put some lemon wedges into it and run cold water through it while you run it. This will leave a clean and fresh scent in your sink.

If you have pets, especially a dog, give it a good wash or send it to the dog groomers for a professional clean. Make sure the pet's bed is washed and aired

Chapter 4. STAGING YOUR PROPERTY

as well and place it in away from the entrance way into the property and main living areas. People generally love animals, but if a prospective purchaser has an allergic reaction, they are unlikely to return.

Keep windows and doors open to air the house so there are no lingering smells. This will ensure that your potential buyers will enter a clean property which will smell fresh as well as look like a show home.

> When I (Geoff) was growing up in New Zealand, an annual working bee at the family beach house started off the first few days of the summer school holidays. The house was painted where necessary and the garden was brought under control. The entire family was roped into this effort, with big bonfires in the afternoon to finish off each day, where everyone subsequently collapsed in a heap, smelling of woodsmoke and paint.
>
> The arrival of the long school's holidays during the Christmas break heralded the 'spring' cleaning in our (Sharena's) home in Fiji. It was one of life's rituals when I was growing up, with my Mother ensuring that this great job was completed before giving her permission for us to enjoy the holidays. The first weeks of the holidays were always donated to cleaning the house from top to bottom.
>
> My Mother (a school teacher) used the term called 'spring' cleaning, but it was the 'wet' season there instead of Spring (which is unheard of in Fiji, where the only other season is 'dry'). During 'spring' cleaning, everything we owned was taken out of its usual resting place, reassessed for usefulness, and an executive decision made by my Mother as to whether it would be retained or disposed of.
>
> This done in each room, the entire house and contents were cleaned from top to bottom. Ceilings, walls, doors, windows, ledges, floors and furniture were thoroughly swept and wiped down. Old clothes were donated, and replacements bought (if necessary). Curtains were brought down and hand-washed before being placed on the washing lines to dry in the scorching sun (the usual 30 degrees, even in the 'wet' season), after which they were ironed and put up again. Other possessions like linen and soft furnishings were put 'in the sun'. Coir mattresses, cushions, pillows and blankets were dragged out of the house and placed onto woven mats in the garden to be aired and refreshed in the sunlight.
>
> Putting our belongings outside didn't just end there. We were under numerous instructions, and were continuously reminded, to keep an eye on the weather in case of the forewarned tropical showers; to make sure we turned over

every single item several times throughout the day so that, rather than overcooking on one side, they were sun-burned on all sides; to keep the birds away from them. But above all, we had to make sure that no one stole these precious possessions because my Mother, bringing up four children on her own, would not have been able to afford the luxury of replacing these.

We completed de-cluttering and cleaning one room per day during our 'spring' cleaning season. And irrespective of whether we had 2 or 3 bedrooms in the home we were in at the time, our 'spring' cleaning season lasted at least the first week of the school holidays, if not more (oh joy, while my friends played and looked on…).

My Mother's life was an indelible crusade and she ran our home, along with our lives, like a military operation. My Mother's 'spring' cleaning has provided me with structure and good practice; this cleaning ritual is now firmly embedded in our own lives. We also enjoy the crisp and bright feeling in the house when we have completed our 'spring' cleaning.

While we follow a weekly, fortnightly and monthly routine of differing levels of cleaning in our home, regularly refreshing items like duvets and covers, mattress and pillow protectors, after the end of each season we have an overall household clean and take the opportunity to de-clutter. Items we have been using which are readily available, e.g. clothes, shoes and linen, are assessed and either cleaned and stored or donated.

The end of each season is also a great time to air out mattresses. Pillows, duvet inners and blankets can be given to your local drycleaner who can clean and return them to you, ready for the next time you need them. Our cleaning during end of season is organised over several consecutive days and we clean out and de-clutter one room per day, e.g. on kitchen day, we empty out all our cupboards and drawers of crockery and cutlery, wash any items that need cleaning, wipe down the surfaces, remove items we haven't used and are unlikely to use in the next 6 months, and keep what we love. From the pantry and fridge, we throw out any food that is past it's use-by-date and clean out all the units. The blinds are wiped down and the curtains cleaned. We continue with the kitchen until we are happy that the we have attended to everything.

While sometimes it may end up taking more than one day per room to complete all the decluttering and cleaning in our home, it's necessary for us to do this so that we happy with what we carry with us to our next property. It's also very satisfying to focus on our achievements, knowing that the results are due to our dedicated labour.

Chapter 4. STAGING YOUR PROPERTY

Give rooms a function

Always think about the type of person who will be purchasing your property and prepare it accordingly. A large family house may benefit from an area designated as a play zone, whereas a small bachelor pad may benefit from an office area.

Remove any excess furniture and rearrange the remaining furniture to maximise space and clearly define what each room's function is. You can also borrow or hire the relevant furniture for the space you are creating and return it after exchange of contracts.

> While it may not appear to be necessary for all types of properties (e.g. new home builds), we always furnish and dress every room in our properties. Up to 85% of people are unable to visualise how a room will look if it is not furnished. The space can also appear lifeless and cool if you don't dress it appropriately.

If you have a room that is just used for storage but is large enough to be classed as a single room, put a bed in it so it has a clear function.

Separate dining rooms have become less common now that open plan living is popular in the UK, but a home should still contain some form of dining space. Provide a clear dining area as it gives it the feeling of communal living, gathering and sharing.

Show how to use awkward zones, such as under the stairs, by transforming it into a small study area or tidy storage space.

Prepare individual rooms

There are different considerations to be taken into account for each room, which is why it's necessary to address each room separately. These are described below.

Hallways

> If your front door opens into a hallway, these areas need to be kept clear of all clutter and detritus. So, remove all coats, shoes, bags, umbrellas, dog leads and other belongings away from the doorway. Ensure the entranceway is bright and well-lit so that when the door is opened, your potential buyers see a clean and spacious passageway rather than standing huddled at the front door.

The interior and exterior areas surrounding the front door will need to be thoroughly cleaned. Place clean or new doormats inside and outside the front door. These will ensure that your home is as hygienic as possible, and dirt doesn't get dragged in. In view of the time and effort spent on cleaning your property, you will want to ensure your labours survive for as prolonged a period as possible. We ask people to remove their shoes when they enter our home and we advise our agent of this as well. Potential buyers don't mind removing their shoes when entering a house because they can see that the property, which they could be purchasing, is being kept clean and maintained at a high standard.

Any other hallways within the property, whether they are upstairs or downstairs, should also be cleared so that viewers don't feel like they are entering over-crowded zones. Cluttered floors in these areas may have items that potential buyers could trip over because they are generally looking up, not down. So, declutter, clean, repair and accessorise all these hallways as well. You can have rugs on the floor as well as decorative mirrors and wall art to make these spaces interesting.

Kitchen

The kitchen is the most valuable room in a house, is worth the most per square foot and can make the difference when buyers are unsure.

Before putting your property up for sale, take the opportunity to clear out the drawers, cupboards, pantries, fridge and freezer and make these more accessible as well as show the amount of space available. Clear the kitchen worktops of clutter and small appliances as this will allow you to show off the counter space. Remove your notes, reminders, shopping lists, children's timetables and fridge magnets.

If your kitchen is looking dated, paint the cupboard, draw fronts and end panels, or replace them. Replace your counter top if necessary because an expanse of this will be in view when your prospective purchasers visit. If you have a grubby kitchen tap which cannot be cleaned to a gleam, replace it with a new one. Paint over a dated tiled splashback or replace with new. Replace any passé lighting with new lights and fittings; LED lights can make a kitchen look modern and provide better visibility.

Apply new silicone around the kitchen sink, where old silicone is looking dirty and damaged. Repair or replace old or cracked tiles and re-grout tiled areas. Consider upgrading the plumbing fixtures and white goods, but keep in mind

Chapter 4. STAGING YOUR PROPERTY

that while that may make your property sell faster, you will be unlikely to recoup their full value.

If you are unable to make your existing floor look fresh and clean, it may be time to replace it. You can have some vinyl flooring fitted over screeded tiles – this will lift the room and make it easier to keep clean as well.

Clean all the blinds thoroughly. If you have curtains in the kitchen, ensure these don't look fussy and old fashioned (unless you are planning for an eclectic, period or cottagey scheme throughout the property). Clean and rehang the curtains or remove and replace them with blinds. If you have a pretty outlook from your kitchen window, don't crowd the window sills with paraphernalia.

Where practical, paint (with the appropriate appliance paint) or replace any appliances that are damaged or not working. Whether you are including these in the sale of your property or not, the brightness of new or almost-new appliances can revitalise a kitchen.

All these changes will completely transform the look of your kitchen.

Lounge and dining rooms

In traditional homes, the lounge (or living room) is typically the first room you will see when you enter. After that, it's usually the dining room. With the UK favouring more open-plan living, these rooms are no longer always left separated. In many cases, they have been opened up for multi-use, allowing for a more casual, social and spacious look and feel.

A lounge needs to be set up for relaxed conversation and have sufficient seating for the size of the household, plus some more. Group furniture together so that it is easy for people to have undisturbed exchanges. There can be more than one conversation area, especially in larger rooms that can afford this space. Put small tables next to the sofa chairs so that your visitors have somewhere to place their coffee or tea cups and saucers, along with any nibble dishes and drinks glasses.

Remove any superfluous or oversized pieces of furniture that will stop you from creating a balanced room and thereby causing a polarising effect. Media and storage should be appropriately sized for the room, like book cases, so as not to take over the rooms. Pack away any books and games that you are not expecting to use in the next three months. Having a low padded chest can be useful for sitting on as well as putting toys and other small items into if you want to clear a room in a hurry.

Soft furnishings like cushions, rugs and throws can add a warm and comfortable, or elegant and sophisticated look to the lounge and dining areas. Assess and confirm the type of effect you are trying to achieve and use the appropriate accessories.

> A dining room needs to have a large enough table for the household. If it's a one-bedroom property, then a small table seating 2 to 4 people is adequate. A four-bedroom property will need to have a table that seats six to eight people, so viewers can see that the entire household is able to come together to share meals.

There also need to be comfortable-looking chairs at the dining table. Remove any items that crowd the dining area so that you can lay the table and move around easily, rather than creating a space where your potential buyers will be squeezing in and out of.

You can group furniture around a fireplace and mantlepiece, or in front of the fire, to provide a cosy atmosphere. If you are putting your property up for sale in the colder months, this is especially important because people will want to enter the house and see where they can be comfortable. Think about seasonal décor and accessories depending on time of year. For the colder months faux fur throws look great in reception rooms and bedrooms, however the effect isn't the same during summer. Stage for the seasons.

Ensure that you have sufficient radiators or place heaters in discrete area of the rooms. We installed a long slimline red electric panel heater in one of our hallways. It not only looked attractive (balanced with the pieces of wall art) but it also produced sufficient heat for us. It could have been easily installed in the lounge or dining areas as well if there had been insufficient heat from the existing radiators.

If you have a working fire, get the chimney swept and ready to use so you are not smoked out if you are using it during a viewing. Remove any unnecessary items in front of the fireplace so it is clutter-free.

Check the lighting as this is especially important in the lounge and dining rooms. Lighting in these rooms should be set up to provide a peaceful atmosphere for everyone. These rooms should not be over-lit, or you may end up with a harsh and sterile environment. Similarly, they should not excessively low otherwise it will be too dark. You're looking for the right balance, especially if the property has been converted from two totally separate rooms to an open-plan space. Replace any old and shabby lamps with what suits your new décor, ensuring that they are placed in the right areas around the room.

Chapter 4. STAGING YOUR PROPERTY

Ensure that your existing furniture and furnishings are fit for purpose. If they are old and need repair, get this done. Otherwise, you may want to consider either hiring or investing in some modern items to provide a more contemporary look in these critical rooms. They don't need to be cutting edge pieces, but they do need to fit the room's décor.

Remove any old and tatty curtains or broken blinds. Window treatments should reflect the image of the room. You can have diaphanous, light panels that create a luxurious and delicate cover in a sophisticated room, or you can have silky sari-like fabrics creating an exotic environment. If you have a beautiful garden to look at, make sure you use your windows to frame this well.

Space is the ultimate luxury, and you can show this by decluttering the main living and dining areas. Invest in some appropriate storage pieces and put away all the remote controls, newspapers, books and magazines so that you can show that there is clear space for people to relax and enjoy conversations and meals.

Bedrooms

Clean out your wardrobes and find a home for clothes you do not want, whether you store it off-site in suitcases (which you can do for seasonal clothing), sell it on eBay or Gumtree, or give it away to charity. Where practical, only put half of the clothing back in wardrobes because this will create a sense of space, which is important to a potential buyer.

Replace dated or damaged dressing tables, cupboards and chests of drawers and bedside cabinets for a more upcycled and contemporary look. If bulky built-in storage is making a bedroom look small, or if it is dated, consider replacing it with free-standing furniture. You can always take this with you when you leave. We have previously used tall standalone pantry units for storing linen in and have sold these with the property.

> Bedrooms should feel light and airy. Ensure windows are not obstructed by furniture. If bedrooms are being used for another purpose, these should be returned to their original functions so that buyers are clear how many bedrooms the property has.

Place double beds in bedrooms that can accommodate a double bed to show that the room is large enough to be called a double bedroom. Similarly, place single beds in rooms large enough to be presented as such, rather than being left as a storage area.

Where possible, show that beds can be accessed from both sides. Complete the setup of each bedroom with accompanying bedside cabinets, lamps, artwork and accessories.

Ensure you have appropriate lighting in the bedroom. You will need:

- Strong lighting so you can see the outfits and colours in your wardrobe and be able dress easily. Centred ceiling lights and internal wardrobe lights are useful for this.
- Adequate lighting and mirrors for daily rituals and to apply creams and cosmetics. A natural light source is considered best for this purpose. Failing that, illuminated cosmetic mirrors are a good standby. According to our Interior Design and Decorating Diploma courses, every Paris style bedroom has a decadent vanity table!
- Good lighting to read clearly by, which can be provided by appropriate bedside lamps.
- Soft or dimmed lights to aid relaxation.

We use dimmer switches throughout our property, so we can control the amount of light required in each room, as well as cater for the mood being set at any particular time.

Mirrors need to be easily accessible and well-lit. If you have sufficient space, using tall decorative leaning mirrors can greatly increase the size, lighting and opulence in a bedroom. Feng Shui and Vastu Vidya laws specify that you should not have large mirrors in the bedroom, and mirrors should not be placed facing beds, so if you are a follower of these teachings, set up your bedrooms accordingly.

Children's rooms should be kept clean and tidy and redecorated in muted colours if they have loud colour schemes on walls and ceilings. Take down wall posters to keep the walls clutter free. In a smaller bedroom that could have been used for a baby or a child, we have placed animal-printed blinds on the windows and soft toys on a single fold-up bed so that the room could be displayed as a single room. So, you can still have a room displayed as a children's room but looking more organised.

> When storing seasonal clothing, bedding, curtains and cushions, use vacuum storage bags. The air is sucked out of these bags using a vacuum cleaner. The bags create a lot more storage space in your home and are fully reusable. They also protect packed items against mites, moisture and dust.

Beds dressed with fresh, neutral and ironed linens, silks or velvet, with suitable scatter cushions, look more inviting than an unmade bed.

Ensuite, family bathroom and cloakroom

> Swap personal hygiene items in ensuites, family bathrooms, wet rooms and cloakrooms with plants or pottery. If you don't have sufficient storage, buy a small drawer set for all your personal items. Stores like John Lewis and B&Q have a wide selection.

Replace damaged or dated bathroom suites with new inexpensive units. Alternatively, replace toilet seats, dated taps and shower heads with new. Replace old shower curtains with new or install a shower screen (which is more expensive). Check the worktops and door handles and make sure you can keep them gleaming, otherwise replace them.

Repair or replace old and / or cracked tiles and re-grout tiled areas where old grout is stained or has broken up. Apply new silicone around the hand basins, toilet, shower tray and the bath where old silicone is grimy and spoilt. Paint over dated tiles with the appropriate tile paint for a fresh look. Install new flooring if necessary; even if you have tiled floors currently, these can be covered up with smart vinyl flooring once the floor is screeded. Keep all the colours in mind and ensure they are cohesive.

Have adequate lighting in these areas. Fitting an illuminated mirror for the daily ritual can show that you have paid attention to details and catered for the entire household.

Open up windows to air the rooms. Make sure the extractor fan fit is in working condition and has a quiet operation. If it is noisy or not working, replace it with a new silent model. Make sure you wipe away all condensation after using these rooms, especially around windows, mirrors and glassed areas (like shower cubicles) so that they are clear when viewings take place.

Home office or study

The home office or study area needs to show it is a defined space with a specific purpose in mind. Most people use the smallest room in a property for a study, so the space needs to be used accordingly.

Declutter the area or room, removing any oversized and extra pieces of furniture, fittings and accessories. Make sure your bookcases are not overflowing with books, photos and collectables. Leave space on the shelves so that this shows there is room for storage.

Clean all the other furniture and the desk, neatly storing computers, books, files and paperwork. Put pens, rulers and stationery out of sight. Put away printers or bulky items in an office cupboard so they don't crowd this space during the viewings. If your desk has a wire management system, make sure you are using it to hide your wires. Otherwise make sure all wires are hidden away where practicable. It's time for that 'clear desk policy'!

Repair any areas damaged or replace as necessary, e.g. if the flooring is damaged beyond repair, look at either covering this area with a large rug or installing new flooring. If you are replacing flooring in a study, carpet is the best option, especially if you have office chairs with wheels. If you had hard flooring, such as wood, tile, concrete, laminate or vinyl use a carpet square or rug to prevent your office chair sliding around.

Clean the room, starting with the ceiling from floor to ceiling, including windows, electrical sockets, lights, light fittings and switches.

> Refurnish the room with office-appropriate items. Include storage cabinets and spare seating if possible as these will indicate that you have paid attention to detail. Home office seating should look appropriate, so use an office chair rather than a dining room chair. If possible, add a pedestal and shelving unit to formalise the space.

Repair and redecorate the area or room according to your cohesive colour scheme. We like to hang fun wallpapers and artworks, along with our certifications and graduation photos, so that the room looks attractive and bright. We love to read so we also have tall bookshelves fitted in our studies, so this creates a 'library' effect.

Lighting is very important in the study, so ensure that you have sufficient natural and artificial lights set up to show that potential buyers can work at any time of the day or night. Replace any fluorescent ceiling lights with modern (preferably LED) ceiling lights. Put table lamps on the desk to shoe that daily work routines are supported.

All this will create an office environment and aptly name the area you have set up. You can have the area photographed and described in your sales and marketing brochure as a home office or a study. This set up is preferable to displaying a study area showing only a small desk and an even smaller chair.

Utility room

Utility or laundry rooms need to be cleared out, cleaning products and other items sorted and stored out of sight. Storage in a utility or laundry room is very important as you don't want to be faced with containers of washing powders and cleaners every time you enter this room. Coupled with this is the smell of all the cleaners, which can become collectively overpowering.

If you keep other items like pet food in the utility room, you will want to have separate cupboards where you can store these away from cleaning products.

> If you have tired or insufficient storage, look to replace these. Places like Howdens, Wickes and Ikea have good storage solutions and differing sizes. We had a boiler boxed in using a kitchen cupboard carcass and door because it looked tidier than leaving it exposed.

Replace the cupboard and drawer knobs and fit a new worktop if necessary.

Any damaged tiles should be replaced and tiled areas re-grouted. Freshen up old tiles by painting, keeping the colours cohesive with the rest of the room and property.

Apply fresh silicone around areas that need this, especially around basin area. Replace the flooring if it's tired, damaged, or you can't keep it looking clean despite trying.

Air the room out by opening the windows in the utility room. If there are no windows, make sure that the extractor fan does a good job of ventilating the room, and is a quiet model. You may be getting a lot of condensation if you don't have a vented tumble dryer. This is particularly important in winter, when condensation can be an issue throughout the property. If there is problem with condensation in the utility room, you may wish to consider buying a new, refurbished or reconditioned condenser dryer. If it is free-standing, you can take it away with you when you move.

Exterior and curb appeal

> Staging and real estate professionals state that the outside of the home makes the first impression and can affect the price of your property. If the landscaping and presentation is presented to a high standard, a property can sell for 4-5 percent higher, while properties which have a poorly presented frontage and landscaping can sell for 8-10 percent less.

The best advice is to cross the street and consider what you see. Can you see the house for all the foliage? If you live in an area where there is an inclination to have very high hedges and trees (e.g. on a private estate), then have these tidied up. If they have overgrown and look untidy, trim or cut back trees and plants, weed flower beds and rake up the leaves and debris. Replace dead plants and shrubs with colourful flowers and vegetation in the front and rear gardens.

Mow and water the lawn to keep it in a good condition. If you have dead patches of grass from a dry summer, burns from pet urine or other damage, consider using a natural and non-toxic green grass repair colourant. This is applied from a spray bottle and will instantly turn any brown grass or spots green again. Select a spray that is biodegradable, non-toxic, non-hazardous, as well as safe for children and pets.

If the lawn is too damaged, look at re-turfing it. Laying a new lawn is more expensive but it will give an instant lift. Laying artificial grass is also a good option if you want a low maintenance lawn. It provides a real grass look but offers greater wear and weather resistance. It is ideal for urban and small gardens; there's no need to water it in dry weather and the artificial turf is porous so will drain off.

Make any required repairs to the roof and guttering. Clean out the gutters and clear out debris and leaves from the downpipe and drain covers.

Clear the driveway of any old vehicles, bikes, caravan, machinery, boats and clutter. Sweep or jet wash pathways and the driveway and remove any oil stains. Repair any cracks in the driveway, and pathways and boundary walls.

Tidy and de-clutter sheds, greenhouses and outbuildings and apply a fresh coat of paint. Store away any toys, bikes or equipment in the garden. Remove any pet toys, accessories and pet droppings, as well as any sign of pets inside the house. Put away the dog chews and cat litter. Ask friends or family if you can leave your pet with them during viewings.

Repair and re-stain any decking. Sweep or jet wash patio and deck surfaces. Stage the rear patio with new outdoor furniture if the old is tired or damaged and display colourful pots with flowering plants or fresh greenery.

Repaint the exterior of the property and jet wash the render / brickwork where moss or dirt is detracting from its appearance. Repaint the garage door and any exterior woodwork if it is looking tired. Replace damaged fence panels and trellis. Paint or re-stain the panels to provide a more uniform and contemporary look. Ensure gates are repaired, painted and oiled so they are working properly.

Clean or repaint the front door, replace the door furniture and fit a clear house name or street number. Make sure the front door bell is in working order.

Hide all bins out of sight or put up some trellis to screen these off.

> Add to the appeal of the property. In a property we sold, we fixed a canopy over the front and back doors which provided modern porch-like structures so that there were large covered areas people could stand under if it was raining. We placed large pots with plants by the front door to make the entranceway more attractive. We also used white pebbles around the sides of the property to make these spaces more striking. We replaced the exterior doormats to newer welcome mats.

Take professional photographs

When you are selling your property, an estate agent will produce a brochure for your property, or at the least will take photos of it for their website and other property sites.

> Try to be at the property when the photographer is taking pictures. Photographers won't always go to the trouble of making final styling adjustments before taking their photos. Being there yourself to make those adjustments means that when the photos are produced, cushions will look plumped; and it will be the table lamp that will get the attention, rather than the wires.

Confirm that you are happy with the photos they have taken and the quality of these. Sometimes, it's only when you see photos that you realise where you need to make changes, especially if they are not cohesive and rooms have a polarised effect. We have seen a range of photos of properties over the years, most of which have been good, but also some really poor ones that have undersold the property for which they were designed to promote and sell. Keep in mind that more than 90% of buyers search online first.

Some home owners are investing in aerial photos and videos of their homes to gain an advantage when selling their homes. These images can be taken by drones for residential estate agents on behalf of the home owner. They can stand out from the crowd on websites like Zoopla, Rightmove and Prime Location. Drone imagery captures the scale of the property, the land, gardens and surrounding area that is not possible with ground-based photography.

If you are marketing your property yourself, ensure you take professional standard photos, or hire a professional photographer to take photos for you. It is really important to make a good impression not only in person, but also online. Double check if your staging work is cohesive and that it connects with your target market and potential buyers.

A note of caution about photographic copyright:

> When you commission a professional to take photos on your behalf, e.g. photographing your home or for any other purpose, the copyright of the images will usually remain with the photographer, or in other instances, the company engaging the photographer. You will need to obtain the photographer's or the company's permission before printing further copies of the images, sharing them with friends or family, or undertaking other acts restricted by copyright, such as posting the images to social media sites, putting them on your own website or using them commercially.

If you do use the images without the photographer's permission, they can sue you for copyright infringement. When you engage with them, ask them to assign the copyright rights to you, or to provide you with written permission to use the photos. If they refuse, don't use them – you will find someone who will agree. You can obtain a contract online, e.g. Find Legal Forms has an easy to follow one-page contract for Assignment of All Rights to Photograph.

Chapter 4. STAGING YOUR PROPERTY   205

Below are examples of professional staging photographs taken at our property:

For more of our staging photos, please visit our website on www.gsansellproperty.com.

Viewing day

> This is meant to be a big day because your potential buyers are walking through the door.

Tidy up the whole house. Put fresh bedding on the beds. Ensure the laundry basket has a lid on it and any clothes lying around in the laundry room or in any of the bedrooms have been put away. Place clean, fluffy towels in the bathrooms and close all toilet seat lids.

In the kitchen, make sure the dishes are washed and put away, with tea towels and hand towels out of sight. Place a bowl of fresh fruit on the kitchen worktop.

Clean and clear away the surfaces, sinks and taps in the kitchen, ensuite, family bathroom and cloakroom and utility. Also clean the floors in all the rooms as required and wipe away all condensation.

Chapter 4. STAGING YOUR PROPERTY

Clear away shoes, coats, bicycles, toys and any clutter from the entrance or hallway. Pets should be either temporarily relocated or moved away from the entranceway to a secure area. Pet food and bowls need to be stored away.

Make sure your framed artworks, pictures and wall mirrors are hanging straight. Having a small spirit level handy is great for this.

Check the home office and ensure you have removed any sensitive and confidential documents from view. Ensure computers are locked away, or at the very least, computer screens are locked.

Turn off the television and any audio systems.

Switch on the lights in all the rooms so that the whole property looks bright and welcoming. Make sure all doors leading off the hallway are open to create a sense of space.

Leave all the doors open, inside and outside your home, so that all areas can be accessed easily, including lofts, basements, sheds and outbuildings. Leave the loft hatch pole in clear sight and the loft ladder down or leave a ladder close by to access the loft.

If it's cold during the viewing, make sure the central heating and fire are turned on (or lit) as this will make your home feel warm and inviting. Open the curtains and blinds to let in natural light and reveal the view. If weather permits, open windows and let in fresh air. Keep the property free of cooking, pet and cigarette smells.

Some buyers are looking for a lifestyle as much as a home. Setting the dining table with placemats, crockery and cutlery sets, attractive napkins and glassware helps people to imagine living there. Put a vase of fresh flowers on the dining table.

> Leave the agent and the potential buyers to view to your property. Go for coffee or lunch and have a well-deserved break away from your property, resting assured that you have done an excellent job with staging your home for sale.
>
> Good luck with securing your buyer quickly and easily!

Checklist – Staging your property

The following Checklist will help you to plan and track your progress through this process.

Key activities and planning

- ☐ Decide on key activities to undertake and where to apply your money, time and effort.
- ☐ Define the type of buyer you are targeting and prepare a cohesive styling plan.
- ☐ Review houses for sale in the neighbourhood to see how you can stand out.
- ☐ Walk through each room, taking notes and photos of areas that need attention.
- ☐ Decide on your budget for staging.
- ☐ Obtain planning permission and quotes from the specific trades for any work required.

Professional versus DIY home staging

- ☐ Educate yourself on home staging or budget for a home staging professional.
- ☐ Obtain input from local agents on improvement and presentation requirements.

De-clutter

- ☐ De-clutter your home inside and out well before your move.
- ☐ Remove bulky items and rearrange furniture for ease of access, flow and balance.
- ☐ Remove all excess items, collectables and books and put surplus items into storage.
- ☐ Sell, give away or donate other items to family, friends and charities.
- ☐ Organise offsite storage space and hire a skip to throw away remaining items.

Repair and redecorate

- ☐ Undertake any repairs required inside and outside.
- ☐ Repair any doors, locks, handles and hinges and clear all doorways, inside and out.
- ☐ Re-grout all tiled areas and apply new silicone to kitchen, bathroom and utility.
- ☐ Ensure all areas can be accessed, including lofts, basements, sheds and outbuildings.
- ☐ If the loft has a pull-down ladder, make sure it is sturdy and works well.
- ☐ Have any damaged or cracked windows repaired and missing putty replaced.
- ☐ Repair and repaint all woodwork, windows and doors as needed.
- ☐ Paint walls and ceilings in all rooms using harmonising neutral colour schemes.
- ☐ Wallpaper feature walls as focal points for colour and interest.
- ☐ Put up wall and floor mirrors, prints and artworks on walls.
- ☐ Use soft furnishings, accessories, plants and flowers to brighten rooms.

Plumbing and heating

☐ Ensure the boiler, radiators and central heating system are all working.
☐ Make sure the water pressure is reasonable, with all showers and taps functioning.
☐ Ensure that the lounge and dining room fires are operating.
☐ Have the heating set to be on for viewings if selling your home in the winter.

Lighting and electrics

☐ Make certain that lights and switches are working properly.
☐ Ensure electrical controllers are functioning and correctly programmed.
☐ Confirm all lamps, electrical sockets and appliances are functioning.
☐ Program security or external lighting to function after dark, especially during viewings.
☐ Add extra lighting if there are dark spots in any of the rooms.
☐ Ensure there is lighting in the loft for the potential buyers to view the loft space easily.
☐ Replace any fluorescent strip lights with LED spotlights.

Flooring

☐ Repair or replace dated or damaged flooring in all rooms.
☐ Clean, sand, paint or varnish wooden floors.
☐ Restore indentations in carpets and floors.

Clean, clean, clean

☐ Engage a professional cleaning company if possible.
☐ Thoroughly clean the interior and exterior of your property from top to bottom.
☐ Clean curtains, blinds and soft furnishings in all rooms or replace them with new.
☐ Fix the source of any smells inside or outside your home.
☐ Screen away bins from the main entranceway to the property.
☐ Send pets to professional groomers where appropriate.
☐ Wash and air pet belongings, placing away from the main entrance and living areas.
☐ Open windows to air the house so there are no lingering smells.

Give rooms a function

☐ Create room functions according to your target market, removing excess furniture.
☐ Arrange rooms with relevant furniture, furnishings and accessories.
☐ Show potential buyers how to use awkward spaces.

Prepare individual rooms

Hallways

- ☐ Make certain the entranceway is bright and well-lit.
- ☐ Ensure you have clear access to the interior and exterior of the front entrance.
- ☐ Place clean or new doormats inside and outside the front door.

Kitchen

- ☐ Paint or replace cupboard / drawer fronts, cracked and dated tiles and splashbacks.
- ☐ Ensure all drawers and cupboards open and close properly.
- ☐ Replace cupboard and drawer handles and knobs with new contemporary fittings.
- ☐ Replace the worktop and kitchen tap.
- ☐ Replace any appliances that are damaged, not working or outdated.
- ☐ Re-grout tiled areas and apply new silicone.

Lounge and dining rooms

- ☐ Replace any outdated furniture and fittings and repair any damaged items.
- ☐ Furnish each area appropriately, ensuring there is good flow, accessibility and balance.
- ☐ Group seating for comfort and easy conversation in the lounge.
- ☐ Ensure you have adequate seating and eating spaces for the size of property.
- ☐ Use soft furnishings and accessories to create the relevant look for your target buyer.
- ☐ Have your chimney cleaned and ensure sufficient heating, especially during viewings.
- ☐ Ensure that window dressing reflects the image you expect.

Bedrooms

- ☐ Clear up wardrobes, bedding and other items, storing or donating possessions.
- ☐ Remove excess items from walls and floors, including children's art, posters and toys.
- ☐ Remove bulky storage systems and replace with suitable (free standing) furniture.
- ☐ Replace dated furniture or repair and paint damaged items.
- ☐ Show bedrooms as light and airy, ensuring windows are not obstructed by furniture.
- ☐ Return bedrooms used for another purpose to their original functions.
- ☐ Use correct sized beds to display room size, confirming number of bedrooms.
- ☐ Complete setting up each bedroom with bedside cabinets, lamps, art and mirrors.
- ☐ Accessorise with scatter cushions, rugs and throws for target age group.
- ☐ Make beds with fresh, neutral and ironed bed linen.

Chapter 4. STAGING YOUR PROPERTY

Ensuite, family bathroom and cloakroom
- ☐ Create sufficient storage in all these rooms for items such as toiletries and towels.
- ☐ Put away personal items, replacing with suitable accessories.
- ☐ Replace damaged or dated suites, worktops and handles as required. Fit wall mirrors.
- ☐ Replace old shower curtains with new or install a shower screen.
- ☐ Open up windows to air the rooms and ensure the extractor fans are working.
- ☐ Wipe away all condensation after using these rooms, and especially before viewings.

Home office or study
- ☐ Declutter the area or room, removing inappropriate furniture, fittings and accessories.
- ☐ Clean and tidy the room, refurnishing according to home office requirements.
- ☐ Store away printers or bulky items in an office cupboard.
- ☐ Make sure all wires are hidden and the desk is free of clutter.
- ☐ Refurnish the room according to size of space and office requirements.
- ☐ Ensure you have sufficient natural and ceiling lights as well as desk lamps.

Utility room
- ☐ Declutter the utility or laundry rooms and cleared out old and damaged items.
- ☐ Repair, replace or create storage areas which can be closed away.
- ☐ Sort through all the items and products, disposing damaged articles.
- ☐ Replace outdated or non-functioning appliances.
- ☐ Store all items in cleaned, closed storage spaces.
- ☐ Air the room out, opening windows or using the extractor fan.
- ☐ Remove all condensation before viewings.

Exterior and curb appeal
- ☐ Cut back and tidy hedges, trees, gardens and lawns, replacing as necessary.
- ☐ Clear, clean and repair or replace gutters, downpipes and drain covers.
- ☐ Clean and repair cracks in driveway, pathways and boundary walls.
- ☐ Paint, re-stain or replace damaged fence panels and trellis.
- ☐ Store away toys and equipment lying in the garden.
- ☐ Ensure any gates are repaired, painted and oiled to work properly.
- ☐ De-clutter, tidy and clean sheds, green houses and outbuildings; repaint if necessary.
- ☐ Sweep or jet wash any patio and deck surfaces and re-stain any wooden decking.
- ☐ Clean, repair and repaint the garage door and exterior woodwork for all outbuildings.
- ☐ Jet wash and repaint the exterior of the property.

- ☐ Clean, repair and repaint or replace the front door and / or door furniture.
- ☐ Affix a clear house name or street number and ensure the front door bell works.
- ☐ Remove any rubbish from the property; clean up and clear away any pet droppings.
- ☐ Hide all bins out of sight.
- ☐ Stage the rear patio with new outdoor furniture, colourful pots and flowering plants.
- ☐ Place pots with new shrubs or flowering plants on either side of the front door.
- ☐ Place clean or new welcoming doormats outside the front door.
- ☐ Add to the appeal of the house; introduce small items e.g. pebbled areas in the garden.

Take professional photographs

- ☐ If possible, be at the property with the photographer to make final styling adjustments.
- ☐ Check the property photos and descriptions to ensure that your staging is cohesive.
- ☐ Obtain the correct rights from the photographer so you can use the images.

Viewing day

- ☐ Ensure pets have been removed and their possessions stored out of sight.
- ☐ Open the windows, curtains and blinds to let in natural light and reveal the view.
- ☐ Keep the property free of cooking, pet and cigarette smells.
- ☐ Wipe off condensation from the windows.
- ☐ Tidy up the house, clear and clean all surfaces, basins, sinks and taps.
- ☐ Make sure the dishes are washed and put away, as are tea towels.
- ☐ Remove any remaining clutter on kitchen worktops; place a bowl of fresh fruit there.
- ☐ Check the dinner table is set correctly with a vase of fresh or faux flowers.
- ☐ Put clean linen on the beds and fresh towels in the bathroom.
- ☐ Close the laundry basket and all the toilet seat lids.
- ☐ Lock away the computer and any sensitive and confidential documents.
- ☐ Check that all wall mirrors and artworks are hanging straight.
- ☐ Turn off the television and audio systems.
- ☐ Leave all the doors inside and outside your home open for easy access.
- ☐ Leave the loft hatch pole in clear sight and the loft ladder down, or a ladder close by.
- ☐ Make sure all doors leading off the hallway are open to create a sense of space.
- ☐ Switch on the heating and fire if viewings are held in the colder months.
- ☐ Ensure the hallway is clear and the light is on before you leave the property.

Chapter 5

SELLING YOUR PROPERTY

Overview

As a seller, there are a number of things you need to be aware of which are likely to affect your sale price, and even when you decide to put your property on the market.

We have found planning to be a crucial part of our sales process. Understand your finances and decide if you can afford to sell and move. Prepare your property for sale for your target market or engage a home staging professional to help you present your home to optimise return. Engage local professionals and stay in touch with all parties. Complete all the activities expected of you to enable the sales process to complete successfully.

Plan the sale of your property

Be proactive and responsive throughout this process and move speedily so that the buyer is not tempted by other offers. Plan well so that you can quickly share the documentation and information you have already collated, e.g. details of your solicitor, planning and building consents. Ask the agent to keep the buyer updated of your progress whilst keeping you informed of the buyer's advancement towards exchange and completion of contracts. If you have direct access to the buyer, keep them updated and follow up on anything that they address that appears to be an issue (happening now) or a risk (may or may not happen in the future).

You don't pay Capital Gains Tax when you sell your home if all of the following apply:

- You own one home and you have lived in it as your main home for the entire time that you have owned it.
- You have not let out any part of your home (excludes having a single lodger).
- You have not used any part of it for business only.
- All the buildings and the ground included are less than 5,000 square metres (just over an acre) in total.
- You did not buy your home just to make a gain.

So, if these apply to the sale of your property, you don't need to do anything; you'll automatically get a tax relief called Private Residence Relief. Discuss this with your solicitor if you have any queries as to whether this applies to you or not.

Chapter 5. SELLING YOUR PROPERTY

The selling timeline and process

The end-to-end selling process timeline can take a considerable amount of time or be relatively fast. The duration of each stage within the selling process will depend on how long it takes you to obtain an offer, and then accept the offer (with any conditions attached). It will also depend on how responsive all parties are, including you as the seller as well as the buyer, solicitor, agent, surveyor and mortgage provider.

The time to get to first offer stage can be influenced by the geographic location, e.g. properties in the Northeast of England may take longer to reach offer stage than those in London and surrounding areas (Greater London).

The diagram below illustrates the approx. timing for the stages within the selling process:

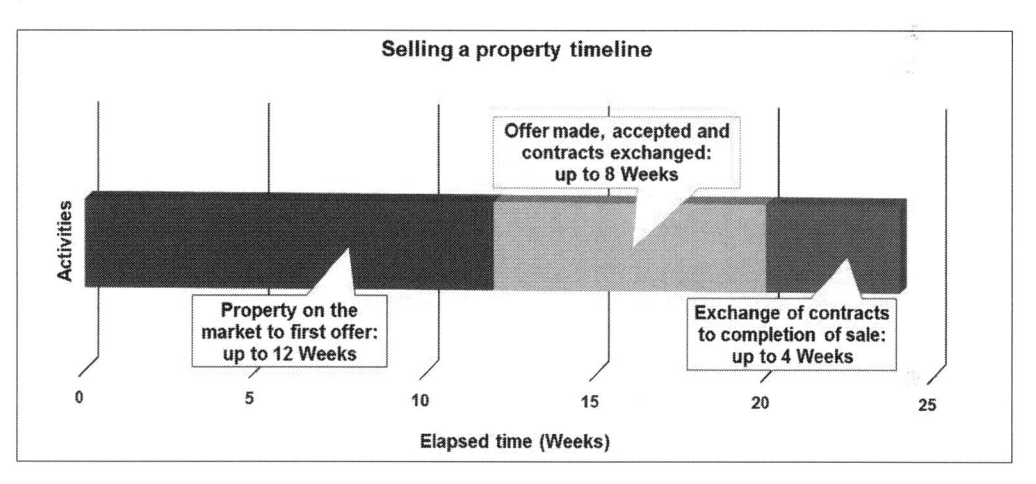

Selling a property timeline

Activities:
- Property on the market to first offer: up to 12 Weeks
- Offer made, accepted and contracts exchanged: up to 8 Weeks
- Exchange of contracts to completion of sale: up to 4 Weeks

Elapsed time (Weeks): 0, 5, 10, 15, 20, 25

From placing your property on the market through to completion, it can take up to 4 months, with each phase taking the time approximated below:

Up to 12 weeks from when your property is initially marketed to receiving your first offer.

Up to 8 weeks for offer acceptance to exchange of Contracts.

Up to 4 weeks for completion of Contracts.

Being aware of how long these processes can take helps you to plan ahead and schedule activities accordingly.

The illustration below provides a summary of the processes for selling a property:

1. DECIDE IF THIS IS THE RIGHT TIME TO SELL
Assess whether moving is right for you at this time, if you can afford to or whether you can develop your current property to better suit your needs.

2. PLAN FOR YOUR SALE
Familiarise yourself with the current property market, obtain market valuations for your property from local estate agents and calculate your finances.

3. DECIDE HOW YOU WILL MARKET YOUR PROPERTY AND FOR HOW MUCH
Decide whether to sell your home yourself, sell via a local estate agent or sell it using an online estate agent. Agree the selling price and the selling fee.

4. PREPARE YOUR HOME TO SELL
Undertake required repairs, freshen it up with a coat of paint, de-clutter and remove all rubbish from the property.

5. ENGAGE A SOLICITOR OR CONVEYANCER
Agree a fee for their legal work to transfer ownership of the property to you.

6. MAKE AVAILABLE IMPORTANT DOCUMENTS
For your Solicitor & prospective buyers, provide copies of Planning & Building Regs Consents, Completion Certificates, FENSA reports, NHBC warranty, etc.

7. VIEWINGS
Confirm who will be conducting the viewings, you or an agent. Make sure the property is well presented and those conducting the viewings are well prepared.

8. OFFER TO PURCHASE YOUR PROPERTY
You are reviewing written offers. You are clear about what sort of buyer's position you will consider. You accept an offer and instruct your Solicitor.

9. OBTAIN QUOTES FROM REMOVAL COMPANIES
Agree a quote and date for the move.

10. EXCHANGE OF CONTRACTS
Contracts are exchanged making the purchase legally binding between the parties.

11. COMPLETION OF CONTRACTS
Legal ownership of the property is transferred, and the parties physically move.

12. POST COMPLETION ACTIVITIES
Your solicitor provides you with an account, the redemption of the mortgage and confirmation that change of ownership is registered with the Land Registry.

Chapter 5. SELLING YOUR PROPERTY

Finalise your decision to sell

> As much as possible, be sure that selling your property is the right thing for you to do. Though you can change your mind part-way through the sales process, a lot of people's lives, and finances will be impacted negatively when you do; cast a thought for them, be authentic in your decisions and careful about your actions.

If you are considering selling because you need more space to better suit your needs, you may instead wish to contemplate building an extension, converting the attic, or digging out the basement to provide the additional space. The cost of buying (particularly the stamp duty charges) and the expense of moving is considerable, so you are more likely to save money by expanding your existing home.

Fast changing house prices may affect your sale price. If property prices are rising rapidly, you may not be able to afford a place much bigger than the one you currently own.

> External influences can have a huge impact, such as the Bank of England base rate changes. Putting your house on the market when interest rates fall means there are more buyers to appeal to; people feel they have more to spend when rates fall. Nervousness with the outcome of the Brexit vote, amongst other things, has caused asking prices to fall in the London market due to fewer overseas buyers. This has caused an excess of high-priced homes, and prices are now adjusting to attract the good buyers still in the market.

On a positive note, infrastructure changes, e.g. the HS2 route and the Great Western mainline electrification, can influence your sale positively if your property is on the planned pathway or located in areas close to these routes and resulting in improved rail links.

You can obtain free valuations from real estate agents and find out if you can afford to sell. Their reports will also advise you if you have positive or negative equity. You can then make a decision about your next steps in an informed manner, knowing what you can expect from the sale of your property, and therefore what you need to spend to buy your next property. Doing a detailed budget by taking into account all your income and expenses will further confirm your affordability and you can decide how much your risk appetite allows you to outlay on a monthly mortgage repayment.

Conveyancing

The definition of conveyancing is the process of legally transferring home ownership from the seller to the buyer. It starts when an offer is made and usually finishes when you hand over the keys to the buyer (although if the property is not left in a satisfactory manner for the buyer, this process can go beyond the date of completion). Conveyancing must be done legally through a solicitor or licensed conveyancer and they will only start the conveyancing work once you have accepted an offer on your property and formally instructed them. It is advisable to have them ready for when you accept your offer. Most agents will have a preferred partner that they work with and can recommend, and they may even be able to offer you discounted rates.

Most firms of solicitors offer a conveyancing service. All solicitors can legally undertake conveyancing, but it is advisable to choose a solicitor who is experienced in conveyancing. If you use a licensed conveyancer, although they are not solicitors, they are licensed by the Council of Licensed Conveyancers.

Do your research and investigate local solicitors and licenced conveyancers and their associated costs. Once you have chosen a professional, instruct them to act for you once you have an offer agreed. Ensure you have been informed of all the costs and fees involved in the conveyancing work, including whether they can offer a Fixed Fee or a No Sale No Fee conveyancing.

If you are selling your property and buying another, use the same solicitor or conveyancer for both where possible as it works out cheaper.

Before deciding who will do your conveyancing, find out the expected cost. Contact more than one solicitor or licensed conveyancer for this, as there is no set scale of fees for conveyancing. Check the following:

- Whether the figure they have quoted is a Fixed Fee or will if more work is required.
- Whether they can offer 'No Sale No Fee' conveyancing.
- If the costs include expenses and VAT and get a breakdown of these charges.
- What charges will be applied if the sale falls through before Contracts are exchanged.

Chapter 5. SELLING YOUR PROPERTY

Ensure your paperwork is in order

You will be asked to provide various items of paperwork when selling your home. You may not have or need all of them but get them ready in advance and there won't be a big panic or delay when they're needed. It will also help things move along more quickly once you've accepted an offer. Also, make available other key documents that might be of interest to prospective buyers to give them early confidence that work done to the property is legal and has been formally approved by qualified trades or Council.

Key documents for the sale of your property include:

- Property details and dimensions.

- Evidence of recent utilities bills, buildings and contents insurance.

- An Energy Performance Certificate (EPC) which provides information on the energy efficiency of a property using A to G ratings. The EPC is produced by an accredited domestic energy assessor and it is a legal requirement that falls under the Energy Performance of Buildings Regulations 2012 which ensures that a valid and up-to-date EPC is available when a property is put on the market for sale, or to let. An existing EPC report which has been carried out within the last 10 years will suffice as long as no material works that may affect the EPC rating have been carried out. If the EPC has changed due to works completed, then a new EPC is required. You must provide an EPC free of charge to potential buyers and within the first 7 days of the property being put on the market.

- Any Planning and Building Regulation Consents, along with the relevant Completion Certificates, for alterations, extensions or work completed on the property.

- An electrical certificate for any electrical work done as part of the UK national standard, BS 7671 (Building Standards Requirements for Electrical Installations). There should be an Electrical Installation Certificate or, where applicable, a Minor Electrical Installation Works Certificate, that confirms the work meets this standard. There should also be a Building Regulations Compliance Certificate that confirms that the work meets the Building Regulations.

- A Building Regulations Compliance Certificate from a Gas Safe registered engineer who has installed a heat producing gas appliance, e.g. gas boiler, fire, cooker or hob.

- Records for the servicing of the boiler.

- Any guarantees and warrantees such as for recent damp-proofing, or for the installation of a boiler and new appliances.
- Details of any maintenance Contracts in place, e.g. for the alarm.
- Certification for the replacement and/or installation of new windows, doors, roof windows and roof lights (FENSA reports) if installed or replaced in the last 10 years.
- If the property is under 10 years old, a copy of the New Home Policy and Warranty documents, including the National House Building Council (NHBC) warranty, or another recognised Certificate (e.g. Architect's Certificate).
- Confirmation if the property is a listed building or is in a conservation area.

Prepare and stage your property for sale

Before deciding on the sale price, consider getting a survey done of your property so you can fix any problems before they appear on a potential buyer's survey (e.g. repairs or re-decorating to improve the presentation of the property). Arrange for a survey especially if you think there are any major problems that might affect the value of your property (e.g. a roof in a bad state of repair, or obvious signs of subsidence that might need remediating before you sell your property). Once your property has been brought up to a good standard, you can use your survey report to attract buyers by demonstrating how good the condition of your house is.

When preparing your home for sale, ensure that there is as much effort put into fixing the outside as on the interior of the property. The front of the house should look welcoming – cleaning up the front gardens and driveways, along with placing a few brightly coloured potted plants by the door, can do wonders to the look of a property. The appearance and condition of the side and back gardens, as well as the outbuildings, cannot be seen to be neglected either. Clear out and freshen any of these areas, especially if they don't look clean and crisp. A coat of paint can transform an area.

Before selling one of our properties, we painted the inside and outside of our garages in white so that they looked brighter and cleaner, transforming the space within and making both the areas look larger and more useable.

Staging your home correctly and appropriately for sale is very important, as are the photos you will use to market your property. Excellent staging and great photos will assist in maximising interest from buyers (especially if they are only able to view online) and will give you the best chance of a quick sale while also obtaining an amount close to your asking price. Before photos are taken, get your property looking its best, making sure it is clean, tidy, free from clutter and that it looks good from the outside (i.e. has kerb appeal).

The buyer for one of our properties was living abroad at the time we put our property on the market for sale, and based on the photos, she made a strong case for us not to sell before she returned to the UK (it was only a matter of a short time). We liked the fact that she was unencumbered and ready to move on the property quickly, so we decided to wait for her instead of taking a lower, conditional offer from another buyer. She came to view the property a day after she arrived into the country, and the offer and acceptance process was completed very quickly because she had already decided that she wanted to buy the house from the way the property was staged, and the photos shown online.

Refer to the *Staging Chapter* for guidance on preparing your property for sale.

If you are unable to present your house for sale, engage a property staging expert to prepare your home for sale so that you have a greater chance of selling your property quickly and obtaining your asking price. You can obtain quotes online and a good place to start is the Home Staging Association UK (HSAUK) website, where you can find professional home staging experts aligned with the association, as well as information and reports on the benefits of staging your home for sale.

Fixtures, fittings and chattels

You should decide in advance if you are prepared to include any extras in the sale, e.g. curtains and carpets, which are known as fittings. A price for these can be included in the asking price, or a separate price can be asked in addition to the sale price. Notify the agent of any items that are not included for sale.

There are items that you are expected to sell as part of the house sale unless you make it clear to the buyer that such items are not included in the sale. These are known as fixtures and include items such as fireplaces and a central heating system. However, in some cases it is not always clear whether something is a fixture or fitting. It's useful if you draw up a list of any items you intend to remove or are prepared to sell separately. Advise the agent of these to manage expectations all around and avoid problems later.

If you are interested in selling any additional chattels, confirm this list so that later you can advise your solicitor, agent and the potential buyers of these items. A chattel is defined as something that can be moved and isn't part of the property being sold. The chattels we have sold with our properties include sofas, bar stools, bedside cabinets, rugs, gym equipment (including a treadmill) and garden furniture.

Disclose material information

> Prior to 2013, the sale or purchase of a property transaction was covered by Caveat Emptor (*let the buyer beware*) when it was up to the buyer to ask the questions, with the seller, or their agent, required to provide honest answers. Since 2013, with the repeal of the Property Misdescriptions Act, the sale and advertising of property has come under the 2008 Consumer Protection Against Unfair Trading Regulations (CPRs) and you are now legally required to disclose material information.

This means that the CPRs require you, as a seller, to inform your estate agent, and any potential buyer, of material information that may affect a buyer's decision to either view or buy your property. No longer can you, as the seller, choose what to tell your agent or potential buyer, or omit information that is material to a potential buyer. You should also ensure that your agent is adhering to disclosing all information provided, otherwise this could leave you and them open to prosecution. Also make sure that your agent knows exactly what the sale price of the property comprises of, including fixtures and fittings.

The National Trading Standards has released updated guidance that all estate agents should be working to. Agents cannot make misleading statements or fail to mention something that may put off a buyer, so if a seller lives next door to a school, a power station or sewage works, this must be mentioned; any photos taken of the property in such a way as to conceal these structures is misleading.

Do not try to hide things and you are not completely transparent about any problems with the property or the surrounding area. A survey will highlight any issues and buyers will do their own due diligence into the local area so if there is anything the seller is hiding is likely to come to light. When it does, the buyer will either withdraw, lower their offer when they get the survey or, worse still, sit on the decision until the last minute and then pull out because they haven't been able to come to terms with the new information, putting you back at square one.

Property valuations and agent's costs

> Invite a minimum of 3 recommended local agents to inspect your home and provide a property valuation, their commission structure and contractual information. You can review and compare the Contracts to inform yourself of what is expected in these agreements.

You can also ask the agents for input if you have not prepared your property for sale and believe it needs attention. In this case, obtain as much information as possible while they are valuing your property and ask them what specific work they believe needs to be done to make it as saleable as possible. Some agents may not be forthright with you as they won't want to introduce any obstacles before you sign the contract with them, but if you have built a good relationship, you can ask them to be upfront about this.

Notify the agent of work that you have done since your purchase, e.g. if you have added or removed any outbuildings or refurbished a home office. As well, if you have had a survey done and completed the fixes and work recommended, share this with the agent so that they are aware of the works completed and can pass this on to potential buyers.

The agents should be able to provide details of comparative houses, so you can see the style and condition of other properties that have been sold in the area at a similar price. These details will indicate what you need to do with your own property to attract buyers at the price level you are expecting to sell at. Find out from the agents what their justification is for the amount they're valuing your property for, along with details of what they are going to do for you to find the right buyer.

When discussing each contract with the respective agent, find out from them what their sales commission and fees are. Most agents calculate their commission as a percentage of the final selling price of the property, generally between 1% and 3, plus VAT. This information will help you to calculate the costs of selling your property through a local high street agent and whether you want to go down this path. You can also use this information to compare costs across all the agents who have provided valuations for you, as well as negotiate a better rate for yourself.

You should also check whether you have to pay extra, or if the following are included:

- VAT (if not stated).
- Advertising costs, including charges for a 'For Sale' board.
- Costs of preparing details of the house, including photos and floor plan.

For the sale of our first property in the UK, we negotiated the fee to 0.75%, including VAT, because we had renovated the property to a high standard (best in the street) and we believed it would be sold within a week without much effort from the agent. Having confidence in the quick sale of your property depends a lot on the condition you are selling it in, so ensure that it's looking it's best. Our property was sold to the father of one of the agents and we have stayed good friends ever since, even getting together for dinner when we have visited Dubai, where he is living now!

You do not have to sell your property at the price the agents valued it at. It is your home, and you can decide what you sell it for, but it needs to be in line with what buyers expect to pay for a similar property, in that condition in that area. Be aware of the stamp duty brackets when you're selling your home. Buyers will normally try to negotiate a discount, so sellers often add on an extra 5-10% to the selling price so that they get what they want to achieve from the sale.

Do your own research and search through online property portals such as Rightmove and Zoopla to see what similar properties are selling for in your area. Educate yourself on the prices of properties recently sold as there is quite often a disparity between a seller's asking price and what a property actually sells for.

Understand your finances

As a seller, you may worry that buyers will hold up the sale whilst going through the many activities during this process, but you should make sure there are no potential roadblocks on your side either, especially by getting your finances in order.

Make sure you understand all the fees presented to you by the agents who are assisting you in the sale of your property. Clarify anything that appears ambiguous, even if you need help from an external source (e.g. your solicitor) to understand the information provided, so that the costs and the terms of the contract are clear to you.

Let your mortgage provider know that you're considering selling your property. Request a redemption figure from your mortgage provider so that you know in advance the amount that is still owing on your mortgage. This is how much you will need to pay your lender upon completion of the sale. It may include an Early Redemption Charge or Penalty Fee if the repayment of the mortgage is earlier than the term initially agreed with the lender.

> If you're within your existing mortgage term, check the fees you will pay when you sell:
> - If you are on your mortgage lender's standard variable rate (the rate your mortgage reverts to when a mortgage deal ends), then you can think about moving your mortgage to your next property without any charges being applied by the lender.
> - If you are buying another property and your mortgage is portable, you're also fine (as long as the lender's happy with the new property and the price and you pass affordability tests). Your existing mortgage moves with you at no extra cost and when that deal comes to an end, you can re-mortgage on your new property.
> - If your mortgage is not portable, you may face Early Repayment Charges (ERC) that can be approximately 1-5% of the remainder of your mortgage debt, making moving very expensive.

Also find out what the costs will be for you to move from your property. Ascertain if you have any external storage requirements (e.g. if you go into a rental property, decide if it is likely all your belongings will fit into the property or you will need to obtain extra storage space for these).

Collate all the fees, commissions, costs and expenses (including those of your solicitor) and have it on hand. We use a spreadsheet to record all these details so that any changes can be updated quickly and easily.

Following the sale of your property, you may wish to rent, or move in with family or friends, before you buy your next property. Or you may decide to buy and move to another property on the sale of your current one.

If the sale of your property is dependent on you buying another one, make sure that you start marketing your existing home and securing a buyer before initiating the search for your new home. This will position you well as a buyer and you will be an attractive prospect for agents. As a well-progressed buyer, you will also appeal to the seller of your next property, otherwise you might risk missing out on a great house you have identified because you have not progressed sufficiently with the sale of your current property.

If you are planning on purchasing your next home using the proceeds of the sale of your current property, also think about the kind of mortgage you'll require for that transaction.

> Refer to the *Buying Chapter* for detailed information to help you buy your property.

Confirm your asking price

> Whether you are finding a buyer yourself or using an agent, decide the price range you will be happy to put your property on the market for, and the least you will be prepared to accept.
>
> Also consider all the costs you have collated and take this into account in making your decision, e.g. if you are paying out £10,000 to the estate agent, £5,000 to your solicitor and £10,000 to your mortgage lender for early repayment charges, you will want to ensure you can cover these costs with the sale of your property.
>
> Buyers want a discount, so consider adding 5% to 10% to the asking price to achieve the sale price you expect.

Use the valuations provided by agents as reference points, along with your own investigations and the comparative property prices in your area. You can also find out about the cost of houses locally by looking at local papers, agents' windows and similar houses in the area. Use online websites such as Nethouseprices, Zoopla or the Land Registry to see what properties have sold for in the area or street you are selling in. This will give you an indication of what buyers are prepared to pay for a similar property. Ensure you are comparing your property equally to others. Be aware that the highest valuation provided by the estate agents may not be realistic to achieve as they may have been inflating the valuation to secure your instruction.

When we were selling our previous property, we found another lovely property in a nearby street that had a similar asking price. But when we looked at the photos, they showed that the building was not finished, and the bathroom had been left undone, so that house took a long time to sell after ours was sold. Make sure your house is up to spec and according to the price you are asking.

Decide how you will sell your property

When selling your property, you can find a buyer yourself or use an estate agent. Before you decide, consider how much each method would cost and how much time you have available. If you use an agent, it will be more expensive, but the agent will take responsibility for advertising, showing potential buyers around, and negotiating a price for the sale of your house. If you want to find a buyer yourself, it will be cheaper, but you will need the time to make all the arrangements yourself, follow the sales process through to completion and deal with any problems, including those in the chain (if this applies).

Selling privately

Although most people will use a traditional high street estate agent to help them sell their home, you can potentially save money by selling privately or using an online estate agent.

Be aware that as buyers have not been vetted by an agent, you are letting unknown strangers into your home. Make sure that for any viewings you are conducting yourself, ask a friend or relative to accompany you while you're conducting the viewing. Agree a prearranged 'code word' with friend or family member so that if either of you feel uncomfortable then you can shut down the viewing as soon as possible.

Be careful if the potential buyer asks about any confidential information such as security systems or how often the house is left empty. This information is best left until contracts have been exchanged. Also, never leave viewers unattended, and make sure that you put away all valuables during house viewings.

Before embarking on this, inform your insurance company of your intension to have private house viewings as they may have some steps you need to follow to ensure security. Otherwise, you may not be covered for theft if you have a burglary and you allowed people into your home knowingly, however unintentional the outcome was.

Selling offline

If you want to avoid using an agent, leaflet the nearby streets, use noticeboards in your local supermarket, advertise in local newspapers and by word-of-mouth. Although these may seem like rather outdated methods of marketing, they are tried and tested, and are often very low cost. According to research, homebuyers in England are most likely to move between 3 and 6 miles away from their current homes. This means that if you're selling your privately, the most likely buyers are going to be in your neighbourhood.

Enquire with the local papers how much they charge for property advertisements and draft your advert on the basis of how much you want to spend. Use existing adverts as a guide to the correct format and wording. It is also possible to advertise in shop windows, although it is advisable not to give the address, just your contact number.

Draw up details of your house similar to that of an estate agent, e.g. give details of room sizes, community charge/council tax, local facilities and fixtures and fittings. Provide these details to potential buyers, either before they call, or at the time they view.

Selling online

More and more home-sellers across the UK are selling their properties privately online. The big online property portals such as Rightmove and Zoopla are only available to high street estate agents and online agents. You cannot sell your property privately on these portals without going through an agent. However, online agents charge a one-off fixed fee if you want to use them for selling your property, so this makes them a lot cheaper than traditional high street agent's fees.

UK homeowners are also finding new ways to sell their homes in a bid to combat high estate agent fees. This, combined with the increasing use of social media, is bringing the following alternative and unusual methods of selling homes:

- Sellers are using Facebook Live and Facebook Messenger to showcase their homes and get the word out. However, due to the limited reach an individual has using their personal profile, they would also need to buy Facebook ads to publicise the sale.

- Gumtree has more than 1,000 property listings, with a large amount of those uploaded by individuals who want to sell their home without a middleman. Sellers simply need to upload a few photos of their home, include a description, and wait for the inquiries to come in. With Gumtree attracting around 16 million visitors each month, the potential reach of each listing is huge

- eBay also has over 1,000 properties listed for sale. eBay users pay a £35 charge, but there is no final fee to pay once a house is sold (although there is a PayPal charge).

- Sellers who are struggling to sell their properties also have the option of swapping their homes with others through sites such as Easy House Exchange and Preloved.
- Sellers are offering raffle tickets to people hoping to win a free property in a prize draw.

The main advantage of selling privately is that you save on agents' fees and take full control of the process of selling. You don't have to wait to see how your house is being marketed or wonder how inquiries are going as it is all down to you. You may be able to speed up the process, as there will be fewer people involved. You also know your own property better than any agent will and you can highlight the benefits (e.g. new boiler fitted) to potential buyers better than anyone else.

Quick house sales companies

There are companies that offer quick house sales which is where a quick house sale provider offers to buy your property, or to find a third party to buy it quickly, and usually at a discounted price. Be careful when selling your home using these organisations. Before the Office of Fair Trading (OFT) closed, it completed a study of companies offering quick house sales. It warned of the risks of using some companies, with these ranging from reducing their offer to buy at the last minute, to lack of clarity on buyer finances. Research the company involved and read reviews before placing your house for sale with them.

Selling at auction

If you're looking for a speedy sale and certainty that a buyer won't pull out, then auctions are a good option. Once the auctioneer's hammer falls, the buyer has to put down a 10% deposit, after which they have a month to provide the remaining funds.

Demand from multiple buyers can help to drive up the price of your property quickly, especially when they're all in the room together and desperate not to miss out on the chance to own the property (i.e. Fear of Missing Out – FOMO). If you have a difficult to sell property, one that is a bit unusual or run-down you may find it hard to appeal to conventional buyers, but auctions are often attended by expert buyers or people looking for a project, and they know enough about the market to understand your property value.

If you need to sell up quickly or you need the money urgently, then an auction may be the right sales channel for you. As long as you've set a realistic price, and there is sufficient interest, your property should be sold by the end of the auction. Expect to pay the auctioneer approximately 2.5% of the price you get for the property. Find out all the costs before starting down this path, e.g. if there will be advertising costs. You will also need to pay a solicitor to help with the legal activities prior to the auction and on the day.

An established auction house can be more expensive, but they are more likely to know how to market your property to the maximum number of potential buyers. Conversely, you might find though that a less established company is more accommodating and cheaper.

The sale is binding from the moment the hammer comes down on the lot, and you will sign and exchange Contracts there and then. So, there is no time for second thoughts or cold feet – if you think an agent is pressurising you, then step back and obtain guidance from your solicitor before proceeding with the auction of your property.

Your auctioneer will help you set your guide price, which is the price that the public is allowed to know, and you can use it to lure buyers in. Your reserve is the lowest price you will accept and is kept private between you and the auctioneer. If all the offers are lower than your reserve price, then the auctioneer will withdraw the property from the auction. If someone offers your reserve price, or above, the auctioneer will drop the hammer on the bid and you won't be able to back out, so think it through carefully.

One of the benefits of selling your home through an auction is that it's quick – it might take just a month to go up for auction, then the sale could be completed within 28 days. But this also means you need to be ready to move quickly once the sale has gone through.

In recent years, a new type of auction has become popular, and this is known as the modern method of auction. Used by some agents, the modern method of auction allows buyers to bid on a property online. The buyer will pay a non-refundable reservation fee but will have a longer completion timescale, giving them time to sort out mortgage finance.

Educate yourself on the different types of auctions on offer, and if this is the appropriate sales channel for you, proceed with the one most suited to you once you have obtained input from your solicitor and have earmarked a place to move to in case there the sale is completed very quickly.

Selling using real estate agents

> An experienced agent with strong local knowledge and providing sound advice is worth their weight in gold. They will know how to market a property efficiently and cost-effectively as it's something they do daily. Good agents have the ability to get houses noticed on publications and powerful online property portals with huge levels of traffic, they turn responses into enquiries from prospective buyers. A confident agent will know how to manage buyers who are just pushing their luck, as well as be experienced in managing the entire chain, keeping everything on track and getting you to that all important finish date.

The power of an agent's high street shop window has yet to diminish as displaying properties in their windows is a strong source of leads for them. Most of us like browsing properties for sale, and a shopping trip to our local high street is a convenient time to do it.

Also, think about people who are planning to move to an area they don't know. After looking for houses on the major property portals, they will visit the area and look round the agents' offices to find the right property.

Another thing an agent does, that no private property site can do, is find potential buyers who are ready to move. If an agent has sold a property similar to yours, they may have had 15 enquiries, meaning they know 14 potential buyers who are still looking for a house!

When you're handling the sale yourself, you'll have to determine the genuine buyers. Agents handle cold callers and enquiries as a norm, and usually vet as well as pre-qualify people financially before bringing them to view your property. This means agents can find out if the potential purchaser has a pre-qualification letter from their mortgage lender showing that they can obtain the requisite funds for the property purchase, or, through the pre-qualification process, check if they can afford to purchase your property.

An agent can also find out if the buyer is selling their property, whether it's already on the market, if they have a potential buyer and if they need the funds from the sale to purchase their next property (early knowledge of this dependency means you can decide whether you want to be in a chain or not).

If the agent has not qualified the potential buyers, you can insist that the potential buyer goes through the qualification process prior to viewing your property. You will then have confidence from the beginning that the buyer can afford to purchase your property, and are ready to do so, rather than finding out at a later stage that they were wasting your time, by which time you may have lost the interest of some genuine potential purchasers.

Finally, when an offer is made, the agent will continue to earn their fee by liaising between you and the buyer. Agents are trained in negotiating and can help to ensure you get the highest price, as they are not emotionally involved. When you're selling it yourself, the temptation is there to take the first offer rather than holding your nerve and obtaining the price you genuinely deserve.

> Some agents will encourage you to sell your home at a lower price to make it easier for them to sell. Others use the pricing range on property channels like Rightmove as this is where pricing criteria is entered by buyers, e.g. £650,000 to £700,000, and where they would want your home to be displayed. For example, if you are selling your property for £705,000, you would be better advised to price it at £698,000 so that your home is displayed in the £650,000 to £700,000 range, rather than the £700,000 to £800,000 range. Ask your agent how they have come to assess the price of your home so that you can understand this. At this stage, you have a chance for input before the price is set and advertised. Increasing or lowering house prices after initial advertising can confuse potential buyers about the property value.

If you have decided to use an agent, choose one who you know has a reputation for being polite and supportive during your sale as you will be dealing with them a lot. If possible, make appointments and visit a few agents and decide if you can work with them (and have the chemistry to want to work with them). If you find that your hackles are up at the first meeting and you don't like the manner in which the agent is communicating with you, or if you believe they are guarded about any part of the discussion (rather than being frank and open), then move on to assessing the next agent.

If it is not possible to visit the agents, either obtain personal recommendations or read reviews on Google to identify who you would like to represent you. Biggest and / or cheapest is not always best. Some agents have short-term attitudes only for the duration of the sale of the property and don't think about when you will be buying or selling again. Others have a reputation for not being in touch again once you have signed the Contract and they have secured your property for sale. Do your research and investigate agents so that you can make an informed decision.

> Once you have selected an agent, review the contract with them. Read the agreement thoroughly, even if you have to obtain input from your solicitor to explain the clauses. Some agents make it very difficult to get out of a Contract and others don't provide the full details at the outset. When we were selling a property, we were approached by an agent who advised us that they would discuss their fee in detail once the Contract was signed – needless to say, we didn't bother to proceed with them! You need to know all the details of engagement and all your financial commitments before you entrust the sale of your property to anyone.

We have heard of agents who sign their clients up to packages and provide a long list of 'things to do' before they will put the house on the market. Some requests are reasonable, e.g. de-cluttering, personal items being put away, kitchen and bathrooms cleaned, and toys tidied away if there are small children living in the property. However, if this list, and the resultant costs of the changes, are too high for you to manage, then make sure you discuss this with the agent before you sign the Contract with them.

If your property is going on sale for the first time, the agent may not be the right one for you if they expect you to use and pay for the services of an interior designer, tiler, plasterer, builder, plumber, painter and every other tradesman before they will promote your property for sale. If the services are genuinely required, then this is very useful. But you need to find out first whether the funds you are expected to outlay will be recouped either by attracting the right buyer and / or if you will recover the costs, compared to what you're expecting to sell the property for in its current condition.

Confirming estate agent's costs

Once you have chosen your agent, re-confirm the agreed commission and any fees and charges. The agent must confirm all charges, rate of commission and any other terms of the Contract and do this before they agree to act for you. Otherwise, don't sign the Contract and look for another agent, one who is transparent and shares information.

Agents we have worked with have been willing not to hold us to the entire specified period noted in the Contract if we are unhappy with the services provided, or if they haven't found a genuine buyer within the timeframe we have specified. There may be other provisos you may wish to have written in the Contract so that it's clear from the beginning where each party stands on all points.

Types of estate agent agreements

If you use one agent to handle the sale (rather than multiple agents), this means it's on the basis of a sole agency agreement. Or, the agent may have sole selling rights. This will depend on the Contract that you have signed. Make sure these terms are explained to you in writing if they are used in a Contract.

Sole selling rights means that the agent has the exclusive right to sell your home. You will still have to pay the agent even if you find a buyer yourself. With sole agency, this is still only using the one agent, but if you do find a buyer yourself, you do not have to pay their sales commission. Negotiate a sole agency agreement for a specific period of time so that you can opt out of your Contract if you need to.

Two agents acting together to sell a property is known as joint agency or joint sole agency. A joint sole agency Contract is where the agents involved share the commission when the property is sold regardless of which estate agent actually finds the buyer.

The commission is usually higher for this type of arrangement because the commission has to be shared, and each agent needs to be able to make the transaction commercially viable.

If you appoint more than two agents on a multiple agency basis, commission is only paid to the estate agent who sells the property. The rate of commission is usually higher than for a sole agency agreement.

Selling by tender

Some agents are selling properties by a tender process where buyers view the property at an open day and make an offer through a sealed bid. The buyer will enter into an agreement to pay the agent's commission as part of the tender process and this is paid on completion of the sale. You are only charged a small marketing fee, or no fee, by the agent.

It is not against the law for an agent to sell a property by a tender process, but it can be confusing for the seller and buyer if the agent isn't clear about the process. You are not obliged to sell your property by the tender process.

The main benefit of selling a property by tender is that the seller won't have to pay the agent's commission, but the tender process may put off buyers as they may not want to pay the agent's fee.

Chapter 5. SELLING YOUR PROPERTY

The Property Ombudsman has guidance for agents for selling by the tender process:

- The tender pack should include:
  - Details of the sale.
  - The agreement to make an offer by tender.
  - The buyer to pay the agent's fee.
  - The bid form.
  - Frequently asked questions.
  - A key features document setting out the pros and cons of the process.
- Sellers must be told at the start that the buyer is agreeing to pay the agent's fee.
- The agent's main duty of care is to the seller and the agent must avoid any conflict of interest between the seller and the buyer.
- Sellers should receive advice about all of the options available to market their property and they should receive complete information about the risks of selling by tender.
- Sellers should be told what happens if the buyer does not want to pay the fee when you want to sell to that buyer.
- Sellers should be told what happens if the buyer refuses to pay the fee.

If you think that the agent is not following the guidance, you should contact The Property Ombudsman, or visit the website for guidance. But agents and their management teams are looking to help you to sell your property, so try working through any issues and settling your differences first before taking it further.

Complaints process

All agents must belong to an approved complaints redress scheme. Any agents that do not join a scheme can be fined. There are 3 approved schemes:
- Ombudsman Services
- Property Redress Scheme
- The Property Ombudsman (TPO)

If you have a complaint about your estate agent and together you cannot sort out the problem, you can make a complaint to the scheme to which your estate agent belongs.

Once you have done your research, determine whether you will sell your home yourself or via an estate agent. If you are using an agent, also decide on the type of agreement you will progress with, and whether you will use a sole agent or multiple agents. Advise the agent or agents of your decision, review the contracts you have with them and negotiate the best commission structure before committing yourself.

Your sales brochure

You will need to have a sales brochure prepared whether you are selling directly, or you have an agent. Before you sign off the brochure and proceed with the marketing process, check that all the details are correct, including the selling price, description of the property, accuracy of the floor plan as well as the quality and quantity of photos.

> Once we receive a brochure from our agent, we review it and re-write the descriptions, adding any specific details or information as necessary. We also review the photos taken, replacing and / or re-ordering the sequence of the photos within the brochure. While we have confidence in the agent as they know what attracts buyers, we also like to provide creative direction in the preparation of our marketing brochure; we have put so much time, effort and money into our properties that we want to ensure its described and displayed at its best and stands out as such.
>
> For examples of sales photos, please visit our website on www.gsansellproperty.com.

Viewings

On each viewing day, make sure your property is clean, tidy and free of clutter to give buyers a good impression and to provide you with the best chance of attracting a buyer. Make sure pets have been secured or relocated, and pet bowls stored away.

Having determined how you are selling your property, decide if you will be conducting the viewings or whether the agent will. Agents are experienced at conducting viewings and will recognise quickly if there is genuine buyer interest, and they have usually pre-qualified the potential buyers prior to the viewing. Agents can also deal with any awkward questions and help you to answer these.

If you are doing the viewings yourself, and letting strangers into your home, ensure safety in numbers by asking a friend or relative to accompany you. Be wary of answering questions about confidential information, e.g. security systems or how often the house is empty. If you are conducting the viewings, be calm, informative and polite. Initial viewings generally take around 10 to 15 minutes and buyers are likely to have some questions. To cover these off, have copies of relevant documents and current bills to hand as evidence.

Typical questions viewers will ask are:

- How old is the property?
- When was the property last re-wired?
- What is the Council Tax Band?
- Do you have insulation in the cavity walls and in the loft?
- What is the average cost of your utility bills?
- How old is the boiler and is it regularly serviced?
- How long is left on guarantees for double glazing, conservatories etc.?
- What school catchments does the property's location fall into?
- Which fence boundaries belong to who?

If your agent is conducting the viewings, ensue they know where all the relevant keys and supporting information is located. Let your agent know if you would like everyone to remove their footwear before they enter the house, especially if it has been raining or is muddy around your property. Leave the property before the viewing so that the potential buyers don't feel awkward during their visit and can take their time looking in each room.

If your agent would like you to be present for subsequent viewings for potential buyers to ask you questions directly, it's best to attend the viewing as there may be a number of queries that only you will be able to answer. It's also a great opportunity to engage with the prospective purchasers and encourage them with your enthusiasm and delight in your property. We have had the chance to meet genuine potential buyers and spend time with them, offering them refreshments and just chatting so they can stay longer and enjoy the experience even more of being in our property.

> When we were selling one of our properties, a potential buyer asked to meet us as she had some enquiries and wanted to discuss the property in detail with us. We were asked by her what work we had done on the property because of the gap between our purchase and sale prices within a relatively short period of time. As we had all the documents, planning permissions and associated information on hand to support our viewings, we were able to take her through each of our undertakings room by room. We also used our laptop to show her a number of photos taken before, during and after the refurbishment, and she concurred that a significant amount of work had been done.

What to do if your property is not selling

If your property has been on the market for a while and you have not received any offers, or any that you would deem reasonable, there are a number of actions you can take to improve your chances of selling.

Once you are sure that you make the property available for viewing when required and that it is well presented and free of clutter and pets on viewing days, discuss your concerns with you agent. Depending on the financial market, your property may require additional advertising. Make sure your property is being shown on Rightmove and Zoopla, on your own agent's website and in their office window. Place your own advertisements and promote your house on social media platforms. You can also undertake some offline advertising by printing and distributing flyers and brochures promoting the sale of your property, as well as distributing or advertising in local stores.

The photos that were taken of your property might be lacking quality and need a refresh. Check all of the locations you have your property listed (both online and offline) and verify that the photos are of sufficient quality. If they are not, make sure you tidy up your property, reduce the clutter and increase lighting in key areas before you have new photos taken. Consider hiring a professional photographer if you are selling directly as this should ensure great shots; if you are using estate agent, they will have their own photographer to take the photos, though if they have already taken photos initially, they may charge you for additional ones. Some agents use drones to take photos from a height for perspective.

> A word of caution on using photos taken by other people. Once you've had the photos taken, you will want to use them on property websites or in publications, to print copies or share on social media. Request for the

Chapter 5. SELLING YOUR PROPERTY

> photo rights to be assigned to you, or at least obtain permission from the photographer to use the images. The person who presses the shutter on the camera is the one who owns the rights to the image, irrespective of who the camera or property belongs to. You will infringe copyright laws if you use the images without the photographer's permission. Copyright law is a minefield, so obtain the correct permissions otherwise the photographer has the right to sue you.

Feedback you receive from potential buyers and your agent should alert you to what is not working for them, or what necessary work needs to be undertaken to improve your property. It is advisable to take your property off the market so that these works can be completed, otherwise it may put potential buyers off – having a skip with discarded plumbing and dirt-encrusted shower trays in front of your property is not a sight you want your potential buyers to be confronted with.

> Consider engaging a home staging professional to stage your home for sale. These experts will be able to provide you with information and assistance and they know what to look out for e.g. if there are too many polarising features fighting with the structure, layout and spatial positioning in a room, this would put potential buyers off.
>
> Refer to the *Staging Chapter* for guidance on preparing and staging your property for sale.

Look at the budget you have and prioritise the list of work that needs to be done (e.g. walls re-plastered, kitchen and / or bathroom re-tiled, dilapidated outbuilding removed and replaced with a garden shed or external office). Discuss this list with the agent before you start on the prioritised list of work so that you can both confirm that there will be sufficient changes in place before the property is re-launched. Make your home look as good as you can, as there will always be competition when you are looking to sell your home and it needs to stand out.

Consider adjusting your selling price as this is one of the main reasons most properties do not sell. Your property needs to be priced realistically otherwise it will struggle to attract buyers. Review the selling price with the agent or do your own research online to see what other similar properties are on the market for in your area and also the price that properties have actually sold for.

If your agent is too busy and not able to dedicate as much time into selling your property, it will not be getting the focus and attention it needs. You may want to ask a friend to call the agent and pose as a potential buyer, describing your home to the estate agent as a property they would like to buy. If the agent mentions your property, then you can at least be sure they are doing their job; if not, it's time to change to another agent, or multiple agents, who are likely to be more energised as your property will be a new listing for them.

Check the exit clause in your contract with your existing agent before you go down this avenue as it depends if there is a tie-in period in the Contract you have signed with the existing agent and if the type of agreement you signed allows this. Make sure you discuss this issue with your current agent so that they are aware of your intention to change. This discussion may put more focus on your property and you may not have to change agents.

Offer and acceptance

Receiving feedback and offers from potential purchasers is exciting! We usually start receiving offers within a week of putting our property up for sale, with the confirmed offer and acceptance stage completed within a month.

> We found it very frustrating when the same viewers turned up multiple times to view one of the properties we were selling. We had to undertake the viewings as the agent was too busy with other properties. Along with taking up a lot of our time, we found out later that they could not afford to purchase the property. We had requested that the agents pre-qualify the viewers to ensure that we only had genuine buyers, however these people resisted providing their financial details for the pre-qualification process. After many viewings, when we pushed the agent again to qualify them, it was discovered that these 'potential' purchasers were unable to afford the property by quite a wide margin; in fact, they had hoped to negotiate the buy price down to their much lower budget.

The aftermath of these types of viewings must also be frustrating and disappointing for the potential buyers because ultimately, they miss out on a property that they aspire to. They should be looking at properties that more closely aligned with their budget and not waste their time and effort. Some agents will blacklist buyers that view properties they can't afford, so eventually they will not be presented with properties that are within their price bracket because they are labelled as time-wasters.

It can be disappointing if the offers are well below your asking price. But having worked out what the lowest offer is that you will accept, you will have a clear idea of how much you can afford to reduce the price of your property if this becomes necessary.

Chapter 5. SELLING YOUR PROPERTY

You may find yourself in the enviable position of receiving multiple offers for the sale of your house. You can sell your property to whomever you choose and not necessarily to the buyer who offers the most money. When you receive an offer, be sure to negotiate as some buyers will offer less than they're willing to pay for the property. It's not only price that you can negotiate on, it can also be time so that you have an agreed exchange and / or completion date to work to from the beginning of the offer and acceptance process.

If several prospective buyers are interested in your home, it's also worth thinking about who is unencumbered, most progressed in their sale and least likely to pull out (perhaps due to nerves, or their own sale falling through), and who can move at the same pace as you, along with the amount each buyer offers. Pre-qualification of potential buyers will help to answer these questions. If you are using an estate agent, they should be able to advise you on the position of each buyer.

If you are using an estate agent, they will negotiate the sale price with the potential buyers. The agent will try and obtain the best possible price for you. If you are not using an agent, you will need to negotiate the selling price yourself, or have someone help you with this (e.g. a solicitor, family member or friend). You are not obliged to accept the first offer put to you and you should not be pressured into making a decision quickly.

If you are selling your own property, it's a good idea to keep a list of all the names and contact details of all the potential buyers who make offers in case the one you accept falls through. If you are dealing with an estate agent, they will have this information, and more.

> In order, the safest buyers to choose, especially if you are time-constrained, are:

- Cash buyers who are looking to move quickly. These buyers don't need a mortgage so will move as quickly as you can through the purchase process.
- Buyers who are in rental, those who have already completed, or at least exchanged contracts, on the sale of their own property. These are serious buyers and will move quickly to get back to owning a property as soon as possible.
- First-time buyers. These are good buyers, although the buying process may be tricky for them, and consequently may take more time, as they learn to manoeuvre through the purchase process. This is an expensive first purchase for them, so the timing factor also depends on whether they are

getting good advice and appropriate support from the professionals they are dealing with during the purchase, and from family and friends.

- Buyers who have sold their property subject to Contract. The attractiveness of this could be influenced by whether there is a chain involved, and if so, the length and complexity of the chain. It also depends on the provisos that the buyer's buyer had put in place before the Contract can be signed.
- Buyers who have had offers but have not accepted any yet. This could mean they have had offers where the timing doesn't suit them or lower than expected offers (which may impact the amount of mortgage they obtain, and consequently their next purchase).
- Buyers who have had their property on the market but have not had any offers as yet. You will be able to gauge the suitability of these potential buyers depending on the length of time their property has been on the market. They may be looking to move but may not want to. We saw a property a few years ago that was on the market for over 18 months. It wasn't selling because it suited the owner's son to live there – he kept the house dirty, the gardens untidy and the property was not readily available for viewings!
- Buyers who have not yet placed their property on the market. Generally, this means they are either confident that their property will sell very quickly, or they are not ready to move yet, and are having a look around to see what types of properties are available within their price range. If you are not in a hurry to sell, they can be good buyers because you may have lots of time to take yourself through the purchase process. These buyers could also suit you if you have not found a property to move to.

Even after you have accepted an offer, there is nothing in law to prevent you from deciding to accept a higher offer from a different buyer. Bear in mind that when an offer is made and accepted the potential buyer can also withdraw or lower their offer, e.g. they may not be able to secure a mortgage, or the survey may show up some structural problem which will need funding. When we are selling, we build the profiles of our potential buyers by using a spreadsheet where we record the buyer's information, particulars of their offers and any feedback. We find it helps us to make the right decisions once the full picture is displayed in front of us.

Once you have a confirmed offer in writing from you agent, provide this to your solicitor and instruct them to start the conveyancing process.

Complete conveyancing questionnaires

The buyer's solicitor will need to make enquires so they have all the information they need to proceed with the purchase and draw up the Contracts. You will need to complete various questionnaires, and these will have questions relating to the boundaries of your property, what fixtures and fittings are included in the sale, whether you've had any disputes or complaints regarding your neighbours, proposed developments, building works, sewerage, utilities, council tax and things of that nature. Read these forms thoroughly and fill them out truthfully and to the best of your knowledge.

> The questionnaires will be provided to you by your solicitor and will include the following:
>
> - The TA 6 (Property Information Form), a general questionnaire that includes information on boundaries, disputes and complaints (such as reported noisy neighbour complaints or boundary disputes), known proposed developments (motorways or railways), building works, council tax, utilities and sewage.
>
> - The TA 7 (Leasehold Information Form), or the TA9 (Commonhold) if you do not own the freehold.
>
> - The TA 10 (Fixtures and Fittings Form) which provides details of which fittings and fixtures you would like to include in the sale of the property.
>
> - The TA 13 (Completion Information and Undertaking Form) which is more technical, but also includes finalisation details including arrangements to hand over the keys, how and where you will complete, as well as ensuring that the house is free of all mortgages and liability claims.

Your solicitor uses the questionnaire information and evidence of your title to the property to draw up a draft Contract which is sent to the buyer's solicitors for approval. There are likely to be negotiations over the draft Contract which will include the date of completion (usually 7-28 days after the exchange of Contracts), what fixtures and fittings will be included in the sale price and how much they pay for other fixtures and fitting.

Negotiate the draft Contract

Once you have received a copy of the draft contract from your solicitor, review it in detail.

It's important to closely examine any discounts or reductions of price you may have agreed. The buyer would most likely have had a survey conducted on your property by this time. If the survey flags up anything major such as the need for roof repairs, cracks to brickwork, or anything else that may cause concern, there may also be a negotiation over who will fix this, or even a re-negotiation over the sale price.

You will be asked to confirm exchange and completion dates, which is usually up to 4 weeks after the exchange of Contracts. Check your personal and business calendars and ensure you can commit to the dates that you proposed and agreed initially.

Also check that the list of fixtures, fittings, chattels and any other items you have agreed to sell to the buyer is accurate and complete and includes the correct amount to be paid to you for them.

Plan your move

> Refer to the *Moving home Chapter* for detailed information on planning for your move.

Make yourself available

Leading up to exchange, as well as between exchange and completion of Contracts, there is an increase in activity, so you need to be available to respond to any queries quickly. To prevent impacting your property sales and conveyancing process, make sure you communicate to your solicitor and estate agent any holiday or travel plans you have scheduled. While you are away, ensure that you are still available via phone or email to respond to any queries or make decisions promptly. Don't ignore any aspect of the purchase that you do not understand – if in doubt, ask.

Also find out when other parties are likely to be unavailable in case this impacts your sale. We were advised by our purchasers that apparently their solicitor had decided to go on holiday for 2 weeks without providing any notice to anyone. It was very close to the date of exchange and it made for an anxious time for the entire chain.

Gazumping, gazundering and gazanging

The terms are explained below:

- Gazumping is when a seller accepts an offer from one buyer, then opts for another higher offer from another buyer. This means that the first buyer is forced to consider offering a higher amount very late on in the process, often leading them to pull out and continue their search elsewhere because their affordability and mortgage application may have been affected by the change in the sale price. Clearly this creates a lot of stress for the already apprehensive, and most probably over-stretched, buyer.

- Gazundering is when a buyer lowers their offer price prior to exchange of Contracts. This can happen for several reasons, including a survey that devalues the property or a downward market. We experienced this when our own buyers reduced their offer just before exchange of Contracts. This was because they had been subjected to the same practice on their own property and wished to pass the cost on. We chose to accept the lower sale price as we were considerably progressed with the sale and we had good buyers. The agent lowered their commission to help offset this, which we welcomed.

- Gazanging is when a seller pulls out after an offer has been accepted, which could be due to a change of heart or if their own purchase falls through and they don't have the confidence that they will find another property by the expected completion date. This forces the buyer to return to their search, often very late on in the process. It also means that the buyer has to bear the costs to date, including any survey and legal costs incurred while progressing the sale. We were impacted by this after our offer was accepted on a property where the seller decided to withdraw her property from the market on the advice of her agent (and friend) because prices were increasing rapidly; the property was put on the market again 9 months later with a much higher sale price, so this was good for the seller. We were informed later that when the property was put up for sale initially, it was just to test the market. Because we didn't know this (the seller and agent were not open and honest about the situation), we incurred costs.

Every year, almost 30% of home sales in England and Wales fall through before completing. A considerable percentage is caused by the use of these tactics. While these practices are allowed, they can afflict one party over the other, and are often played out late in the transaction process. We would encourage you to be authentic and avoid these practices by treating others as you would like to be treated, irrespective of whether you are selling or buying a property.

Avoiding these practices

Of course, things don't have to be like this, and we're seeing more and more buyers and sellers looking for an assured way for the property transaction to take place. There are a few ways you can manage these unsavoury practices.

Meet your buyer and / or seller in person and stay in direct contact throughout the whole transaction. Good things can happen when people come together and are genuine with each other. By opening up this uninterrupted channel of communication, not only is more trust built, but both parties assist to move the process on. Communications are up to date and you are in more control. If relationships are built authentically, with parties exchanging regular dialogue, its less likely something underhand like gazundering will occur.

You could also opt into a scheme where both seller and buyer secure an offer with a refundable deposit. This agreement binds the two parties together and cements the agreement, markedly reducing the chances of a fall-through.

Additionally, you may choose to accept offers from chain free buyers. However, if you are receiving good offers, you are not automatically going to reject buyers just because they're in a chain. But if you're in the fortunate position of being inundated with interested parties with offers, then favour those who are chain-free as they are more likely to be able to move to completion quicker.

Set a date for exchange. As soon as possible, agree a date in place for when you'll aim to exchange Contracts. This is a good way of keeping involved parties focussed on the delivery date, giving everybody something to work towards, which keeps the pressure on.

Move quickly. Keep in regular contact with your solicitor and ensure that your property sale is being pushed through. Your agent should also stay in touch with the buyer's solicitor to ensure things are moving smoothly on that side. Communicate your activity to all parties so they can see you are on top of all requests.

Be realistic about your price. If you set your house price way above what it should be, there is a higher chance of a buyer lowering their offer. If a buyer falls in love with your property, they may rush into making an offer matching your asking price, or even above asking price, in an attempt to secure the sale. Once surveys have been carried out and the buyer has had time to think, they may decide to reduce their offer. Set a fair price so there's less chance of being gazundered.

Get a good agent. A skilled and knowledgeable agent will know how to handle buyers who are just pushing their luck. They will be experienced in keeping everything on track and getting you through to the end of that all-important sale process.

Do not try to hide anything. If you are not completely transparent about any problems with your property or the surrounding area, you are potentially setting yourself up for a fall. A survey will highlight any issues and most buyers will also do their own due diligence into the local area, so if you are hiding anything it is bound to come to light. If it does, the buyer may withdraw from the sale immediately, lower their offer as a result of the findings in the survey or pull out at the last minute, putting you back to square one.

Do your sums and work out your finances. If you're in a chain and you know you will need to move from your property, even when a good offer has been accepted, work out what the lowest offer is that you would accept. If in the event the buyer does reduce their offer, then you will already have a clear idea of how much you will accept, and you will make the right decision for yourself during these challenging negotiations.

Exchange of contracts

In any house sale or purchase, everyone is usually focused on two key events, the first being exchange of contracts and the other being completion of the sale. At any point up to the exchange of contracts, the agreement to buy or sell a property is not legally binding. This means that the seller or buyer can withdraw from the transaction at any time, and this is a key reason why it's important to exchange contracts quickly.

Exchange of contracts can only take place when:
- Your solicitor has received the mortgage offer and all finances are in place.
- Your solicitor has completed all relevant searches for your next property.
- You have organised building insurance for your new property (after exchange you are liable for the property).
- You are aware that if you are in a chain, your solicitor will only exchange if all the other parties in the chain are in a position to, and agree to, proceed. If one party pulls out or delays, the entire chain is held up or the sale can be aborted.
- You have agreed on a date and time to exchange Contracts and that your solicitor will exchange Contracts for you.

- You have agreed on a completion date, which will be written into the Contract.
- You have read and understood the Contract and signed it.

The actual process of exchanging Contracts is dealt with in a telephone conversation between the solicitors, the terms of the Contract are confirmed (including the sale price), and the buyer's solicitor will confirm the amount of the deposit being handed over on completion. This is usually 10% of the purchase price.

Once exchange of Contracts has taken place, both buyer and seller are legally committed to the sale of the property. If the buyer does not proceed with the purchase after exchange of Contracts, they could forfeit their deposit, and if a sum lower than 10% of the purchase price was paid on exchange of Contracts, then they could be asked to make up the amount up to 10%.

If you refuse to go ahead with the sale following exchange, the Contract could potentially be enforced through the courts and you can be forced to vacate, or the buyer could be awarded damages. The buyer's deposit will be returned to them and legal action can be taken against you for damages. Alternatively, the buyers may make an application to the Court for "specific performance of the Contract" and compel you to sell to them.

When Contracts are exchanged, and before completion, the buyer may wish to visit the house to undertake various activities, e.g. measure up for curtains, or get an estimate for carpets and building work. You should not allow any work to be undertaken on your property by the buyer before completion.

We were promised by the agent of a property we purchased that we would have access to it after exchange to undertake similar activities, but the seller reneged on this and we could not visit the property again until after completion. We asked the owner of the estate agency to assist the process as we felt that the agent needed support with dealing with the hostile vendor, but he wasn't interested in helping us, even though we had previously bought and sold properties through his company. Sometime life throws you these types of people but remain measured in your response and keep your eyes on the prize because your dealings with them will come to an end and you'll get the house you wanted.

After exchanging contracts

Following exchange of Contracts, the remaining conveyancing activities that need to be undertaken will be dealt with by the solicitors. The buyer is now entitled to purchasing the property and you are legally bound to proceed with the sale. If the property is leasehold, ensure that the freeholder is notified of the exchange of Contracts.

Just prior to the completion date, consider meeting your estate agent at the property again so that you can both confirm that all the fixtures, fittings and chattels you agreed on are still present and that their condition has not changed.

Prepare for your move

Refer to the *Moving home Chapter* for information to help you prepare for your move.

Completion of contracts

This is the day when the property officially changes ownership. The keys to your property will only be released once the money has been received in your solicitor's bank account.

Make sure your solicitor can contact you easily and keep you updated on the completion activities. If the payment for the purchase of your property is delayed, "completion" may be delayed, and it may not be possible for the monies to redeem your mortgage, or payable on any related purchase, to be transferred by bank transfer. So, if you are involved in a chain, and if one of the links falls through, the whole process will come to a standstill.

Sometimes exchange and completion are transacted on the same day. This has become increasingly common and the advantage for the buyer is that they don't have to pay a deposit earlier than on the exchange and completion day. However, the downside is that it is incredibly stressful, with all the parties involved not knowing that they are definitely moving until that particular day as they await the hour of completion. This also complicates the process of arranging removal companies and forwarding post. If anything does go wrong, none of you will have any time to put things right. And while you are waiting to hear that Contracts have been exchanged and completed, you will need to have your house all packed up, with the removal team ready to go.

The residual monies (generally 90%) will be transferred from your buyer's solicitor to your solicitor's account and any deeds for the property are transferred between solicitors.

Your mortgage provider will have given you and your solicitor the precise figure for the redemption of your mortgage on completion day. Following the receipt of the balance of the purchase monies, your solicitor will pay off your mortgage for you from the proceeds.

The estate agent's fees will be payable at this stage and your solicitor will make this payment out of the funds received from the sale of your property.

Your solicitor will provide you with an account covering all their costs and disbursements, the sale price of the house, the payments made for the redemption of the mortgage and the agent's fees. Pay your solicitor's invoice if you haven't already made arrangements for the deduction of these costs from the remaining funds from the sale.

You can advise the agent to hand over all the keys to the property once your solicitor has confirmed that payment has been received.

> Congratulations on the sale of your property – remember to celebrate your achievement!

Moving

> Refer to the *Moving home Chapter* for detailed information on moving home.

Chapter 5. SELLING YOUR PROPERTY

Checklist – Selling your property

The following Checklist will help you to plan and track your progress through this process.

Plan the sale of your property

- ☐ Be aware of the external influences that may impact the sale of your property.
- ☐ Obtain free valuations from agents to assess your options before you decide to sell.
- ☐ Familiarise yourself with the selling process and timeline to complete each stage.
- ☐ Choose your solicitor or licenced conveyancer for the legal work.
- ☐ Obtain an estimate of the costs from your chosen solicitor or licenced conveyancer.
- ☐ Make important documents available for your solicitor and potential buyers.
- ☐ Instruct your solicitor to act for you once you have agreed an offer.

Prepare and stage your property for sale

- ☐ Obtain a survey on your property to confirm the work required.
- ☐ Read the *Staging Chapter* to help you prepare your home for sale.

Fixtures, fittings and chattels

- ☐ Decide what fixtures, fittings and chattels you will include in the sale.
- ☐ Notify the agent of any items that are not for sale.

Disclose material information

- ☐ Ensure that you inform potential buyers of material information.

Property valuations and agent's costs

- ☐ Obtain 3 agent valuations, their commission structure and charges.
- ☐ Ask the agents to recommend and prioritise any required work to be completed.
- ☐ Do your own research through online property portals for similar properties in your area.

Understand your finances

- ☐ Obtain the size of your outstanding mortgage and any early redemption penalties.
- ☐ Obtain and collate all the estimates, costs, fees, commissions, and expenses.
- ☐ Refer to the *Buying Chapter* for detailed information to help you buy your property.

Confirm your asking price

- ☐ Use the agent's valuations, and your investigations, to confirm your asking price.

Decide how you will sell your property

- ☐ Determine whether you will sell your home yourself or via an estate agent.
- ☐ If you are using an agent, decide whether you will use a sole agent or multiple agents.
- ☐ Review the agent's contracts and negotiate the best commission fee before committing.

Your sales brochure

- ☐ Check all the particulars fully before you sign off and start the marketing.
- ☐ Check the price and descriptions are correct, and the photos do justice to your home.

Viewings

- ☐ Ensure your property is clean and tidy, with pets secured or relocated.
- ☐ Be calm and informative during viewings and have appropriate documents available.
- ☐ Ensure your agent knows where the keys and supporting information is located.

What to do if your property is not selling

- ☐ Confirm with your agent your property is being marketed appropriately.
- ☐ Review the photos of your property and have new ones taken if necessary.
- ☐ Assess whether the price needs adjusting.
- ☐ Refer to the *Staging Chapter* to ensure your property is appropriately presented.
- ☐ Consider moving to another agent, or multiple agents, if you are not in a tie-in.

Offer and acceptance

- ☐ Review the offers you have received and discuss the buyer's position with your agent.
- ☐ For an offer that is presented, either accept it, negotiate on it or reject it.
- ☐ Instruct your solicitor to start the legal work.

Complete conveyancing questionnaires

- ☐ Complete all the required forms to allow your solicitor to draw up a draft Contract.

Negotiate the draft contract

- ☐ Review the contract and ensure everything you have agreed to is reflected accurately.

Plan your move

- ☐ Refer to the *Moving home Chapter* for detailed information on planning for your move.

Chapter 5. SELLING YOUR PROPERTY

Make yourself available
- ☐ Make yourself available throughout this process and respond swiftly to any queries.
- ☐ Communicate to your solicitor and agent any holiday or travel plans you have.
- ☐ Respond to any queries or make decisions promptly while you are away.
- ☐ Obtain details of when other parties will not be available.

Gazumping, gazundering and gazanging
- ☐ Reduce being affected by these practices by staying in touch with all parties.
- ☐ Educate yourself how to avoid these tactics and take preventative action.

Exchange of contracts
- ☐ Ensure you have read, understood and signed the Contract.
- ☐ When you exchange Contracts, you become legally committed to selling the property.
- ☐ Be alert to requests by the buyer to re-visit your property to carry out any checks.

After exchanging contracts
- ☐ Make your property available to your buyer and agent prior to the completion.
- ☐ Update the freeholder about exchange if the property is leasehold.

Prepare for your move
- ☐ Refer to the *Moving home Chapter* for information to help you prepare for your move.

Completion of contracts
- ☐ Ensure your solicitor can contact you regarding the completion activities.
- ☐ Advise your agent to release the keys on confirmation from your solicitor.
- ☐ Ensure your solicitor's fees are paid.
- ☐ Celebrate selling you property!

Moving
- ☐ Refer to the *Moving home Chapter* for detailed information on moving home.

Chapter 6

MOVING HOME

Overview

In planning and preparing for your move, you will need to think through the entire move process and undertake activities early in readiness. This will include investigating removal services, obtaining insurance quotes and looking into mail re-direction. Coordinate your move once you have formal notification of your exchange and completion dates from your solicitor. You will be well organised for your move day once you have undertaken detailed planning, preparation and coordination.

Plan and prepare for your move

When you are planning and preparing for your move, try to do this as early as possible as there are so many activities to organise. Whether you are moving into a rental property or into your own home, you will need to undertake similar moving tasks.

We start planning as soon as we have decided to move so that we have a plan on hand and an easier time when we are preparing to move.

Your preparations for moving can start when you are closer to your moving date and can put your moving plan into action, though it is dependent on your circumstances:

- If you are selling your property, start preparing for your move once you have accepted an offer from your buyer.
- If you are buying a property you are moving into, your preparation should start once your offer to purchase has been accepted and your initial legal work, survey and mortgage application is underway.
- If you are moving into a rental property, start your preparation as soon as you have signed a rental agreement. While there may be a gap between the contract being signed and your move date, you can still undertake some tasks that will make your move day easier.
- If you are already in a rental property, begin your planning process either when you have decided to move, or as soon as notice is given for the termination of your tenancy. Even if you have a long notice period, you may choose to move as soon as you secure a suitable property.

Moving services

Assess your belongings and decide whether you will hire a van and do the packing and moving from your property yourself, or if you will pay for this to be done by a professional removal company, or even a moving services provider. Once you have made this decision, determine if you will utilise the latter 2 services either fully (packing and moving) or partially (moving only, so that you are responsible for all the packing). This will help you to determine what you have the budget and appetite for.

Van hire companies

If you are undertaking the packing and moving yourself, you will need to do all the packing yourself as well as heavy lifting yourself, at least twice – firstly when loading, and then when unloading the van. After that, you will be carrying and moving all your possessions into your new property to place in the various rooms. If you then don't like the placements, you will want to move them somewhere else. Moving yourself also means you may place yourself in positions where you could injure yourself as your focus is to get the work done, rather than your posture (e.g. bending properly when lifting heavy items). Furthermore, you will need to disassemble and disconnect the necessary furniture and whiteware, before re-assembling and re-connecting them when you have moved to your new property.

If you are comfortable with doing all the packing and moving yourself, obtain 3 quotes from recommended van hire companies. Discuss your requirements in detail with the hire companies so that you can confirm what you need on the day. There may be things that come to light during your discussions, e.g. whether you require a van with a low kerb height, or with a tailboard that you can lower so that it's easier to load and unload the van.

> Estimated costs for moving range from £100 to £200 if hiring a van. Find out the total costs for the hire and insurance of the van, and whether there are any penalty payments due if you change the date of the van hire. Confirm how and when your payment is due.
>
> Check that you have the correct driver's licence 'entitlement' for the category of vehicle you are intending to hire. If the van you hire weighs more than 7.5 tonnes once it's loaded, you will require a Heavy Goods Vehicle (HGV) licence. Investigate the process, timeline and cost of obtaining the HGV licence or find someone who already has this and can assist you on your move day.

Once you have received the 3 quotes and have had time to review and compare them (call each of the companies and obtain clarification if you need to, e.g. on costs or the contract), make your decision on which van hire company is going to be your preferred supplier. Call the company and advise them of your decision. Reserve the required sized van or truck with your chosen company for the target move date and advise them that you will be in touch when your exchange and completion dates are formally confirmed by you solicitor.

Start making arrangements with people who will be assisting you with disconnecting, moving and re-connecting white goods (e.g. washing machine), along with any other help you will need on the day of your move, including disassembling and re-assembling large pieces of furniture. Narrow stairs can also be tricky to manoeuvre around when carrying heavy or awkward shaped items, so it's likely you will need support on your moving day.

Removal companies

Securing the services of a good removal company means that you have professionals that are properly trained. We have been very lucky to have found a brilliant removal company near us, Clarkes of Amersham removal specialists. They have been really great to deal with and their removal teams are professional, courteous and careful. Even when we asked for a large and heavy dresser to be placed in different places in a room to check where we would like it best (then to move it back to the original position!), the movers were very patient and polite!

A removal company can pack your belongings correctly and appropriate to what they are, limiting breakages and damages, along with doing all the lifting and carrying. Furthermore, these professionals will disassemble and disconnect the furniture and whiteware, before reassembling and reconnecting it when you have moved to your new property.

> If you are paying for a removal company, personal recommendations are a good place to start. Also, sites like Which? provide an endorsement scheme by assessing traders and making credit, reference and administrative checks, along with a personal interview with a trained assessor, to ensure they are a reputable removal company before giving the company the official seal of approval.
>
> Choose 3 recommended removal companies for a quote from websites such as Which?, Checkatrade, Rated People. Prior to contacting them, check whether they are members of the British Association of Removers (BAR) and therefore meet the BAR's criteria on training, insurance, capacity and experience. Check that they are fully insured themselves and that they also

cover your possessions and valuables during transit (one does not necessarily preclude the other). Ensure you have the right level of cover from your removal company or ask to increase this if it is necessary. Some companies will not insure your move, or provide transit insurance, if they don't pack the items, so find out about this.

Estimated costs range from £400 to £1,200+ for a removal company, and £150 to £400 extra if the removals company is packing for you (increases depending on number of bedrooms). Ask for a quote from the 3 removal companies for either their packing and moving service, or just packing; request a quote on both if you haven't decided yet (on receipt of the quotes, you can compare the costs of each of the services). Each company should send people to your property to assess all your possessions, discuss your expected move date and confirm where you are moving to so that quotes can be prepared.

When the assessors are at your property, discuss the following:

- Any access issues with both properties (your current property and where you are moving to) and any parking issues there may be on the day.
- The move of frozen and chilled food from your fridge / freezer. Some removal companies will not take these due to removal conditions, so you may need to make separate arrangements for these. Or you may be allowed to move these items intact in your fridge / freezer, so find out what the guidelines are for each of the companies giving you a quote because they all have different rules. It's a good idea to deplete your fridge / freezer stocks as much as possible before a move, and not to re-stock anything other than necessary items, so that it's less of an issue when you move.
- Valuable or fragile items requiring special handling (e.g. artworks, musical instruments, and wine collections).
- Extra-large, unexpected or awkward to move objects (e.g. curtains, treadmill, fridge / freezers and fish tanks).
- Furniture or whiteware that will need to be disassembled and re-assembled (e.g. wardrobes) or disconnected and re-connected (e.g. washing machines).
- Any items stored in the loft, basement, shed or other outbuildings.

Once you have obtained and reviewed the quotes, if there is anything that is not clear, call the relevant removal company and ask for further information or clarification. Decide on whether you will proceed with a move only service and undertake the packing yourself, or the pack and move facility, then choose your preferred company. Let the relevant company know of your decision to proceed and reserve the date for your move, confirming that they can still meet your targeted move date. Advise them that you will be in touch to confirm your arrangement once exchange and completion dates are formally agreed.

Other moving services

Some real estate agents provide a moving service for buyers and sellers which includes providing meter readings, closing or transferring utility accounts, changing locks and furniture auctioning. Depending on your estate agent, this service could be free except for supplier charges (e.g. locksmiths).

A moving services company (rather than a removal company) is useful if you wish to pass all the moving activities when downsizing for yourself or for other people, whether it's to a smaller independent property, or to a retirement home, care home or sheltered accommodation. This will ensure you have assistance as well as help with counterbalancing the stress and effort of this activity. You should be able to obtain a no-obligation quote from companies that can provide the full package, from finding you a new home, planning your home move, re-organising personal and household effects and packing, to moving and unpacking. You can contact Age UK for contact details of trusted companies in your area or look up the Age UK Business Directory on the internet. You can follow the same process for finding the right moving service company as written in the section above for removal companies.

There are also specialist moving companies that can manage the entire relocation process, from finding you a property to move to, packing, moving and unpacking your belongings, selling your previous property, to auctioning surplus items. This service is chargeable, so contact the specialist moving companies directly for the services they offer and their prices as these vary from location to location.

External storage

Ascertain what additional storage requirements you have. If you require more storage space for your possessions than what your new property will provide, investigate the availability of storage depending on if you will need regular access to your belongings. Get quotes from 3 recommended storage facilities companies, having obtained confirmation that they have the appropriate storage available at the time you are planning to move.

Buy locks for self-storage units in advance of your move day. While most storage facilities have 24-hour access, they may only be manned for a limited time during the day, so if you are looking to purchase items from them (e.g. dust covers or packing material) you may need to purchase these in advance if arriving at the storage unit outside of normal business hours.

Insurance

Check that your contents insurer covers your possessions, including all your valuables, during your move (while you are transit). Find out what the value of the cover is and ensure this is the right amount as all your possessions will be in transit at the same time. You may be required by your insurers to pay a premium for this house removal transit insurance, or goods in transit insurance. Also check how long the transit cover period is; you don't want to be opening packing boxes a month after your move only to discover fragile items have been damaged and you can't claim for these because your transit cover only lasted for the first 5 days of your move. Consider cancellation protection for your van hire, removal company or moving services for any last-minute changes to your move.

Confirm with your Buildings and Contents Insurance what standard of locks need to be fitted to be compliant with the insurance policy. If you are having the locks changed in the property you are moving to (excludes rental properties), convey that information to the locksmith in advance of their scheduled fitting date.

If you have external storage, you will need to notify your contents insurance company of the type of external storage facilities you are intending to use. Check with your contents insurer if you are covered for this additional storage. If not, obtain quotes for the extra storage and decide on the best policy for your cover.

Local council services

> Contact your local council to find out what you will need to do to obtain permission to temporarily suspend parking bays or yellow line dispensation, so you can park the removal van in front of the house you are moving from, as well as in front of the house you are moving to, on the day of your move.

Confirm details of the temporary suspension cost (including the administration fees), timeframe and application process so that you can diarise this and make the application in a timely manner. Also find out what the refunds and change processes are in case your move date changes following the submission of your application. Some councils provide a refund if you advise them within the assigned timeframe but don't refund the administration fees because they need to cover the cost of the application, change and refund processes.

Find out what the refuse bin collection days and times are for both properties and check if you will be impacted by this. It can be a real nuisance when you are interrupted and having to shift a vehicle several times when you are in the middle of packing and moving.

Check when council tax payments are due, as well as details on obtaining bins, along with the correct stickers for bin collections, in case these are not in place at your new address.

Advise the council that you are expecting to buy the property in question. Find out how much notice they need you to provide them to make arrangements for your change of address and payment for council tax (these are usually transferred from one property to the next if both properties are in the same area).

Utilities

> Utility services include gas, electrics, water and telecommunications. Investigate what you will need to do to either move the utility services from your current property to your new address, or close existing accounts and start new ones with new suppliers.

When you are moving into a property, you do not need to use the same energy providers that are already supplying services to that property (unless you are moving into a rental property that has a stipulation in the rental contract is that the existing utilities providers cannot be changed). The same goes for TV, internet and telecom services - use online comparison websites to compare broadband packages and mobile deals for the area you are moving to. Check in advance the quality of mobile phone signal in the property you are moving to. If the signal is poor, it would be worth finding out who the best provider is for that area.

You can find out who the utilities providers are for your new property. Your solicitors, the agent or the current owners / occupiers of the property you are moving to can provide this information if you don't already have this (refer to the documents for the purchase of your new property).

You will need to choose a new telephone number if the telephone exchange is different from your existing one, otherwise you may want to retain your home telephone number as it's known to all your contacts. Your service provider will be able to check the existing line at your new address and advise what facilities you will need in case these are not available there currently. You may need your supplier to visit your new address, in which case, this will most likely need to be booked for a certain day and paid for.

If you are moving into rental a property, check this with the letting's agency or landlord.

Cleaners and gardeners

> While people may have intentions of leaving properties clean and tidy after they have vacated a property, it's not always possible to do this given the challenges of moving day and availability of time. We always have professional house cleaners for carpets, windows and ovens booked in advance to clean the entire property once it's been vacated by us so that the property is looking it's best when our buyers move in.

Newly refurbished properties can continue to have a lot of dust settling over a long period of time. Before we move into our own property, after it has been refurbished, we arrange for two separate professional house cleans to be undertaken – once shortly after the refurbishment has been completed, and then on again the day before we move in. Because we are in rental properties in between owning our properties, we are able to do this, but it may not be as convenient for you. We also have a professional general house clean done a few days after our move because there is so much traffic in and out of the house on move day, along with boxes being unpacked and dust settling everywhere.

Obtain quotes from reputable cleaning companies in your local area or through personal recommendations. Discuss your requirements and tentatively schedule all the cleaning services you will need for your move. Booking them in early means that they have a placeholder for your property cleaning as good cleaners tend to get booked up quickly.

Tentatively book your gardeners in advance for the final tidy up of the garden. They may be able to remove rubbish that remains on the property as professional gardeners can have access to places to leave their waste material.

Locksmith

We always have a locksmith booked on the day of completion to change and upgrade all the external door and window locks so that we have peace of mind regarding who has keys to enter our new property. You may wish to identify a local locksmith and discuss the doors and window locks you would like to have changed on the day of your move and ascertain how long they will need to spend at your property as well as the cost of the work. Ask them to tentatively schedule you in and let them know you will be in touch closer to the date, and at the latest, as soon as your move date is confirmed. Ensure you have spoken with your insurance company beforehand, so you can advise the locksmith of the British Standard locks required.

> You may want to wait until the end of your moving day before you have your locks changed so that the locksmith is not getting in the way of the movers and vice versa.

Mail redirection

It is worth familiarising yourself with the process to redirect your mail. You can apply for your mail to be redirected up to 6 months before, or 6 months after, your moving date. At this early stage you don't want to pay for the re-direction to take place in case there is a delay or a change in your purchase, but you want to find out what you need to do to re-direct mail and what evidence you will need to supply for this.

It takes 5 working days for mail re-direction to take effect, although it's best to apply 3 weeks before relocating. There are separate processes for redirection of personal and business mail. There are also different documents required for personal and business mail re-direction, so ensure you have these to hand and they don't get packed away.

The process and documents for mail re-direction are as follows:

- Personal mail redirection can be applied for online. You may not be required to provide any evidential information, but you will be asked security questions, so have access to documents such as bank/credit card/loan information or mobile phone contract details.
- Business mail re-direction cannot be done online. If your business address is the same as your home address, then you will need to complete the redirection and either post your form or visit a post office to lodge your application. Either print the online business redirection form or pick it up from a post office in readiness.

    When completing the form, you will need to provide evidence of company name and proof of address as follows:

    o A company bank statement, building society statement, or credit card statement.

    o Two different utility bills (not mobile phones or bills printed from the internet) or two different company invoices, or a rates demand.
- Sole traders also complete the business redirection form, but they can provide personal information for evidence e.g. personal bank account statements.

Documents for your move

Create a labelled file box containing all the documents you will need on the day of your move so that these don't get packed away. These include:

- Change of address forms and evidence documents for personal and business mail.
- The Fixtures and Fittings form and the Chattels list (if this is relevant) to check that all the items you have agreed as part of the purchase remain on the property. If any items are missing, they will need to be returned, replaced or compensated for.
- The floor plan with the sticker labels showing the rooms, locations of your furniture and where other possessions will be placed. Keep a few photocopied spares to hand out on the day. It's useful to have a readily available copy of the floor plans on every floor in the house so people can refer to it easily.

- Any contracts that are relevant for the day e.g. for the van hire or removal company.
- Utility meter locations so you can take the meter readings. Take the contact details of the utility companies, and the reference numbers for the move of your utilities, to your new property in case you find there are issues.

Handover to you

If you are moving into a property you have just purchased, keys to your new property will be made available to you once the buyer's solicitor has advised your solicitor that the full purchase monies have been received. You solicitor will then advise you and the agent of this so that the keys can be released to you.

Discuss with your solicitor, and confirm with the agent, how and when the keys to your new property will be made available to you. Where the keys are held by the agent, it is easier for them if you pick up the keys from their offices. However, it is always helpful if the agent can meet you at your new property to hand over the keys to you. This not only saves you time on a very busy day (especially if you are moving on that day), but it also gives you and the agent the opportunity to have a quick look around the property and ensure everything is as expected and in order before you move in.

When we are selling a property, we prepare a labelled Handover box for the new owners containing the following:
- Guarantees and warranties for recent damp-proofing, new boiler and appliances.
- Instruction manuals for the boiler, alarm, central heating, smart meters, underfloor heating, solar power controller, oven and white goods which will remain in the property.
- Details of any maintenance contracts in place currently, e.g. for the alarm.
- Locations of the gas, electrical and water meters, fuse box, water stopcock, security light switching, and any other electrical controllers.
- Allen keys and various window and door keys for the property on labelled key tags.
- Remote controls (e.g. for electric fires, air-conditioning, cooker hoods and garages).

Then just prior to us moving out, we also place any unattached sink, waste disposal unit, handbasin or bath plugs in a bag inside the box so these don't get packed by mistake. Ask the sellers to prepare a similar handover box for you so that it makes for an easier entry into your new property.

If you are moving into a rental property, keys to your new property will be made available to you on the first day of your new tenancy by the letting's agent or landlord. An Inventory Check-in Report is also most like to have been provided you.

Read this thoroughly and return it with any changes you have in the required timeframe. We usually accompany the Inventory Clark when they are going through the property, on our entry and exit from a rental property, so that we are aware of what is in the report.

In an apartment we rented in the City, we accompanied the Inventory Clark as she did the report on our entry into the rental property, but she was not happy with us being there so rushed through it. Later, we took photos of finely cracked tiles in the bathroom (which were not noted in the Inventory Report) and submitted these to the rental agent. The landlady and rental agent came to visit the property and couldn't believe that the damage wasn't done by us, but the dated photos provided irrefutable evidence that they were taken very soon after we arrived at the property, and even they could see that the cracks were old.

During our stay at the same apartment, we moved a sofa from against the wall into the middle of the lounge and noticed that it had radiator burn marks on it. The sofa was not placed against the wall radiator when we arrived at the property (it was against the opposite wall), so we were puzzled how the burn marks got there, but we decided to dismiss it and took no further action, thinking that the landlady would have known about it from the Inventory report done when the previous tenant left. When we moved from the rental property, the Inventory Report showed the damage to the sofa, and although we were not responsible for it, we were liable for the damage because we couldn't prove that we hadn't damaged the sofa. So unfortunately, we had to pay for it and the money was taken out of our rental deposit. Just as well we had taken photos of the cracked bathroom tiles because we have no doubt we would have had to pay for these as well!

Handover from you

> Prepare a Handover box for the new owners similar to what you have requested from the sellers of the property you are moving to. Refer to the section on *'Handover to you'*.

Like the handover of keys to you for your new property, you will need to make similar arrangements for handing over the keys for the property you are moving from. Ensure that there isn't a clash in the times for when you are providing keys to your existing property, obtaining keys to your new home or when you are moving.

Dependants

If you have small children, elderly relatives, anyone who is nervous about the move, or has special needs, consider how you will manage their move to minimise anxiety and disruption for everyone. You may want to make alternative arrangements for them to stay elsewhere while the move is underway. Discuss any plans with them where appropriate and make decisions together so that everyone is involved and informed, and expectations are managed. Your children may want to have sleepovers with friends, whereas elderly family members may want to have a quiet time with other relatives.

> If a decision is made that everyone will move together, make arrangements so that there is someone to keep an eye on the children as they will be unfamiliar with the new surroundings, as well as the people around them. Ensure that the remaining dependants can manage on their own while you are busy with the move, otherwise make arrangements for assistance.

Pets

> Having nervous pets around you on the day of the move can be distracting for you and troubling for the pets. Consider making arrangements for your pets so that they are accommodated elsewhere on the day of your move, otherwise they will get overwhelmed and anxious.

It may be prudent to arrange to relocate your pets for a few days before and after your property move. Once they have been relocated, and in the days leading up to your move, check in on them to help them feel more settled. You can also confirm they are comfortable and well cared for, so one less worry on the day of the move.

If you decide to take your pets with you on the day of your move, then consider taking advice from your vet, especially if your pets are anxious when travelling. Depending on how your pets will be transported, you may also need to consider sedation, especially if your pets are going overseas. Ensure you have the leads or leashes, as well as the correct carriers to place your pets into for transportation and confirm that their surroundings are well-ventilated while they are travelling.

Remember to take the relevant foods for your pets and have these easily available on the day of your move. You will also need to take into account feeding times as your vet may recommend not feeding your pets up to 12 hours before travelling so that they don't get ill.

Identify an area in your new property where you can place your pets, so they don't run away from their unfamiliar surroundings.

Make arrangements to update their identity tags and microchips so that if they do go missing, they can be found and returned as quickly as possible. You may also wish to keep a recent photo on hand in case it's required.

De-clutter

De-cluttering is part of planning your move so that you have fewer possessions to move. Otherwise you will move unnecessary items and need storage space for possessions that are superfluous. De-cluttering can help you to decide how much space you will need in your next property.

> We start our planning and de-cluttering as soon as we have made the decision to either sell our property or move out of a rental property. If we are selling, we usually rent a skip and declutter the entire property, disposing of unnecessary items and identifying possessions for donations. And if we can do without certain items until after we have moved, we start wrapping and packing these away, including personal items like photos and collectibles, or more general items household like crockery, pots and pans.

Pass redundant or surplus items on to charities, family and friends, or dispose of them either by selling or auctioning them off. Once they are out of sight, they will also be out of mind before long. You may also need to make space for new fixtures, fittings or chattels in your next property, which is a fun thing to look forward to.

Plan your de-cluttering time into your daily timetable so that you are not taken unawares as this activity can take up a vast amount of time (it's dependent on how often you stop to reminisce about each item!). If you spend 30 minutes a day on this task, starting in the smallest or easiest room, or area, you will be able to see quite an improvement in your clearance rate each week that passes.

Tools

Having a small set of tools on hand for the move is really useful, especially if you are undertaking the move yourself. You might need it for things like taking furniture apart and reassemble it at the other end, or to screw shelving units to a wall. Also make sure your cordless drill is charged up for moving day. A set of Allen keys may also prove handy. Buy what you need now so that you can have them at hand as you start your packing.

Packing material

If you are undertaking the packing yourself, identify the best places you can get boxes and packing materials. Obtain all your packing material as soon as possible and start your packing. You can find recycled removal boxes at Sadlers and Eco-boxes.

You can buy large wardrobe / garment removal boxes and transfer clothes from your wardrobe straight into these for your move (rather than packing them all and finding you have to re-iron them after they have spent a few days in suitcases or smaller boxes). These can be purchased online, e.g. at Packing Boxes and Argos.

If you are utilising a removal company for your packing and moving, ask them to deliver some packing boxes, vacuum storage bags, bubble / tissue wraps and tape to you in advance, so you can start with the small items you would like to pack (e.g. personal items and moving day boxes).

Protective flooring

We place mats on the ground to protect our floors and carpets as there is so much traffic through the doors when moving, particularly if it's a wet day. They are re-useable mats, so we pack them last when we are vacating a property. Then these are the first things out of the moving vans so that they are in place when the move starts at our new property. We use Proplex or Corex surface protection sheets as they stay flat on the ground and don't get tangled around legs like drop cloths do. You can buy these at Wickes, Corex or Universal Site Supplies.

Your shopping list

Start preparing a shopping list so that you can action it as soon as the exchange and completion dates, or your rental contract, are formally confirmed. Necessary items may include food, bedroom curtains, temperature-controlled packing, tools, pots and pans (including those for induction hobs where required), moving boxes, or protective flooring, so start your search for these items now and locate the best suppliers. If you may not have a lot of time between exchange and completion, consider buying these items now. In the unlikely event that you don't move to the property you have made an offer on this time, you will most probably still need all the items on your shopping list for your next property, so buying the items sooner rather than later means you can start your packing.

Valuables

Make on-hand or off-site arrangements for a safe place for all your personal and valuable items, e.g. sensitive documents, business contracts, share certificates, bearer bonds, passports, jewellery and watches. Pack and store these as early as possible, and you don't have to think about them again until you have moved into your new property.

Essentials for your move day

> We try and plan for as many things as possible to make our first night comfortable and to help settle in as quickly as we can. During our last move to a rental property, we tried to cook some eggs on the hob for a quick dinner, but the pan wouldn't heat up. After some time, we realised that we were using a pan that was not suitable for an induction hob. We had not used this type of hob previously, so this was a lesson to be aware of for next time. The following day we ordered a set of induction pots and pans and re-packed all our cookware (which had been carefully unpacked, re-washed and placed in the cupboards!).

If you are moving yourself, travelling a long distance, and it's a hot time of the year, then it will be necessary to consider how you will transport chilled and frozen food during the move. Consider buying some temperature-controlled packaging or gel packs for your move day. You can buy these at Chilled Packaging and JB Packaging. If you are unable to move the necessary foods, rather than throwing these out, plan to donate them to a nearby shelter or soup kitchen; you can search online and find out where the nearest ones are. You may be able to arrange for them to pick up the items a few days before your move, so it will be one less thing for you to think about on the day.

One of the first boxes we pack is the medical box, and this has all the medicines that may be required on the day of the move, as well as anything we will need for the first few days, so we don't have to search for any medicines. It includes a first aid kit in case of any small accidents. So, pack a medical box with all the necessary items that you and your family are likely to use, according to your needs, such as nebulisers, nebules, mouth and nose inhalers, hay fever medication, eye drops, ibuprofen, paracetamol, migraine tablets, plasters, bandages and antiseptic wipes.

We also pack a linen box especially for the first night of our move and have this on hand for ease of settling in after a very busy day. This box has the essentials for the bedrooms and bathrooms, including sheets, pillow cases, duvets, duvet covers, hand towels, towels and bath mats. You may want to include bedroom curtains for the main rooms so that you have privacy (in case these any of these rooms, e.g. the master bedroom, is overlooked).

We pack an overnight bag too for each person in the household to cover us for the night of the move. The bag contains a toothbrush, toothpaste and change of clothing so that we don't have to search for these in the multiple boxes in the various rooms.

Additionally, we always pack a separate survival box for the day of the move with a spare kettle, cups, spoons, tea, coffee, sugar, snacks, fruit, energy bars, cold drinks, cleaning materials, tea towels, hand towels, paper towels, loo rolls and rubbish bags. You and your helpers will need fuel on the day, along with all the other necessities, to keep you going. In case you don't have the facilities or power on at your new accommodation (or the kettles been packed!), also pack a full thermos with hot drinks or soup to sustain you.

Think of what you can have on the table quickly for dinner for your family and pets. You may choose to cook and freeze food for a few days in preparation for your move. Keep in mind that you will need to transport these so buy temperature control packaging if the property you are moving to is located a significant distance away.

Floor plan for your new property

> Now that you have de-cluttered, check that you can fit your belongings into your new property. If you have a floor plan for your new property, this will have the room sizes. Identify a space for each of your large pieces of furniture, then work through all your possessions until you have a home for everything. If you do not have a floor plan, see if you can obtain access to your new property, and draw your own rough floor plan. Using a tape measure, identify where your larger items will fit and mark these on your floor plan.

If you cannot fit all your possessions into your new home, determine whether you will need to let some or all the extra items go and de-clutter even further, or if you wish to store them for the foreseeable future (in which case you will need to make arrangements for these to be kept somewhere, whether with family, friends or in a paid storage unit).

As you are reviewing the floor plan, identify an area you can set aside for those boxes that don't appear to have a designated area of storage as there are always homeless items (e.g. you may not know which rooms your artwork will go into, so store these together in an area which will not have a lot of other furniture or other items so that you and others are not constantly falling over these items. Be wary of placing artworks, photos and books in an external storage area or garage as these could end up being damaged).

If you have dependants and pets moving with you on the day, consider allocating an area or room where you can locate them so that they are not disturbed by the move and the hectic nature of the day. Ensure this space is well aired. You may need a separate space for pets where you can place their food and water within the confines of the area, and without worry that the area may be soiled. Prepare a sign notifying people not to open the door otherwise they may escape and get lost.

Colour coding and labelling

Now that you know what you are taking with you, you can start packing up the rest of your house. If your removal company is packing for you, then sort through your possessions and place all the similar items together. You may decide to start wrapping and storing the items that are not necessary until you have moved.

If you are doing you own packing, then start wrapping and packing these possessions anyway. Items you can start on include collectibles, ornaments, toys, books, cookware, utensils and spare cutlery.

> On your new property's floor plan, colour code the rooms so that the colours on the boxes match. So, if you have a pink sticker on all the boxes for your bedroom, have a pink sticker denoting your bedroom on the new floor plan. This will help everyone involved in your move to know where to place all your possessions on moving day.

You can use the same colour stickers on the rooms you are vacating so that your removal company or those helping with your move know where to place boxes and items the (e.g. the pink sticker can also be placed on your current bedroom door). So, everyone will be aware that items from room with a pink sticker on the door go into boxes with pink stickers, and according to the new floor plan which also shows the placement of the pink sticker, which are then placed in the room with a pink sticker on the door in the new property.

Label all your boxes so that you know what is in them. If there are fragile or dangerous items in a box, these should be clearly marked as such. A room full of boxes with pink stickers will not tell you what the boxes contain, and you always end up with more boxes than you expect.

Removal companies generally label the box on top, writing on the box tape itself. You can re-use the boxes if you are able to do this. But if boxes are placed on top of each other, you will need to remove the top boxes to identify what is in the lower boxes. So, you may want to write a short label on the side of the boxes to identify them from both top and sides. This will take more time, but it will make for an easier identifying process when you have a whole house full of boxes to unpack. You can then choose the most important boxes to unpack first before tackling the rest of them. Knowing how long your transit insurance covers you for also helps as you can focus on unpacking boxes that have fragile or special items to check for damage and breakage before the insurance runs out.

It's also useful to place an arrow showing which way up a box should be placed while loading, unloading or storing.

Chapter 6. MOVING HOME

Coordinate your move

The following activities follow on after you have completed your planning. Organising your move is easier and more fluid once all your planning has been properly and completely finished and you have attended to as many of the details as possible.

Finalise your move date

Once your exchange and completion dates have been formally agreed by your solicitor, you can start the process of coordinating for your move.

Confirm the date with your chosen removal company or moving services and check that they can still meet your move date. You will need to make the payment for this now if you haven't already done so to reserve the vehicle.

If you are hiring a van to undertake the move yourself, confirm the date with the van hire company and ask them to verify that the right sized vehicle is available for you to pick up on the date it's scheduled for. Make your payment as required.

If you are obtaining help with your move (e.g. for disassembling, moving and re-assembling furniture or disconnecting, moving and re-connecting white goods), confirm the availability of the people concerned because you need to know that they will be there on the correct date, and at the right time, to assist you.

If you are utilising removal services or specialist moving services, contact them to confirm your requirements and make the required payment to secure your move date.

We make sure that we let our neighbours know the date on which we are moving and that we will have large trucks parked outside our property so that they can move / use their vehicles accordingly. It helps to minimise the risk of damage to relationships and vehicles!

If you still require storage externally after you have de-cluttered, confirm with your chosen offsite storage company that they still have the appropriate storage available for you on the required date. Pay for this facility in advance, if necessary, and consider starting to move items into the storage locker before your actual move date. This will make it easier for you on the day of your property move as you will only need to move into your new home then, instead spending the additional time and effort in moving your belongings into your storage locker as well on the same day.

Contact your utility service providers and either move your utilities suppliers from your current property to your new one for the required date or open accounts with new suppliers. Advise the relevant suppliers to close your existing accounts on your last day so that you don't continue to be charged, and therefore end up paying bills for two properties.

> At a previous property, the sellers didn't advise the gas and electricity companies of their new address, or that they had moved, and the utility company thought we were responsible for paying for the services supplied to the previous owners. We updated the utilities companies of the situation and the bills were then re-sent to the correct users. So, when you receive the first few utility bills, check that the correct name is on the invoice (i.e. yours), the supply address is for your new property (and not the new address for the previous owners) and the right date is applied to the bills (starting on the day that you bought the property or when your rental contract started).

Advise your local council of the date of the change in property ownership and confirm arrangements for the delivery of any bins and stickers required. You may also want to ask for details of the bin collections days so that you are aware when these are.

> Confirm any insurances that you need and make the payment for these, e.g. for while you are in transit, or for any additional storage.

Confirm the dates with your professional cleaners, gardeners and locksmith so that everyone knows your move is still taking place on the date it was booked for. If you are unable to meet them at your property on the planned dates for each of these services, make arrangement for keys to be delivered or picked up, or for someone else to meet them and show them around and confirm the work to be done.

Check and verify that the arrangements you have made for your dependants are still workable and in place (e.g. friends are still able to have your children stay for a sleepover). If any of your dependants are going to stay with friends or family earlier than on the day of the move, confirm this now so that you can put together the necessary 'away' bags as well as pack any surplus items. If everyone is moving together, ensure they all know and understand what they need to do leading up to the move and on the day of the move (e.g. the children's favourite toys and books have been selected to be available during the move, while packing the rest of the possessions in preparation for the move. On the day of the move, put those selected toys and books into one room until you are ready to take them to your new home. This will ensure they don't get packed into the various boxes.

Move your pets out of your property according to the arrangements you have made, and as soon as possible. You can then label and pack all the items belonging to your pets. If you are not going to move your pets before your home move, ensure that they're secured or restrained (e.g. a lead on your dog) and fed at the appropriate time before moving.

Make arrangements for any frozen or chilled foods that you are moving. Consider buying extra chiller boxes and packaging that can provide thermal protection so that your food does not defrost in transit. If you are donating food you are unable to take with you, confirm that someone from the shelter or soup kitchen is either able to pick the items up, or you can drop the food off at a local foodbank or supermarket collection point, on a day that is suitable for you.

Refer to your shopping list and complete your shopping for any necessary items you still need e.g. food, bedding, curtains, packing and garment boxes.

> Pack and store away your valuables, e.g. jewellery and important documents.

Change of address notices

Once you have exchanged, and the completion date is confirmed by your solicitor, or if you are moving into a rental property, when the start date of your rental contract is confirmed, organise the re-direction of your personal and business mail to your new home (at least 5 days before your move date if possible).

Use the Royal Mail postal redirection service for your home move (and for your business move if it's also the same as your home address). It's also worthwhile using organisations such as 'iammoving' to assist you with your change of address (this is an online change of address service via which you can notify over 1500 organisations).

> If you find that you have less than 5 days between exchange and completion of contracts and your move becomes imminent, you may want to provide your new address to the people moving into your property and ask them if they could forward your mail to your new address for the initial days after the move. If this is an issue, perhaps they could just put your mail into a post office box and within a week the redirection will take effect.

If you have sufficient time between exchange and completion of contracts, start to inform all the relevant authorities of your new address. This may take some time with all the other activities you are undertaking to prepare for your move, but if you have the re-direction in place, your mail will be sent to you at your new address for the period of time you have selected for the redirection services (e.g. 3, 6 or 12 months).

We have found that opting for paperless communications with as many organisations as possible helps to minimise our postal mail, so this makes address changes easier for us.

The list below shows where your change of address details may need to be advised. It includes a range of services, but is not exhaustive:

- Your solicitor
- Your employer
- Bank
- Credit card
- Pension
- Benefits (child benefits)
- Savings and investments
- Shares
- Insurance (vehicle, home, building, business, travel, medical, life, pet)
- Vehicle (DVLA for driver's licence and registration, breakdown services)
- Professional services (doctor, dentist, accountant)
- Schools, college, nursery
- Oyster card
- House alarm company
- Vet and pet identity tags
- Inland Revenue
- Electoral Register
- Mobile phone company
- Landline phone company
- TV & satellite service provider
- Internet provider
- Utility companies (water, gas, electric)
- Local council (council tax, refuse collections)
- Store and loyalty cards
- Library
- Clubs & associations (gym, football, golf, wine, coffee, scouts / girl guides
- Catalogue providers / subscriptions
- Paper and / or milk delivery
- Other

Pack your belongings

Refer to the *'Essentials for your move day'* section in this book.

Keep the Handover box you have prepared for the new owners in a safe place as you have important documents, labelled keys, Allen keys and remote controls in the box which will provide for ready access to anyone if the box is lost.

Keep your 'Documents' box on hand so that you can access it quickly and easily when you get to your new property.

> Also pack the following boxes separately so that you can access all these items collectively and as required during your move:
> - A medicine box with all the requisite medication.
> - A linen box for the first night of your move, with the basics for bedrooms and bathrooms.
> - An overnight bag for each person in the house, with essentials and clothing.
> - A survival box with the necessities required in the kitchen and WC for you, your family and all your helpers on the day.

Confirm that your valuables are already packed and in a safe place.

If your packing is going to be done by your chosen removal company, then you may want to accumulate similar items as these become available (e.g. mirrors and photos which are being taken off the walls) if they are going into different rooms in your new property. It's always easier choosing from a group of items collated rather than utilising the first thing that comes to hand. You may also wish to stay on top of your rota for delivering refreshments while directing the packing and coordination of what will go in which room.

If you are doing your own packing, continue with this and keep to the same colour stickers with your labelling and boxing that you set up initially so that you have the remaining boxes coordinated, make unpacking easier.

Move clothes from wardrobes into the garment boxes and pack away any other items in wardrobes (e.g. shoes), drawers, tallboys and bedside cabinets, clearing out each bedroom as much as possible so that you only have essential items remaining in these rooms until the day of the move.

Pack the remaining items and clear out all the rooms, emptying kitchen cupboards, drawers and bathroom cabinets. Don't overfill boxes when packing; keep in mind that you will be lifting all the boxes when you're moving and / or unpacking, so keep the box weight manageable.

Similarly, don't put heavy items all together in a big box (e.g. a large box of books). Items that are delicate or scratch easily need to be wrapped individually and placed in smaller boxes marked 'Fragile'. You may want to invest in plastic storage boxes to pack your fragile items, which you can find at Big Dug or Ryman Stationery.

Dangerous items and liquids should be placed in separate boxes and split up according to where they are used (e.g. cleaning supplies for the kitchen and bathroom should be separated from plant fungicides). They can then be placed in the relevant areas when unloading. Ensure these are clearly labelled and not able to be tampered with or opened by small children or pets. Lockable plastic storage boxes are useful for packing dangerous items. You can buy these from places like Solent Plastics and Amazon.

Box up any items that are outside in the garden, including pot plants. There may also be things that are in outbuildings, sheds or garages that need to be packed and ready for removal. If things are too big to pack (e.g. lawnmowers) then these need to be placed together with any other items outside the house so that they can be all loaded in the removals van collectively and moved to your new property.

While dismantling or disconnecting any items, ensure that all the related fixings are kept together (e.g. nuts, bolts, screws, fasteners and any tools required) in a bag and fix or tape it to the item so that everything required for re-assembling or re-connecting is available. Label the bag of fixings and tools in case it comes away during the move. We left Allen key sets for our buyers so that it would be easy for them to put curtains in their new home.

Try and have an early night before your move day!

Activities for your moving day

It's going to be a long and frenetic day, so start with a healthy and hearty breakfast! Expect today to go smoothly because you have done a vast amount of work to ensure this.

Keys to your new property

Ensure you have access to a set of keys, or you are meeting the agent (who will have the keys) at your new home, in time for when your removal van arrives at your new property. Otherwise a lot of time can be wasted waiting for keys. Some companies charge overtime if people do not have their property open for unloading within a certain timeframe because it means their movers are being held up. If you are moving yourself, then you may be asked for extra money if you are late in returning the vehicle you have hired.

Leaving your current property

Check that you have the *Handover* box for the property buyers in a safe place, so it doesn't get packed away. Place any last-minute items in the box, e.g. waste disposal plugs. After we have moved all our possessions out of a property, we leave this box on the kitchen benchtop so that it is visible and easily accessible by the new owners.

Ensure you have your *'Documents'* box to hand. It will have copies of your floor plan, locations of meters for the new property, chattels list and furniture and fittings form.

Before your helpers and the removal people arrive, place mats on the ground so that your floor is protected as much as possible.

If you have dependants moving with you, see if you can arrange an area for them away from the upheaval where they can be until you are all ready to leave for your new property. Make sure any pets are fed as required, secured and placed in an appropriate place, ready for transportation. Take your pet foods and have these easily accessible.

If you are moving yourself, pack any remaining boxes and load them onto the van. Empty out your fridge and freezer, putting them into temperature-controlled packaging. If you are using a packing and moving service, ensure all your possessions have been packed and moved into the removal van, including food from the fridge and freezer. Thaw out any meals already cooked and frozen in preparation for dinner on the night of your move.

Once all your possessions have been packed and moved into the removal van, do a final check over. You will not have free access to the property after you have moved out and handed the keys over, so this is the last time for you to confirm that you have thoroughly examined the entire property before leaving. Ensure that everything, inside and outside, has been packed by checking all the cupboards, drawers, pantry, outbuildings, garages and sheds. Pay attention to out-of-reach areas like high cupboards and loft spaces.

Check that all the necessary whiteware has been disconnected and is on the van or truck. You may want to ask your movers to load your fridge / freezer last on the van so that it's one of the first items to be unloaded and switched on – this will allow you to place all your frozen items back in quickly. Pack the protective covers for your floors last so that these are easily available for your use again before the van unloading starts at your new property. Also, if you have dependants who need seating as soon as you arrive at your new property, arrange for some garden or foldaway chairs to be packed into the truck last so they will be first to be taken off the truck at the other end.

Ensure all the rubbish has been removed from the property because this is your responsibility and you can be liable for the cost of removal and cleaning if the property is not left in a suitable condition.

> When we purchased our previous property, the sellers left a large amount of rubbish outside the front door, including old mattresses and boxes. We rang our solicitor and the agent, advising them both that we would be calling a removal company to take away the garbage and that the sellers would be expected to pay for this. Very shortly afterwards, the seller's removal van arrived to take away the rubbish.

Take your exit meter readings in case there are any disputes in future. We usually take a photo on our phone's camera so that there is date and time stamp evidence on hand. Close the property, ensuring all the windows and external doors are locked properly. Remember to set the alarm.

Hand over the keys as arranged (e.g. to the real estate agent, new owners or rental company). Leaving keys in the house through a mail slot may not be a good option if they can be seen or reached.

Arriving at your new home

Pick up the keys to the new property as arranged or meet the agent at the property so that you can both go through the house together and ensure everything is in order.

As soon as you have access to your home as the new owner, check against the Fixtures and Fittings form, and Chattels list if this is relevant, to ensure that all the agreed items have remained at the property. Let your solicitor know as soon as possible if any items are missing so that they can be returned, replaced or compensated for by the sellers. During a move, items can be packed away unintentionally, so the sellers need to be advised what items are missing and to either return them or recompense you for them.

> We had a situation where it was agreed that the cooker in the kitchen was to remain, but in fact it was removed, causing damage to the surrounding kitchen cupboards. Lights were also removed, leaving dangerously exposed wires at head height. These items were not removed unintentionally!

Check that no changes have been made to the property from when you agreed your offer. This could include the removal of expensive floor tiles which have been swapped with vinyl flooring, or the removal of a shed or outbuilding. Make sure that the sellers have left the property (including the loft, basement, garage and / or outbuildings) clean and tidy, otherwise they can incur costs for the removal of their rubbish if you have to arrange it.

Have your solicitor's report on the Land Title to hand as this will provide you with the location of the water stopcock, electricity and gas meters so you can identify the location of these utilities and meters. Take all the meter readings at your new property in case of disputes later on. Using your phone is a good way to record the details as this provides photo evidence. You will then have the correct details to hand if your first utility bills at your new property show different readings.

You may want to provide a meal for your movers and helpers as an act of thanks and goodwill because everyone has worked hard to get you to this place. We bought fish and chips to feed and invigorate us all before the unloading of our possessions began – the shop was on the way to our new home and everyone approved of the choice of food!

When you open the doors and enter your new home, keep in mind that it's most likely to have been recently vacated and that it may not be cleaned and presented to your satisfaction – after all the place is empty, and there may be some resultant scratches or small damage from people having moved their belongings out, leaving furniture marks and previously unseen stains. Don't let these things be the overriding factor in your arrival at your new home. You will be living there now and will have the opportunity to put on a coat of paint and personalise it to your heart's content. So, enjoy the moment you have arrived at and feel the joy of owning this property and making it your home. You've made it!

> If you have dependants moving with you, ensure that they are out of the vehicles and fed as quickly as possible. Then move them into a room together, along with the necessary toys, books, games and gadgets, so that they can keep a look out for each other as well as keep away from any harm while the move is in progress.
>
> Similarly, with pets, get them out of the vehicle and settled in as a matter of priority. Provide food and water as appropriate and keep them in a closed room so they don't run away. Place a sticker on the room door so that people (including children) don't open the door and let your pets out.

Check that all the rubbish has been removed from the property. You should have 'vacant possession' of the property, as noted in the Property Information Form exchanged between all parties, and it should have been left in a clean and tidy condition. If this is not the case, and the property has not been left according to how you expected it to be, contact your solicitor and the agent as soon as possible. If you are moving into a rental property, the landlord or previous tenant should have organised the cleaning of the property. If it has not been cleaned, contact the lettings agent / landlord and get it rectified.

> Also confirm that all chattels, furniture, fixtures and fittings have remained on the property as agreed – you can check these against the lists you have on hand in your 'Documents' box or folder. Again, if there are items missing or not left as agreed, contact your solicitor and the agent as soon as possible.

Ensure that all the utilities are also working as expected (e.g. lights and heating) otherwise if you have no lights, hot water, heating, or telephone signal, you will need to call the utilities services companies (details of each of these are in the *'Documents'* box you have).

Place mats on the ground to protect your floors and carpet in your new property. Place a sticker on the doors of the relevant rooms, isolating the 'spare' room where all the extra boxes which may not have a home yet, or the areas for which may be overflowing, have a space for placement.

Take your removal people and helpers into your new property and show them each of the rooms. If you have pets on the property, alert them to this so that they don't open the door to that particular room or area. Share the floor plan with them before they start unpacking so that they know where all your furniture, chattels and other items will go. The floor plan should be easy to follow as it will be colour coordinated and labelled. Provide a spare copy of the floor plan to the removal company team leader and leave a copy in the first room to be entered on each of the floors in the property so that it's available to check against.

If the fridge and freezer are already in the property, check that these are switched on and are working properly. If you are transporting the fridge and freezer to the property, make sure they get plugged in as soon as possible (and are working properly) once they are unloaded from the truck. While it's advised that gas systems need 24 hours to settle after being moved, you may not have much choice in the matter and may need to re-stock at the first opportunity so that your chilled and frozen food remains unspoilt.

We unpack the fridge and freezer boxes first. Then we unpack the bigger boxes in our kitchen as quickly as possible on the day of the move (while the movers are still there), so that the kitchen is set up quickly and they can take the empty boxes away with them.

Locate and unpack your essential boxes, making sure they are in the right rooms. Place the medicine box within easy reach (but not accessible to children) and remember where you have placed it (you may want to let other household members know so that they can remind you later if necessary).

Beds which are going to be used that night are also made up quickly as one of the initial tasks before too many other items are placed in the bedrooms.

Big boxes are unpacked as quickly as possible, even if things are not stored away yet, to remove the boxes from the house. It's much easier to put things into place later on when you can see them, rather than having to manoeuvre through the mountain of boxes.

> Whether your move is being undertaken by a removal company or you have help with your move, check the following before everyone leaves and ensure these are done
>
> - Furniture is re-assembled.
> - Whiteware is re-connected.
> - The boxes are in the correct rooms, otherwise ask for them to be moved to the appropriate room.
> - Boxes which have already been unpacked are removed from the property. Removal companies are happy to take away their boxes because they can re-use them. After the move day, you can call them to pick up the empty boxes when you have a significant enough number for them to collect.

If you have the locksmith there at the end of the day, advise exactly which locks on the property need to be changed. Confirm with the locksmith that British Standard locks are being secured so that these are in line with your home insurance policy.

Once your helpers and the removal people have left, take a deep breath and stop for a cup of tea! You have now moved in and can take as long as you like to unpack and get settled in. See to any dependants and pets to ensure they are comfortable. Everyone will get more familiar with their new home in the next few weeks.

Congratulations and well done! We wish you all the very best in your new home and hope you love living there!

Checklist – Moving home

The following Checklist will help you to plan and track your progress through this process.

Plan and prepare for your move

☐ If you are undertaking the packing and moving yourself but need to hire a van to move:
　☐ Obtain 3 quotes from recommended van hire companies.
　☐ Choose your company and reserve the required sized van.
　☐ Check that you have the correct driver's licence 'entitlement' for the vehicle.
　☐ Make arrangements for people to assist you on moving day.
☐ Obtain 3 quotes from the removal company and reserve the date for your move.

External storage

☐ Organise additional offsite storage and reserve the storage locker or facility.
☐ Collect storage instructions and buy locks for self-storage units in advance.

Insurance

☐ Confirm with your contents insurer you are covered during your move and in transit.
☐ Obtain cancellation protection for your van hire or removal company for any changes.
☐ Confirm with your insurer what BS locks are required by your insurance policy.
☐ Check with your insurer if you are covered for external storage facilities.

Local council services

☐ Obtain details on temporarily suspending parking bays or yellow line dispensation.
☐ Check with your council when tax payments are due.
☐ Obtain information on bins, bin stickers and collection days for your new address.

Utilities

☐ Contact all your utility providers (gas, electric, water, etc) and find out details for:
　☐ Closing the relevant accounts at your current property.
　☐ Opening these accounts at your new address.

Cleaners and gardeners

☐ Book cleaners and gardeners for the house you are leaving and moving to (if needed).

Locksmith

☐ Book a locksmith and advise the British Standard door and window locks you need.

Chapter 6. MOVING HOME

Mail redirection
- ☐ Find out how to redirect your personal mail and what evidence you need to provide.
- ☐ Print the online business redirection form or pick it up from a post office in readiness.

Documents for your move
- ☐ Fill a labelled file box with all the documents you will need on hand for moving day:
  - ☐ Change of address forms and evidence documents for personal and business mail.
  - ☐ The Fixtures and Fittings form and the Chattels list (if purchasing a property).
  - ☐ A floor plan with the sticker labels showing the rooms and locations of your items.
  - ☐ Any contracts that are relevant for the day e.g. for the van hire or removal company.
  - ☐ Utility meter locations, contact details of utility companies and reference numbers.

Handover to you
- ☐ Confirm with your solicitor and agent / landlord how and when you will receive the keys.
- ☐ Request the sellers prepare a Handover box for you which contain the following:
  - ☐ Guarantees and warrantees for damp-proofing, new appliances and boiler.
  - ☐ Instruction manuals for appliances, electrical systems and controllers.
  - ☐ Details of any maintenance contracts in place currently, e.g. for the house alarm.
  - ☐ Locations of the utility meters fuse box, water stopcock, security light switching.
  - ☐ Window and door keys for the property.
  - ☐ Remote controls (e.g. for electric fires, cooker hoods and garages).

Handover from you
- ☐ Prepare a Handover box for the new owners.

Dependants
- ☐ For any dependants stressed by the move, plan for them to stay elsewhere on the day.
- ☐ If everyone is moving together, make arrangements for assistance with dependants.

Pets
- ☐ Make arrangements for your pets to be accommodated elsewhere during your move.
- ☐ If they are moving with you, have ventilated transport, carriers and pet food.
- ☐ Identify an area in your new property for your pets to be secure during the move.
- ☐ Take a photo for ID and arrange to update their identity tags and microchips.

De-clutter
☐ Begin de-cluttering well in advance and donate or sell items that are no longer needed.

Tools
☐ Have a set of tools and Allen keys handy in preparation for your packing and moving.

Packing material
☐ If packing yourself, get the boxes and packing materials and start packing.
☐ If using a removal company, ask for boxes / tape / paper to be delivered in advance.

Protective flooring
☐ Investigate where you can buy re-useable protective flooring and buy these now.

Your shopping list
☐ Prepare a shopping list for food, curtains, cool boxes, cookware for induction hobs, etc.
☐ Start your search for these items and buy now, including non-perishable food items.

Valuables
☐ Arrange a safe place for your valuable items – documents, passports, jewellery, etc.

Essentials for your move day
☐ Buy temperature-controlled packaging or gel packs for your chilled and frozen food.
☐ Pack a medical box for the first few days of your move and have this on hand.
☐ Pack a linen box for the first night of your move and have this on hand.
☐ Pack an overnight bag for each person in the household for the night of the move.
☐ Pack a separate food, drink, toilet, cleaning, pet food survival box for moving day.
☐ Cook and freeze meals in advance.

Floor plan for your new property
☐ Confirm large pieces of furniture will fit by measuring and marking them on a floor plan.
☐ If any will not fit, sell or give them away or organise to have them stored.
☐ Allocate on the floor plan a separate safe space for dependants or pets for moving day.

Colour coding and labelling
☐ On your new floor plan, colour code the rooms and match with the moving boxes.
☐ Label the boxes with their contents as well as any delicate or dangerous items.

Coordinate your move
- [ ] Start this once exchange and completion dates, or new tenancy dates, are agreed.

Finalise your move date
- [ ] Confirm with the van hire company the right sized vehicle is available and pay for it.
- [ ] Confirm with the people helping you with your move they are still available.
- [ ] Inform your neighbours the date you are moving and of the trucks parked outside.
- [ ] If using offsite storage, pay for the facility and start moving items into it.
- [ ] Arrange with your utility providers to close, open or move accounts for each property.
- [ ] Advise your local council of the change of ownership and arrange for bins and stickers.
- [ ] Confirm the dates with your professional cleaners, gardeners and locksmith.
- [ ] Confirm any insurances that you need and make the payment for these.
- [ ] Confirm the arrangements you have made for your dependants are still in place.
- [ ] Move your pets into their alternative accommodation as soon as possible.
- [ ] For any frozen or chilled foods buy additional chiller boxes or donate any food.
- [ ] Refer to your shopping list and complete your shopping for any necessary items.
- [ ] Pack and store your valuables, e.g. jewellery and documents.

Change of address notices
- [ ] Re-direct your personal and business mail once exchanged, or rental contract signed.
- [ ] Provide your new address to those moving into your property for forwarding your mail.
- [ ] Inform all the relevant authorities of your new address.

Pack your belongings
- [ ] Refer to the *'Essentials for your move day'* section earlier in this book.
- [ ] Keep the Handover box for the new owners in a safe place.
- [ ] Keep your Documents box on hand for when you get to your new property.
- [ ] If you haven't already done so, pack a medicine, linen, survival box and overnight bag.
- [ ] Confirm that your valuables are already packed and in a safe place.
- [ ] Keep to the same colour stickers with your labelling and boxing for easier coordination.
- [ ] Pack, leaving only the essential items remaining in rooms until the move.
- [ ] Pack all remaining items, clear out each room, including kitchen / bathroom cupboards.
- [ ] Put dangerous items and liquids in separate boxes according to where they are used.
- [ ] Keep all nut, bolts, fittings together when dismantling or any items.

Activities for you moving day

Keys to your new property
- [ ] Ensure you have the keys to your new home in readiness for you and the movers.

Leaving your current property
- [ ] Have the *Handover* box for the new buyers in a safe place with any loose sink plugs.
- [ ] Have your *Documents* box to hand, with the floor plan, chattels list and meter locations.
- [ ] Place protective flooring or mats on the floor to protect it during the move.
- [ ] If you have dependants moving with you, locate them in a safe place until you all leave.
- [ ] Ensure any pets are fed, secured and in a safe place ready for transportation.
- [ ] Thaw out any frozen meals in preparation for dinner on the night of the move.
- [ ] Do a final check everywhere – pantry, loft, outbuildings and garage.
- [ ] Check that all the necessary whiteware has been disconnected and on the truck.
- [ ] Have your fridge freezer loaded onto the truck last to be first off at the new property.
- [ ] Pack the protective covers for your floors last so they are available for unpacking.
- [ ] Pack several chairs last to be unloaded first for any dependants needing seating.
- [ ] Ensure all the rubbish has been removed from the property.
- [ ] Photograph the meter readings when you exit the property.
- [ ] Lock all windows and doors, set the house alarm and hand over the keys as arranged.

Arriving at your new home
- [ ] Pick up the keys to the new property as arranged.
- [ ] Allow time for a meal break and rest for everyone – shout a round of fish and chips!
- [ ] Settle in your pets, provide them food and water and keep them in a safe place.
- [ ] Check that all rubbish has been removed from the property.
- [ ] Confirm that all chattels, furniture and fittings have remained at the property as agreed.
- [ ] Photograph all the meter readings at your new property.
- [ ] Ensure that all the utilities are also working as expected (e.g. lights and heating).
- [ ] Place mats or protective flooring on the ground to protect your floors and carpet.
- [ ] Identify a 'spare' room for all extra boxes that do not have a home.
- [ ] Place a colour coded sticker on the door of each room for the boxes for that room.
- [ ] Have the fridge / freezer are unloaded, switched on and re-pack the contents.
- [ ] Locate and unpack your essential boxes, making sure they are in the right rooms.
- [ ] Place the medicine box within easy reach (but not accessible to children).
- [ ] Make up beds before too many other items are placed in the bedrooms.
- [ ] Check whiteware is connected and furniture is re-assembled before the movers leave.
- [ ] If a locksmith has been booked, confirm they are fitting the required BS locks.
- [ ] Congratulate yourself on a job well done and enjoy your new home!

Chapter 7

MANAGING STRESS, ISSUES AND CONFLICT

Overview

Each phase of the property process brings stress, issues and conflict to some level.

In buying and selling, you have advocates in the form of your solicitor or conveyancer who can assist and advise you through each matter. With moving, you have advice from organisations on how to best direct your efforts and obtain help. Though you still need to manage the extent of it, and how it impacts you, these structures and advocates advise and assist you to deal with stress.

> Generally, the longest period of major anxiety occurs when renovating a property. Then your stress, issue and conflict management skills really need to come to the fore. The Q&A section at the end of this chapter deals with issues arising during property refurbishments projects and aims to assist you by providing guidance for resolution.

Managing stress

How do we manage stress and emotional upheaval during this time? We are usually working full time in the city while simultaneously undertaking one of these phases, so we have to make certain that we keep on top of everything, whether it's our projects and assignments at work, or our personal ventures.

Buying, undertaking a renovation project, selling or moving home can be a time of great anxiety and pressure, so it's a period where planning well in advance has proven to be invaluable for us. Having a plan also ensures that we have a view of the entire process, end-to-end, otherwise things can easily slip off our radar during these times of heightened activity. Additionally, it helps us in managing our time and efforts in an efficient manner. Invariably, advanced planning helps us to manage stress and undertake the numerous activities required during these very busy months.

So, have a plan. If you haven't planned to be at a certain place or time, then how will you know when you've arrived? Not having a blueprint to manage the process and the outcome is planning to fail. You don't need to over-think or over-plan before you take any steps, but just make sure that you plan appropriately, relevantly and sufficiently.

When you have costed out your property purchase or renovation project, you need to ensure it is going to fit with your available budget. Nothing creates stress and strain faster than financial worries. Decide how much you have to spend and stick to that figure. Step away if you need to and save more before you purchase or renovate.

There are always unanticipated stresses, either affecting us directly or indirectly during any of the phases. There are so many activities and people involved, with everyone having their own area of expertise and say in any matter. During these times, it is really important to ensure that we keep communications open with all the relevant parties. We step in where necessary, whether it's getting information to our buyers by contacting them directly or following up on goods deliveries that other people are responsible for.

We have found that the most important thing for us to do during these periods of high activity and strain is to remain aligned with each other and maintain our focus as a couple.

We try and keep to a good diet, continue with our exercise schedule, and get as much rest as possible so that our stamina is maintained in order to deal with all the activities and decisions required during these constrained and exhausting periods.

But it's not always possible to stay focused and well managed. If you find that things have become unmanageable, you can decide to step away from most things at any time, including your property purchase and sale (unless you have got past the stage of exchanging contracts). Sometimes you just have to move away to gain perspective.

When it all becomes too much for us and we feel that we have entered a never-ending story during any of these phases, we take a break for a few days and get away from it all. Then we can return energised to pick things up again in a better state. It also means that this allows a short separation from the relevant parties (buyers, sellers or builders) and the time apart permits all parties to obtain some space as well as time to gain clarity.

> It's important not to spread yourself too thin during these months. Frayed nerves and exhaustion will take their toll, relationships can suffer and falling out with your employer is also a real possibility if you're burning the midnight oil.

Get as much advice as you can before you finalise your plans on any of the phases, asking friends, colleagues and anyone else you know who has completed a similar or recent purchase, sale, renovation or move. Join online forums to obtain advice; people are likely to have some useful tips on surviving each of the phases while maintaining sanity!

Get help where you need it and outsource what you can so it's beneficial to all parties. Having someone cleaning your house helps you out and provides the other person with the opportunity to earn a living.

A property project is exciting, but it can also be stressful. There can be cost overruns, delays, issues and disputes with trades, planning permissions dragging on or denied, redundancies, and so on. Where possible the stress needs to be managed because at some point you'll feel the strain, and so will those around you. However strict and structured your plan, build in some time to take a break. If money is tight, plan a day out away from everyone and anything demanding your attention. Hop on a plane and recharge your batteries for a couple of days if this is affordable. One of us goes fishing for the day and the other paints – you can surely guess which one of us does what!

Issue management and conflict resolution

If you are having work done on your property, and there is a problem caused by the builder or contractor, you expect to be able to discuss this rationally and professionally in the first instance. You should also be able to have the problem resolved by the contractor, or at least get some of your money back. This is not always the case.

> To deal with issues and conflict resolution with your build team, try your best at all times to maintain a good relationship with all the trades involved because this helps everyone. It's not always easy, as some contractors don't need help to give themselves a bad reputation. You may decide not to work with them again, so see this as sufficient recompense. Keep your eyes on the prize because you will reap the benefits of having a renovated property with an increase in valuation!

Renovations are notorious for overspends and getting out of hand. One of the major concerns is costs and available budgets. Once you have collated all the costs for your renovation project, confirm your budget and make sure that you stick to it. It's your responsibility and not the contractor's fault or problem if you don't manage your finances well. If they have completed the work as agreed, then it's really important that they get paid quickly. Otherwise, if there are issues and conflict arising from lack of payment, then they could take you to court to obtain relief.

If you need to, delay your renovation project until you have sufficient finds to complete it, rather than over-dependence on overdrafts, credit cards and other loans. To save money, many singles and couples live alongside their renovation

Chapter 7. MANAGING STRESS, ISSUES AND CONFLICT   295

work, or perhaps worse, in a tiny caravan on site. This can be really stressful, especially if it is getting close to winter time, and there are young children involved. If you can afford it, move out while the bulk of the renovation work is in progress. Rent an apartment or stay with family. This provides you with much needed privacy and space to think, as well as a more pleasant and hygienic environment to live in, rather than inhabiting a dusty and constrained space and being overrun with contractors during a prolonged period of time.

> Make sure you obtain your contractor's full contact details before any work starts, as having this will make it easier to deal with any issues or disputes quickly.
>
> Whatever the problem is, take it up with the main contractor who arranged the work, even if they sub-contracted all or some of the activities out e.g. to a tiler, bricklayer or another builder. Do this as soon as the issue arises.

Prepare for your discussion with the contractor in advance. Gather any related paperwork and receipts and take photos that you can use as evidence of the issue. Ensure you have made detailed notes about what's caused the problem, including dates and times, as these will aid you in communicating and focusing on the specific problem.

Speak with the contractor and ask for the issue to be put right. Try and come to an agreement about how the problem will be fixed. If necessary, put the issue and fix in writing and email the problem and resolution to the parties involved. Do this at your earliest opportunity so that everyone has a copy of the agreed next steps.

Conflict management in property projects largely come into play during refurbishment. If you have found that there is no end to the increasing cost and / or delays from your building and contracting team, and you are constantly managing the fallout and growing hostility from these service providers who are not treating you fairly, then it may be time to call it quits, rather than put up with further damage. In these cases, you may wish to take formal action and either contact their trade association in the first instance for resolution for breach of contract, discuss the situation with the Citizens Advice Bureau (CAB), or obtain legal advice from your solicitor.

> Make sure you have evidence of the matters that have brought your complaint forward, e.g. documented proof of quotes compared to payments made to date, contractual delivery dates versus actual deliveries, and photos if the standard of work has not been completed as expected. These documents and

photos will also be necessary if you decide to go to court for compensation for the contractor's breach of contract.

When we are undertaking a project, irrespective of the phase it's in, we have an Issues List that we keep, adding any new items and removing those resolved. This gives us one collated document to work from. There are so many things to deal with just within a renovation project, let alone when buying or selling, that we need a structured approach so that everything is done, as well as completed on time for the following activity or phase.

When there are a lot of issues and conflict during a renovation, we find that getting away from it all for a few days makes all the difference. This allows all parties to be in a better state to address the areas of conflict and find resolution collaboratively when we re-group.

How you manage conflict will depend on the type of problem you have.

There are several scenarios noted in the *Q&A section*, with guidance offered for resolution.

To help us stay on top of everything and protect all parties from misinterpretation or misunderstandings, we record everything we can for evidence and reference.

We get as much communication in writing as possible, such as decisions and next steps, and follow up on these as regularly as necessary. This can be in the form of a written quote or letter, emails or texts. This includes agreements from real estate agents early in the process of buying or selling, confirming things like exchange and completion dates so that expectations are managed for all parties across the entire chain.

We contact our broker or mortgage provider directly to obtain updates on our mortgage application if they have not been provided as agreed and expected. We are also in contact with our solicitor regularly. Capturing agreements and decisions made with the builder or main contractor are vital in case of disagreements or issues later in the project.

We stay on top of our finances by keeping an updated spreadsheet detailing our budget, listing costs and expected expenses so that we are aware of the spend and available funds during all the phases. This helps to keep us on top of our budgeting and funding.

Chapter 7. MANAGING STRESS, ISSUES AND CONFLICT

We also create a spreadsheet to capture timetables for deliveries of materials that we are responsible for, whether they are appliances, tiles, bathroom suites or an entire kitchen, and share these with our renovation contracting team. This also means that the appropriate people are at the property to receive these goods and check that the entire delivery has been made before signing off on these.

We document our detailed requirements for a refurbishment and obtain signoff from our builder so that everyone is aware of what is expected.

An example of the template we have created is provided in the *Renovating Chapter*.

Questions and answers (Q&A)

What if the contractor has not done a good job?

The contractor should have undertaken the work taking reasonable care, as well as taking into account the amount they are charging you. If they have not done this, then they have broken the law. You're legally entitled to either ask them to fix the problem or get a refund and stop them doing any further work. Let them know you understand what you're entitled to and use the Consumer Rights Act 2015 (which states that reasonable care and skill must be used while working).

The contractor should then remediate the problem within a reasonable length of time and do so without causing you added inconvenience. The law does not say what counts as reasonable, so this will have to be agreed between the two of you. If they cannot or will not fix the problem, you can request a partial or full refund depending on the severity of the problem. You will then have to come to an agreement about how much refund you should receive. Suggest a figure and explain why you think it is reasonable. If you can't agree on a refund amount, or you are not sure what to do, contact the Citizens Advice Bureau (CAB) consumer helpline. This service is free and may save you a solicitor's fee.

What if the contractor has not done what was agreed?

When you gave the contractor the go-ahead for the work, you technically made a verbal contract with each other, even if it was not a written one. If they have not done what was agreed, they have broken the contract and you can request that they put things right. Make sure you check exactly what was agreed, reviewing any paperwork that they have provided to you, or you provided to them.

Ask the contractor to do whatever is necessary to get the work done properly, giving them sufficient time to complete. They should cover all of the costs, including any extra materials required. If the contractor declines, or you haven't been able to agree to your satisfaction, you may wish to take formal action. You can then contact their trade association for resolution for breach of contract, discuss the situation with the Citizens Advice Bureau (CAB), or obtain legal advice from your solicitor.

Chapter 7. MANAGING STRESS, ISSUES AND CONFLICT

What if the contractor has not completed the work on time?

Give the contractor another chance to complete the work and ensure you make it very clear that it is important that the work must be finished by a specific date. Put this in writing, as it reinforces and formalises the urgency of your request.

If you said the work had to be completed by a certain date and it isn't, and you would like the contractor to remove themselves from your property, tell the contractor you do not want them to carry on with the work they are doing for you. Put this in writing, so you have got a record. Pay them for any work they have done so far, agreeing a discount to make up for the inconvenience they have caused. If they have done very little or no work at all, you may choose not to pay them anything. If you have already given them money (or a deposit) and you think it is too much for the work they have done, suggest a figure and request they refund you the difference.

If they refuse to refund you, advise them you will contact their trade association, and then do so. Also contact the Citizens Advice Bureau (CAB) consumer helpline for assistance.

What if the contractor has charged you a lot more than you expected?

If you agreed a price with the contractor, but they have charged you more, your rights depend on whether you were provided with a quote or an estimate. Verify this against any paperwork you have been provided. A quote is a promise to do work at an agreed price, whereas an estimate is the contractor's best guess as to how much the work will cost.

If you have been provided with:

- A quote, the contractor cannot charge you more than what they have quoted. The exception to this could be if they told you they would need to do extra work, and you agreed to pay more. Therefore, it's obvious to all parties that the price in the quote is not correct because of the additional work done. They cannot charge you more if their costs have gone up since they provided you with the quote. Even if they made a mistake with their quote, if it was not obvious to you when you got the quote, you have a legal right to have the work done for the price stated in the quote. If they cannot provide you with a good reason for raising the price, tell them that you will only pay what was quoted. Put that in writing, so you have a record. Don't be pushed into paying more. If you're unsure about what to do, contact the Citizens Advice Bureau (CAB) or your solicitor.

- An estimate, and the final bill is a lot more than what you were expecting, you can dispute it as the final price should be reasonable. Review the estimate you agreed to, along with any reasonable changes as to why the price may have increased, including events beyond the control of the contractor (e.g. bad weather, or the cost of materials going up if the work has been completed over a lengthy period of time). Let them know that you're unhappy with the price and provide them with a figure that you think would be reasonable to pay. Again, put that in writing so that you have a record. It's likely you will have to negotiate with them, but don't let them bully you into paying more.

  To assist you with deciding how to proceed, you could ask another contractor for an estimate for the same work. Also find out if the contractor is a member of a trade association and contact them for advice, or get an expert opinion, which you will probably have to pay for. Contact the Citizens Advice Bureau (CAB) to discuss this.

What if the contractor has not installed properly, such as a kitchen or boiler?

If you have had something installed at your home and it has been done badly, you are entitled to have it fixed or obtain a refund. For example, if the installation is not where you agreed it would go, or if it is dangerous or unsafe. Again, when you gave the go-ahead to the contractor to do the work, you both entered a contract. If they have not done what was agreed, they have broken the contract and you can request that they put it right. If you can, verify any agreements on any paperwork you may have been provided by them, or to them, including any emails, even though it's irrespective of whether the contract was in writing or not. As you are both under contract, you are legally entitled to request that they either fix the problem if they provided you with the goods as well as the service or obtain a refund and ask them to stop doing any more work.

Inform the contractor that you know what you are entitled to. Take up the problem with whoever arranged the installation, even if they sub-contracted the work to another contractor or business. Ask for a reduction for any inconvenience caused, for example 5% off the cost, as a goodwill gesture. They might refuse, but it is worth asking. If the contractor does not fix the issue within a reasonable amount of time, see if you can come to an agreement about a partial or full refund. If you can't agree on the fix or the refund, contact Citizens Advice Bureau (CAB) to discuss your options.

What if the contractor has done something dangerous or unsafe?

> Immediately stop using anything that you believe is dangerous or unsafe. If it is an electrical appliance, switch it off and unplug it if possible. If it is a gas appliance and you can smell gas, call the National Gas Emergency Service.
>
> Report a dangerous building or structure to your local council immediately, even if it is outside of their normal working hours. This can be done online in England and Wales. If you live in Scotland, you will have to contact your council directly. Leave the building if you think your life might be in immediate danger.

It is really important that the contractor is reported to Trading Standards if they have done anything that is dangerous or unsafe. You cannot usually report the contractor directly to Trading Standards but contact the Citizens Advice Bureau (CAB) consumer helpline and they will contact Trading Standards on your behalf.

The adviser will ask you several questions, such as:

- Who did the work and whether you have their contact details?
- What was the work and what did it involve?
- When did you give the go-ahead for the work to be done?
- How much did the work cost and how you paid for it?
- Have you already raised a complaint with the contractor?

See if you can agree next steps with the contractor directly. If the work can be fixed quickly, you may allow the contractor to do this. Or the contractor may agree to refund you.

If you cannot come to an agreement with the contractor, you can take the following steps:

- Use a template complaint letter, such as the one provided by CAB. The letters provided contain legal terminology that should alert the contractor that you know your rights.
- Check if the contractor is a member of a trade association. You can look on the contractor's website or ask them if you cannot find this information. Contact the trade association and explain the situation, discussing next steps with them.

- Ask the contractor if they are a member of an Alternative Dispute Resolution (ADR) scheme as this is a way of solving disagreements without going to court. If they do not respond or will not use an ADR scheme, keep a record of the fact that you asked them, including the date.
- Choose an ADR scheme yourself (filter by country to select United Kingdom) to try to solve the problem more informally. This will assist you later if you end up going to court.
- Claim compensation from them if you have to get someone else to complete or re-do the work. This could mean asking the contractor for compensation or it could involve taking them to court, which can be costly and time consuming. If you lose the case, it's likely that you will end up paying for court costs and solicitors for both parties.

Checklist – Managing stress, issues and conflict

The following Checklist will help you to navigate your way through challenging situations:

- ☐ Partners need to remain aligned with each other to maintain focus.
- ☐ Keep to a good diet, exercise and get rest to keep up your stamina.
- ☐ Take a break for a few days and get away from it all so you can return re-energised.
- ☐ Document your requirements and obtain signoff on it from your main contractor.
- ☐ Record everything and obtain all agreements in writing.
- ☐ Be aware of your rights and how to resolve any issues with the trades on your project.
- ☐ Prepare for discussions and gather all paperwork, receipts, photo evidence and notes.
- ☐ Keep in touch with all the parties, especially when issues and conflicts arise.
- ☐ If initial discussions with the contractor break down, contact their trade body or CAB.
- ☐ If you decide on a more formal action, contact your solicitor.
- ☐ Keep evidence of all matters relating to your complaint in case you need to go to court.
- ☐ If there is no end to the increasing cost or delays, fallout and hostility, walk away.
- ☐ Use the Q&A guidance for resolving issues with contractors.

Chapter 8

USEFUL LINKS AND RESOURCES

Reference list

For your convenience and ease of access, we have collated in one chapter those links and resources which have been useful to us over the years while we have been buying, renovating, staging, selling and moving home. Included are suppliers we have used or considered for sourcing products, but our rolodex is inexhaustive, so we have provided a small cross-section of these to suit most budgets. We hope you find this list useful during your property journey. At the time of printing, these links were up to date. If they have been changed or moved since, please search for the words below in your web browser.

Age UK

https://www.ageuk.org.uk/

https://www.ageuk.org.uk/about-us/what-we-do/age-uk-business-directory/

Alternative Dispute Resolutions (ADR)

https://www.gov.uk/alternative dispute resolution for consumers

Architects

https://find-an-architect.architecture.com/FAAHome.aspx

Auctions

http://www.allsop.co.uk/our-services/auction/

https://www.auctionhouse.co.uk/

https://www.propertyauctionaction.co.uk/

http://www.ukauctionlist.com/

Builders and trade's people finder

https://www.checkatrade.com/

https://www.mybuilder.com/

https://www.ratedpeople.com/

https://www.trustatrader.com/

https://trustedtraders.which.co.uk/

Building Control Body (BCB)

https://www.gov.uk/building-regulations-approval/how-to-apply

https://www.planningportal.co.uk/how and where to get approval

Chapter 8. USEFUL LINKS AND RESOURCES

Chattels

https://www.gov.uk/hmrc-internal-manuals/stamp-duty-land-tax-manual

Complaints handling

www.tpos.co.uk

- On 06 Feb 2018 the Ombudsman Services for Property (OS:P) advised that after 06 August 2018 they will not be acting as an independent redress provider for Estate Agencies, Residential Lettings, Property Management, Auctioneers, Chartered Surveyors, Surveyors and Valuers (Enquiries function will remain until the end of 2018). After 06 August 2018, another approved provider will be picked to cover complaints in estate agency and lettings. Currently other redress providers are The Property Ombudsman and the Property Redress Scheme (approved like the OS:P).

- You can contact an ombudsman to assist you with your complaint when:
  o The dispute between you and your service provider has not been resolved after giving the company 8 weeks to provide a full response, or
  o You receive a deadlock letter from your service provider informing you that your complaint will not be taken any further.

- Listed below are the main ombudsmen to contact for property-related complaints:
  o enquiries@legalombudsman.org.uk/

    The legal ombudsman is responsible for dealing with disputes with lawyers and can instruct compensation of up to £150,000, along with payments for interest and unlimited costs.

  o https://www.ombudsman-services.org/sectors/energy

    The energy regulator, Ofgem, has approved the energy ombudsman to manage disputes between energy suppliers and their clients, awarding up to £10,000, though largely the amount paid is approximately £100.

  o https://www.ombudsman-services.org/sectors/communications

    The Communications Ombudsman independently handles disputes between communication companies that are signed up to their scheme, and their customers, including providers for mobiles, land lines, broadband and pay-tv.

Conservation area

The Local Planning Authority (LPA) or District Council for your local area.
https://historicengland.org.uk/owning-historic-property/conservation-area/
https://www.ricsfirms.com/glossary/living-in-a-conservation-area/

Conveyancing

https://www.moneysupermarket.com/conveyancing/
https://www.ratedsolicitors.com/
http://solicitors.lawsociety.org.uk/

Credit score checks

https://www.clearscore.com/
https://www.experian.co.uk/

Crime statistics

https://www.crime-statistics.co.uk
https://www.streetcheck.co.uk/

Donating items

http://www.9livesfurniture.org.uk/
https://furnituredonationnetwork.org/

Early Redemption Charges (ERC)

An ERC is a penalty payment that is charged by the mortgage provider if you pay off your mortgage earlier than the repayment term agreed with the lender. Check with your mortgage provider if this applies to you if you are paying off your mortgage early.

Electric vehicle grant schemes

https://www.gov.uk/grants for low emission vehicles

Estate agents

https://www.allagents.co.uk/
https://bestestateagentguide.co.uk/
https://www.getagent.co.uk/
https://www.primelocation.com/find-agents/estate-agents/directory/l
https://www.rightmove.co.uk/estate-agents.html
https://www.zoopla.co.uk/find-agents/directory/a

Chapter 8. USEFUL LINKS AND RESOURCES

Estate agents (online fixed fee)
https://www.emoov.co.uk/
https://www.purplebricks.co.uk/
https://www.tepilo.com/

Federation of Master Builders (FMB)
https://www.fmb.org.uk/

Flight path checker
https://webtrak.emsbk.com/

Flood zone checker
www.environment-agency.gov.uk/

Floor plan creating software and apps
https://floorplancreator.net/
https://www.ihomeregistry.com/
https://www.roomsketcher.com/

Google maps and Streetview
https://www.google.co.uk/intl/en_uk/earth/
https://www.google.co.uk/maps
https://www.instantstreetview.com

Help-to-Buy and other incentive schemes
https://gov.wales/topics/housing-and-regeneration/?lang=en
https://www.helptobuy.gov.uk/equity-loan/find-helptobuy-agent/
https://www.helptobuy.gov.uk/
https://www.moneyadviceservice.org.uk/Help to Buy and other housing schemes
https://www.mygov.scot/Help-to-Buy/overview/
https://www.smartnewhomes.com/government-incentives/

House price information
http://landregistry.data.gov.uk/
https://nethouseprices.com/
https://www.zoopla.co.uk/

Inspiration

https://images.google.com/
https://www.pinterest.co.uk/

Insurance comparisons

https://www.confused.com/home-insurance
https://www.money.co.uk/home-insurance.htm
https://www.moneysavingexpert.com/insurance/home-insurance/
https://www.moneysupermarket.com/home-insurance/

Listed properties

https://britishlistedbuildings.co.uk/
http://www.english-heritage.org.uk

Mail redirection

https://www.iammoving.com/
https://www.royalmail.com/business redirection
https://www.royalmail.com/personal/receiving-mail/redirection/

Mortgage comparisons

https://www.comparethemarket.com/mortgages/
https://www.money.co.uk/mortgages.htm
https://www.moneysavingexpert.com/mortgages/best-buys/

Moving home for the elderly

https://www.ageuk.org.uk/about-us/what-we-do/age-uk-business-directory/

National Gas Emergency Service

0800 111 999 (UK) / 0800 002 001 (Northern Ireland)
https://www.nationalgrid.com/group/safety-and-emergencies
https://www.sgn.co.uk/Safety/National-Gas-Emergency-Service/

Packaging (recycled) for storing, stacking and moving

https://www.amazon.co.uk/
http://www.argos.co.uk/
http://www.bigdug.co.uk/
http://www.chilledpackaging.co.uk/

Chapter 8. USEFUL LINKS AND RESOURCES

http://www.eco-boxes.co.uk/
https://www.jbpackaging.co.uk/
http://www.packingboxes.co.uk/
https://www.ryman.co.uk/
https://sadlers.co.uk/
https://www.solentplastics.co.uk/

Paint matching

https://www.duluxtradepaintexpert.co.uk/trade paint expert (paint matching app)

Pantone colours for home interiors

https://www.pantone.com/fashion-home-interiors

Pet's microchips

https://www.petlog.org.uk/

Photos and assignment of rights

https://www.findlegalforms.com/free-forms/files/assignment-of-rights-to-photograph.doc

Planning permission

https://www.gov.uk/planning-permission-england-wales
https://www.planningportal.co.uk/info/where and how to get approval

Property Information Form

http://www.lawsociety.org.uk/support-services/documents/TA6-form-specimen/

Property ownership, inheritance and intestacy rules

https://www.citizensadvice.org.uk/
https://www.gov.uk/inherits-someone-dies-without-will

Property search websites

https://www.gov.uk/government/organisations/land-registry
https://nethouseprices.com/
https://www.primelocation.com/
http://www.rightmove.co.uk/
https://www.zoopla.co.uk/

Property search websites for private sales

https://www.ebay.co.uk/b/Property/10542/bn_1838208
https://www.gumtree.com/
http://www.home.co.uk/
https://www.houseladder.co.uk/

Protective flooring

https://www.corex.co.uk/
https://universalsitesupplies.co.uk/corex-sheets.html
https://www.wickes.co.uk/

Removal companies

https://bar.co.uk/
https://clarksofamersham.co.uk/
https://trustedtraders.which.co.uk/

School catchment areas

https://admissionsday.co.uk/

Shopping sites and suppliers

https://www.amazon.co.uk/
https://chilternbookshops.co.uk/home/chorleywood-bookshop
https://decorexi.co.uk/
https://www.decortiles.co.uk/
https://www.diy.com/ (B&Q)
https://www.ebay.co.uk/
https://www.gumtree.com/
https://www.howdens.com/
https://www.ikea.com/
https://www.johnlewis.com/
https://www.marksandspencer.com/
https://www.next.co.uk/
https://www.poggenpohl.com/
http://www.porcelanosa.com/uk/
https://www.pronorm.de/?L=1
https://www.screwfix.com/
https://en.shpock.com/

Chapter 8. USEFUL LINKS AND RESOURCES

https://www.stylelibrary.com/zoffany/
https://www.travisperkins.co.uk/
https://www.wallpaperdirect.com/
https://www.waterstones.com/
https://www.whsmith.co.uk/
https://www.wrenkitchens.com/

Surveyors

http://www.esurv.co.uk/
https://www.ricsfirms.com/
https://www.rics.org/uk/

Stamp Duty calculator

https://www.stampdutycalculator.org.uk/

ABOUT THE AUTHORS

Both writers were born in idyllic tourist destinations – Geoffrey in New Zealand, and Sharena in Fiji. They met in Wellington in 1992 and married a year later. In 1998, they decided to voyage across the world to the UK for their big overseas experience (or OE, as it's known in NZ, which is usually undertaken by young people in their late teens and twenties, rather than adults in their thirties!). Their families were left bemused by their decision to move to a land so far, far, away, but felt safe in the knowledge that they would only be abroad for 2 years because…that's what most people did.

On arrival in the UK, Geoffrey and Sharena established an IT consultancy company, specialising in project management and quality assurance. They have since delivered a number of IT contracts, working in the UK, France, Spain, Portugal, Italy, Channel Islands, The Netherlands and Malaysia. Their client list includes KPMG, PWC, Royal Dutch Shell, Barclays, Lloyds, BNP Paribas, Merrill Lynch, UBS, RBS, MUFG, TfL and Unilever.

In the last 15+ years, they have been developing properties in parallel. In 2017, after almost 20 years of consulting in the City, they decided to take a break and evaluate their options. At that stage, they were both burnt out, physically and mentally.

In 2018, they embarked on another career, doing what they were both passionate about. Combining their skills and expertise in consulting with their love for buying, renovating and selling properties, it was an ideal choice to have a property consultancy business. At the same time, they wanted to share their knowledge by writing this book about their experiences in the property market. Following the processes and checklists in this book, Geoffrey and Sharena have secured an average of 31% uplift on the prices they have paid for their properties. This has occurred within 9 to 24 months of buying, renovating and selling each property. Anyone can benefit similarly by following their formula.

Geoffrey and Sharena currently live in Middlesex. In his spare time, Geoffrey enjoys cooking, fishing, model making, DIY, listening to music and anything to do with cars. Sharena loves reading, writing, drawing, painting, listening to music and new stationery. To visit their website, please go to www.gsansellproperty.com.

Printed in Great Britain
by Amazon